PERSONAL AND P

FEMINISMS, SOCIOLOGY AND FAMILY LIVES

Personal and Political

Feminisms, Sociology and Family Lives

MIRIAM E. DAVID

Trentham Books
Stoke on Trent, UK and Sterling USA

Trentham Books Limited

Westview House	22883 Quicksilver Drive
734 London Road	Sterling
Oakhill	VA 20166-2012
Stoke on Trent	USA
Staffordshire	
England ST4 5NP	

First published 2003

British Library Cataloguing-in-Publication Data
A catalogue record for this book is available from the British Library

ISBN 1 85856 305 4

Designed and typeset by Trentham Print Design Ltd., Chester and printed in Great Britain by Cromwell Press Ltd., Wiltshire.

*To my children - Toby and Charlotte Reiner – in the hope
that their personal lives will be enriched by feminist and
socialist struggles for political change*

*Also to my step-children –
Rachel, Simon and Matthew Duckett*

*They are all young adults of the generation who have been
both privileged, and pressured, to take new perspectives on, and
identities in, family and education*

*For them all, the public and political gaze on personal
issues is indeed a reality*

Contents

Acknowledgements

There are many people – family, friends and colleagues – who have helped to make this book possible. Given that it is about my intellectual journey from childhood to the present, it is hard to acknowledge all my personal and professional debts and I hope that those who are not named personally will not feel offended by the omission.

I particularly want to thank my 'sisters', despite the fact that this has been seen as a controversial concept as I show in the book. First, my two sisters – Judy Berle and Anne Sultoon – have been so very important throughout my life that it is impossible for me to identify clearly and precisely my debt to them and my wider family of origin. Secondly, I need to thank all the feminist friends, colleagues, students, counsellors and mentors, across the globe, with whom I have worked and had fun over the last 40 years or more. Without the international women's movement and feminism, this book would not have been possible.

I also must thank all my academic colleagues, over the years, and especially those at the University of London – Institute of Psychiatry, LSE, Queen Mary and the Institute of Education – the University of Bristol, South Bank University and Keele University. I have also spent many happy and fruitful times abroad in universities, in particular Harvard Graduate School of Education, University of California at Irvine, University of New York at Buffalo, University of Wisconsin, Madison in the USA; Ontario Institute for Studies in Education, University of Toronto, York University, Toronto, and UBC in Canada; Deakin, Melbourne, UTS, UNISA, University of Queensland and QUT, Brisbane in Australia; the universities of Auckland, Waikato, and Canterbury in New Zealand; Umea University in Sweden and the Hebrew University in Jerusalem, Tel Aviv and Haifa universities in Israel.

In the final stages of putting together the manuscript, several colleagues at Keele have been particularly important, including Graham Allan, Nafsika Alexiadou, Pam Alldred, Ian Butler, Davina Cooper, Ken Jones, Chris Phillipson, Angela Packwood, Farzana Shain, Pat Smith, Stephen Whitehead, Carol Hough and especially Gladys Pye. My doctoral students have been very supportive and I thank all my GEMs, Barbara Cole and Gillian Forrester for being so enthusiastic. Dr Gillian Klein of Trentham Books has been an absolutely brilliant publisher.

More recently, my – dare I say it? – husband, Jeff has been a constantly amazing source of succour and support. In April 2002, while staying with Jeff's friend and colleague Roberto Ligrone and his family, Jeff and Roberto managed innumerable botanical excursions whilst I put the finishing touches to the manuscript. I am grateful to Roberto and Gabriella for this Italian family hospitality. It was a really important way for me to be reminded of continuity and change in family and personal lives. Finally, I do not know how to thank Toby and Charlotte who have lived, breathed and argued about the themes of the book for as long as I can remember. Our personal and political lives have been the better for such stimulating challenges.

CHAPTER ONE

Introduction

An intellectual biography as a feminist sociologist of family lives

Introduction

This is my intellectual biography as a feminist sociologist in the academy; a personal perspective on the origins and development of a feminist sociology of family lives in late modernity. The book has been a long time in the making and has many origins. After considerable personal anguish and struggle I have arrived at a conclusion about the importance and, indeed, necessity of writing about my personal, political and professional odyssey as a sociologist and feminist.

I am one of the first generation of feminist sociologists to have been able to enter universities and struggle to contribute to a feminist perspective on aspects of sociology and family lives. Our political and intellectual struggles were around feminism, theorising and deconstructing perspectives on women and women's studies, sex, gender and the nature of the family or family lives. We wanted these issues and questions to become part of the curriculum in higher education but it was not without immense struggle and contestation that we were able to develop such theoretical perspectives. Our concerns derived from the wider political, social and economic contexts of our own lives over the last 35 years. We were part of a growing social movement for political change around women's lives in and outside the family; what was then known as the women's movement or women's liberation and what subsequently has been termed second wave feminism to distinguish it from first wave feminism. First wave feminism was the fight for women's rights and women's suffrage. Second wave feminism has been the more complex struggle for women's liberation from diverse forms of oppression. Our wishes and desires for personal and social changes translated into attempts to develop collective understandings and new ways of learning and teaching about them. We also tried to develop new approaches to understandings and to how we might study and research these vexed questions. They also influenced how we thought about how to introduce such new approaches to teaching and learning, developing new pedagogies for higher education. We gradually became more reflective and thoughtful about how our wishes and desires could become an essential part of the curricula and pedagogies of higher education. I argue that there have been at least three phases in our collective endeavours linked with the wider political context of liberalism as an ideology and social transformations. I illustrate how these three phases have influenced the part played by feminists in the theoretical and methodological developments in sociologies of the family.

This book represents a review of these changing themes and developments in the academy and, specifically, the contributions made by feminists politically, academically, methodologically, theoretically and epistemologically. In particular, I highlight the contributions to changing understandings by feminists, expressed collectively although there is considerable diversity and even differences between types of feminists. The question is however how we know what we know, and how we now teach about this in higher education – in other words, how the pedagogies of higher education have been modified by shifting epistemological concerns. Collectively, reflexivity and subjectivity have become the hallmarks of such developments, although their origins in relation to feminist perspectives have not always been acknowledged. However, some of the more recent British textbooks on sociologies of family life have acknowledged the importance and influence of feminist perspectives, notably David Morgan (1996), Jon Bernardes (1997) and Graham Allan (1999).

Feminisms, sociologies and family lives

As a sociologist by training and feminist by inclination, I want to present a particular perspective on family life in late modernity. My aim here is to present a feminist perspective on family life through the lens of sociology as a discipline in the era increasingly referred to as post- or late modernity. The changes that have taken place in the global socio-economic context, liberalism as a political ideology and their influences on family lives are seen as so dramatic that they constitute a break with the past period of modernity. What I argue is that sociology as a discipline or subject in higher education has developed over the same 35 to 60 year period as family lives have changed. The impact of economic and political globalisation – that is the changes with respect to information and the knowledge economy – has been especially important in influencing our ideas and practices (Peters, 2001). The evidence that we now have has been influenced by the ways in which we have experienced and theorised wider changes and how we feel that they impact upon all of our lives and the choices we have to make. Ethnographies as ways of collecting evidence or conducting social research have become a particularly influential approach in our understandings. This research and evidence is now drawn from a diversity of sources and not just those located within sociology but, increasingly, post-structural critiques of sociological, social scientific or cultural theories. Understandings have drawn from everyday perspectives and interpretations and the ways in which these percolate down into popular writings, biographies, autobiographies, novels, and detective fiction, movies and other material such as cultural, literary and media studies and ephemera. Increasingly, our understandings drew on our autobiographies, our identities and how we interpret and re-interpret them in relation to our positioning and reflections on our views of ourselves. Being a critical feminist ethnographer is a characteristic approach.

Deconstructing the family and family life is therefore crucial to our understandings and interpretations of the social changes and transformations that have taken place. I take family to mean those intimate personal, sexual and emotional relationships that frame our lives in terms of gender and generation; that is, relations between and within the sexes for love and procreation and for caring for us throughout our lives, from cradle to grave. These relations have been regulated by material circumstances, economic policies and by legal and social policies. How our lives are now lived have been crucially changed by the global economic, technological and social changes that have taken place, as well as by legal, social and political reforms. Deconstructing the family has influenced how we understand and interpret the changes and our different involvements across the generations in those transformations.

Feminism as a political, social and intellectual movement has been at the forefront of challenging traditional structures and processes in modern societies and working towards transforming political, economic, social and particularly family life in terms of women's rights, roles, responsibilities and regulation. However, as feminism has developed and become influential in academia, diverse theoretical and political strands have emerged and it is now difficult to talk of one feminism. Feminists of all social classes, ethnic diversities and sexual orientations have become involved in providing critiques of all aspects of life. For my generation of feminists, becoming feminists in the late 1960s, as part of the second wave of the women's movement, our initial concern was with what we then called women's liberation as a political rather than a social or educational movement. It was part of the attempt to provide for women's equality in both public and private life, by means of dealing with sexual liberation, (sex) discrimination against women and women's oppression (see for example Michèle Barrett, 1980). In particular a political slogan was coined which addressed the question of the power relations between men and women in the privacy of the family, namely 'the personal is political', and this was used as a basis for drawing women to an understanding of feminist consciousness.

One of the central arguments of this book is about the way in which these notions of 'the personal is political' have become transformed and incorporated into our academic analyses. Personal matters – privacy, intimacy, sexual relations – are now crucial to our public understandings. Within public discourse the notions of what are called personal responsibility have also become central to public policy debates and, indeed, legislation in several 'modern' states (e.g. Temporary Aid to Needy Families (TANF) 1996 in the USA and Tony Blair's speech at the London School of Economics (LSE) March 10, 2002). There has been a notable shift from objective accounts to taking account of our subjectivities, our agency in relation to social processes and structures, and our personal feelings and accounts. How these shifts have occurred and how influential they have been is the subject of this book.

It was only slowly that we, as feminists, began to account for discrimination and oppression and provide theoretical interpretations that could be used in educational settings, as we moved into the academy and away from more overt political campaigning. Even so Hirschmann and Di Stefano (1996) argued:

> We are also aware that feminism in the academy and in the world at large continues to underrepresent the needs and aspirations of many women. We are painfully aware of the fact that the contributors to this volume do not represent an accurate or full sampling of women's emancipatory aspirations; and indeed, this may ironically be due to our own personal location in the disciplinary norms of political theory, our struggles notwithstanding. (Hirschmann and Di Stefano, 1996: 20)

Eventually this theoretical work became known in the academy as feminist pedagogy. Our interpretations have become incorporated into aspects of education and especially higher education or rather academic life, differentially in different disciplines or subject areas, but prominently within sociology. Hence my desire to present a sociological perspective and approach to our understanding of the changes that have influenced all of our lives in families and in the wider political, economic and social worlds.

I focus on how feminist perspectives have influenced, and yet, at the same time, been influenced by, education and what we now call pedagogy, particularly in the academic world, linking our understandings of family life to wider schools of thought, and the academy. In this respect there is a clear and complex relationship between families and education. For women, and especially women who grew up in the second half of the twentieth century, education, particularly adult and/or higher education, has provided the means for us/them to change aspects of their lives including within the family and employment. Similarly feminist perspectives are now beginning to take root in the academy enabling and interpreting such transformations. (Morley, 1999) Feminists have slowly become part of the academic community and have begun to contribute to analyses within the disciplines as well as in specific areas such as feminist or women's studies.

Such academic feminist perspectives have concentrated on the creation and construction of notions of what it is to be a woman, socially and sexually – daughter, mother, grandmother, sexual being – through family, through babyhood and childhood and into adult life, in relation to men and other women. The wider cultural influences of social and political life have also begun to permeate our complex understandings and challenge our notions, theoretically and methodologically, of sex and sexualities. Understanding our lived experiences, our being, our essence, our difference or our sexual and social identities can only take place through broad understandings of family and its location in relation to other social and economic structures and processes, whatever perspective or school of thought we adopt.

Most traditional sociological writings on family and family lives did not touch upon these issues. They were concerned to explore how families and family lives have changed structurally and the implications for family processes so to speak. The majority of such texts were, inevitably, produced by men, given their predominance within academia. It is fascinating to note how they focused on adult relations and how they discounted children, child-care and education. Where they dealt with issues across the generations, questions about parenting tended to ignore the gendering of such relations. Thus these texts have had a particular bias or focus that I wish to modify/rectify, despite the fact that occasionally a pro-feminist stance (Lingard and Douglas 1999) was taken.

However, many more recent sociological accounts have acknowledged the influences of feminism and the women's movement on developments within sociologies of family. David Morgan not only adapted but also adopted these feminist personal perspectives in his ways of theorising and developing work in the sociology of family life methodologically (1993, with Miller) and in *Family Connections*, (1996) the sub-title of which is '*an introduction to family studies*'. An understanding and sympathy with feminist perspectives was threaded through the book. Gender, as a concept, is the subject of a chapter, with an explicit emphasis on the relation between families, households and employment or work. Morgan drew on a particular genre of feminist scholarship that focused on adult relations and did not deal directly with the question of children, and their care and education. Caring as a concept was explored but mainly in relation to the care of 'dependents', meaning elderly people rather than children. It is striking, and yet perhaps absolutely understandable, that historically some feminist scholars and early campaigners avoided focussing on issues to do with children, worried about the lifeboat principle – women and children first. This is a lacuna that I wish to fill. There is in fact other feminist literature on children and their care and education which foregrounds mothers and motherhood and develops the concept of caring in relation to this. This particular focus on motherhood has been seen as a somewhat essentialist approach to families and concepts of caring.

However, Morgan did not deal with this literature or the complexities of the concepts of caring. Morgan (1998) also explored more recent methodological approaches to studying family life in his address as president of the British Sociological Association, where he explored questions of auto/biography, including his own. This developed out of a self-conscious use of auto/biography in sociology, signalled by a special issue of the journal *Sociology* in 1993, in which Morgan with his colleague Miller wrote about 'the CV as an autobiographical practice' (1993: 133–144). Taking up the methodological shifts and turns, initiated by feminists, towards a more personal and autobiographical agenda, David Morgan (1996) introduced *Family Connections* with his professional and personal developments within sociology. He noted how it was only when his interests intertwined with concerns drawn from the women's movement and feminism that these issues came to the fore again within sociology, and sociology of the family was resuscitated.

Bernardes took up a similar personal and autobiographical stance, at the end rather than beginning, of his book. He identified being involved with family studies as tending towards the 'effeminate' and ended his textbook on the following rather forlorn 'personal' note:

> I long ago became accustomed to being regarded as faintly odd, studying 'family life' usually seen as rather dull, boring and even uninteresting. 'Family life' is thought of as being about (horror of horrors!) (*sic*) women and children, essentially non-economic subjects that do not directly involve trendy issues of social class, capitalist domination or revolution. 'Family living' is regarded as 'already understood' and as peripheral to 'real issues' in politics, business and industry and social science. Perhaps all this is true . . . (Bernardes, 1997: 193)

However, he tried to show how those soft edges can be put in the service of rather more fundamental political rather than personal issues, by trying to present a strong theoretical argument for such studies and politics:

> . . . we have simply failed to employ critical intellectual endeavour in those areas of life we think of as intensely 'private', that is, 'family lives'. It is time to change this . . . The most obvious thing to change is the general belief in 'the family' for a sensitivity to the existence of many different kinds of family practices and pathways . . . [It is time to abandon faith in 'the family'] and begin working instead towards improving some practices and pathways whilst discouraging others . . . (Bernardes, 1997: 194–5)

Interestingly, as he himself noted throughout the book, the sociology of family life, or family life *per se,* has been seen as of central significance to our understandings and our everyday lives. In the early days of the growth and development of sociology, and allied subjects such as anthropology, politics and economics, families and family life were central to the development of theoretical concepts, even amongst major theorists and theoreticians, such as Parsons.

There has been a 'turn' back to these issues in recent times, such that Allan (1999) argued that this is integral to the sociology of the family, and not separate from feminist studies.

The shape of my book – its characteristics, contents, chapters, form, methods – has been through many gestations and includes several abortions. I had been invited to write a textbook on the sociology of family life for a very prestigious publisher in the mid 1990s. However, I found that I could only write in a more personal vein, interweaving my own biography in much the way that Morgan, Bernardes and Allan had done rather than by presenting a dispassionate account. I had originally intended to present the argument in terms of chapters relating to the life course, from childhood through to old age, and using Shakespeare's 'seven ages of man' (*sic*) as a way of so doing. But this did not allow for the presentation of theoretical and methodological developments and did not allow for reflection on my subjective interests and developments, and so I abandoned this approach.

Critical moments, pedagogy and theories of family lives

The birth of this version has come from many sources, including presenting several international seminars on aspects of the book,[1] and teaching aspects of the material on a variety of undergraduate and post/graduate courses both in England and in the USA. In particular, I developed the broad outlines of the argument of the book for my (second) inaugural professorial lecture, given in Keele University on November 22nd 2000. The date turned out to be fortuitously significant as it linked with two other key moments that also fell on November 22nd. The first was President John F. Kennedy's assassination in 1963. The second was Margaret Thatcher's resignation as British Prime Minister after over ten years in office in 1990. Both of these, for those of us alive then, became an occasion for collective but also deeply personal memories. I used them as signals of political and social transformations and shall do so again as a way of threading the themes of this book. This kind of approach – selecting key or critical moments as pegs to hang our personal biographical accounts and critical reflections – has become commonplace within social and educational research or ethnographies.

Another such epiphany for current generations were the events of September 11, 2001 (9/11). One issue that unfolded was around antisemitism, although in the immediate aftermath this was rarely acknowledged. But as the international conflict developed and in particular moved to the Middle East, my political ideas and humanitarian values derived from my Jewish family background in respect of the prospects of further war and conflagration, became deeply enmeshed in renewed feminist political activities. I return to illustrate this later.

Prior to these various international presentations and teaching in Britain and the USA, I had given much less credence to my own personal odyssey, although I had always intended to include references to my intellectual developments and their links with my family and auto/biography. I had also planned to create a different narrative focussing on family rather than education and pedagogies in higher education. However, the shifts in my research and teaching towards questions about the intimate links between personal and public such as around sex and relationship education and deconstructing changing discourses of social welfare forced me to reflect upon my positioning in relation to these issues. Several other personal and private matters made me reflect upon the personal significance of living patriarchy and family. I had to examine the relation between my developing theories and methodologies and my life course and interests. Explaining aspects of my intellectual autobiography – my memoirs – would provide an explanation for the kinds of methodologies and theories that I wanted to explore. Making myself familiar with material for an international audience, both as a teacher and a writer, reading more recent feminist work in the USA and engaging with the topical political debates about family values also persuaded me of the efficacy and, indeed, necessity of locating myself in the methodologies and materials to be considered. I was eager to understand and use some relatively new and somewhat unfamiliar approaches, such as life histories, narratives, biographies and autobiographies, 'marrying' them with more tradi-tional but qualitative research methods, which explore concepts such as diverse voices from interview material. These would all be made relevant to their policy contexts but be rooted in largely British material and methodologies. I was particularly eager to explore reflexive, autobiographical and psychoanalytic accounts as intriguing and innovative. Reflexivity and/or self-assessment seemed to demand or cry out for this personal and, at times, painful journey through the highlights (and lowlights) of the associations between the twin themes of family and education; or rather the complexity of the relationships between family life and my educational or intellectual developments.

The processes of teaching about family and education from a feminist perspec-tive to groups of mature students who were extremely able but relatively untutored in sociology and/or feminism also forced me to think more clearly about what it was I wanted to argue. This also crystallised how I wanted to think about these ideas about family and family life in late modernity as we entered the new millennium. I also had to find a way to explain my particular predilections that were, at times, somewhat at odds with theirs. At the same time there had been a developing new genre of memoirs and intellectual biographies, in particu-lar in the USA, which addressed these issues and made these questions more salient and pertinent for me. Reading, comparing and contrasting the ways in which such narratives, stories and accounts were constructed and contextualized gave an immediacy to the importance of education, in the broadest sense, to these issues. Moreover, it is also important to note how these kinds of bio-graphies, life histories, narratives and stories are also increasing the materials for classes and for teaching and learning in the widest sense.

In seminars, talks and teaching mature students in Britain and in the USA I found I had to situate myself in my family and the broader social and cultural context, and so tell my story. I had to justify why I had chosen particular theories, methodologies and perspectives to the mature students (all in their late 30s and early 40s) who were also practising teachers and/or professionals. In particular, I had to legitimate myself as a teacher of students who were not familiar to me and were quite unlike what I expected when I planned the courses. I had to show familiarity with their concerns and explain my 'difference' as educationally useful. Otherwise I appeared as a Star Wars character; someone 'a long time ago, in a galaxy far, far away', with a somewhat tangential relation to their studies and a digression from their own work for a masters or a doctoral dissertation. For instance, in giving seminars abroad and teaching summer schools in the USA I assumed that it would be important to select readings from the USA and other English-speaking countries such as Canada, Australia and New Zealand rather than rely entirely on British material.[2] My experiences and my research expertise had already led me to consider, compare and contrast American (both Canadian and from the USA) and British material on family and education and in relation to policies and state and family practices. In any event, I see myself as something of an 'USAphile' (rather than Anglophile). I have spent a considerable amount of time in the USA both professionally as a visiting academic and teacher and I have also personally tried to steep myself in its culture.

However, one of my groups of students turned out to be quite different from my expectations, especially in that the majority of them were men rather than women. This had not been my experience in my thirty plus years of teaching. My own experiences, first as an undergraduate and later as an academic, had led me to expect that the majority interested in and involved with these subjects and topics would be women. Of course the more conscious realisation of these gender dimensions was a relatively slow process. It was in part my classroom experiences, as I became a feminist, that had led me to my particular perspec-tives, seeing and teaching or working with female students. A majority of female students had led me to want to bring in their situations, concerns, and position-ing into my materials, my research and my evidence. Thus I became familiar with the now routine use of personal experiences and reflections as a way to organise material. Moreover, biographies are one of the main ways to provide detailed material about personal experiences of aspects of family life. My various groups of students have been eager to present their own personal experiences of

family and family lives as a way to understand and interpret their own developments in context. It has felt safer for all of us to share such accounts rather than
my remaining in the more powerful, teacher position, although it should be
acknowledged that even when sharing I remained in a privileged and more
powerful position. Starting from personal experiences has usually been the case
with feminist studies as I endeavour to show throughout the rest of this book. It
was this kind of material that we as creators of the first British text on women's
studies *Half the Sky* (Bristol Women's Studies Group, 1979; 1984) took as
central.

These and other events gave me permission to think about memories and
anniversaries as part of my own intellectual biography and as a way of codifying
my personal academic development and interests in family and education from a
feminist perspective. This kind of approach of ethnographies, narratives, life
histories, auto/biographies and family memoirs has developed into the key
methodological approach (Chamberlayne, Bornat and Wengraf, eds., 2000).
Indeed, such approaches to writing about women's lives have become central to
feminist pedagogies in sociology, social sciences, education and courses in
women's studies. Recent examples of personal biography and education in
Britain include Rosemary Deem (1996), Valerie Walkerdine (1997), Sally
Tomlinson (1990) and Pat Sikes (1996). There are abundant examples in the
USA – some noteworthy accounts from a diversity of family, social and sexual
backgrounds include Liz Ellsworth (1997), Deborah Britzman (1997), Kathleen
Weiler (1998) and Patti Lather (1991). This is also the case for such feminist
accounts post-colonially. An interesting take on these issues is Sue Middleton
(1999) about her experiences in New Zealand. Jane Kenway's work with
Elisabeth Bullen (2001), Jill Blackmore (2000) provide further instances of
this kind of writing in Australia and there are numerous such accounts from
feminists in Canada, (Sandra Acker, 1999; Jane Gaskell, 2002; Dorothy Smith,
1990). All of these illustrate crossing the boundaries between sociology, education and feminisms.

However, some of the earliest attempts were those by women trying to develop
feminist methodologies prior to its fashion within the academy. For example,
Denise Riley (1992) provided an intriguing insight into her own politics and
practices and struggles in Britain, as did Valerie Walkerdine (1997). But one of
the earliest, and best known, book in this genre is Carolyn Steedman's *Landscape
for a Good Woman*. Here Steedman reflects upon her life and that of her mother,
presenting us with a memoir/biography of her mother's life refracted through
her own concerns. Inevitably her account of her mother's life can only be how
she, rather than her mother, pieced together the elements which have had an
influence on her own life, seeing that as important to her own formative identity.
Published in 1986, at a time when many biographies and memoirs by feminists

were beginning to appear, the book, with its mixed narrative and interpretations, became a classic. As Steedman put it:

> The childhood dreams recounted in this book, the fantasies, the particular and remembered events of a fifties childhood do not, by themselves, constitute its point. We all return to memories and dreams like this again and again . . . interpretation of it can only be made with what people know of a social world and their place within it . . . So the evidence presented here is of a different order from the biographical; it is about the experience of my own childhood, and the way in which my mother re-asserted, reversed and restructured her own within mine . . .
> (Steedman, 1986: 5 and 8)

Significantly, this book lead on to consideration of the ways in which we reflect upon our own family lives and analyse our methods of approaching these subjects. In sociology this has become known as the 'double hermeneutic' (Giddens, 1990). In other words, changes in society and the ways in which we conceive of them can only be understood if we consider ourselves a part of them. We have, constantly, to reflect upon their meanings and make choices in ways we did not have to in the past.

Personal reflections on generations of family lives

It is evident that our lives today (and since the Second World War) as women within families – as mothers, grandmothers, daughters, sisters, granddaughters – are very different from those of our forebears – mothers and grandmothers alike. The opportunities, and yet constraints, on our abilities to be involved in public and private lives have themselves been successively transformed by these wider changes. This is the case for successive post-war generations whose understandings and experiences have increasingly been influenced by those struggling to transform their own lives from the constraints and burdens of past social and economic responsibilities and family and/or sexual obligations. This is not to say, however, that there has been a one-way march of progression and, thus, modernisation. On the contrary, both our experiences and understandings are complex and rooted in complicated experiences, relationships and interpretations, whether of a cultural, political or social construction.

Nevertheless, at a personal level and one mirrored for women of my generation, changes have been profound in balancing family, education and paid-work lives compared with previous generations in the twentieth century. Like Steedman and Walkerdine, I grew up in the 1950s, but unlike them came from a middle class 'ethnic minority' and immigrant background.[3] I was born in 1945 in the shadows of Hiroshima and Nagasaki, according to my mother, and became a relatively privileged member of the first post-war age cohort. Although I was born and lived until my teenage years in a small relatively working-class town, Keighley, in the then West Riding of Yorkshire, my family was cosmopolitan, not local.[4] My parents were Jewish and from different generations of immigrant families. They introduced their children to a particular intellectual middle class culture, despite the problems caused by the war. However, there was a singular split between home life in an intense Jewish family and the outside world of a relatively working-class culture. When we had moved to Shipley, a town nearer to Bradford, I became more familiar with ethnic diversity and various cultural perspectives. Given that my parents were both University-educated – my mother studied at Manchester University and my father at a Technische Hochschule first in Darmstadt[5] and then in Berlin – they planned for their three daughters to be the beneficiaries of educational opportunities up to and including university. As a teenager, at my parents' instigation, I joined a socialist-Zionist youth movement [Habonim]. Then, Zionism was not a dirty word, and the main aim of the movement was to get us to go to live on a kibbutz in Israel.[6] Habonim was an intellectually vibrant movement in which we debated socialist and collectivist forms of living that provided alternatives to the traditional family. Some of these debates led me to choose sociology as a subject of study at university and laid the ground for subsequent interest in the politics of family life.

I attended university in the early 1960s, reading sociology at the University of Leeds, together with more than 50 other young women and about half a dozen young men (mainly middle class and all white though of varying religions and cultures). I started out as an undergraduate in the autumn when Kennedy was assassinated. With the benefit of hindsight, and as I go on to argue, this framed my political and personal biography, in common with others, especially women of my generation. The gender balance amongst the students at the time was remarkable yet not remarked upon. Sociology was only just becoming fashionable and none of us really thought through the consequences of what we were choosing and doing. Serendipity played a major part. Neither the women's movement nor second wave feminism could have contributed to our ideas or thinking at that time, given that these ideas had been dormant since the first wave of feminism. However, these ideas were beginning to be reconsidered across countries of the western world. Simone de Beauvoir had already published *The Second Sex* (1951) and novels in France, and these were being read in Britain, although not yet commonly on academic courses. Betty Friedan's *The Feminine Mystique* was published in the USA in 1963 – the year I started university.

Sociology was probably chosen by most of us either because it was not a school subject or because of its possible links with a career in social work or the social services (see also Deem, 1996, *Border Territories: a journey through sociology, education and women's studies* pp 5–19). Interestingly, many of us continued within both the social sciences and the academy for most of our working lives or 'careers'. The men, inevitably perhaps, were relatively more successful in traditional occupational career terms, with one who became a Vice Chancellor of a new university and another appointed as a Professor of Sociology at Cambridge University. Nevertheless, we the women mostly continued to pursue working rather than family careers, albeit that some of us had career breaks on either marriage or birth of children. Marriage was the destiny for the majority of our cohort of women. The academic year in which we went up to university, the Robbins report into higher education was published (1963) and it confirmed that this was the expectation for women, even for those attending university. Indeed, it showed how more than 45% of the cohort of women born in the middle of the Second World War had married by the age of 21 – the age around which we were expected to graduate from university. Arguments were also presented there against student loans to replace student grants, on the grounds that they would constitute a *'negative dowry'* for women and make them relatively unmarriageable (quoted in David and Woodward, 1998).

But, curiously given how unplanned most of our lives in family and paid work were, careers in education as (school) teachers or 'doing' sociology beckoned. Indeed they emerged as a pattern for many of us, the women, as have changes in sexual and marital relationships with many of us experiencing marriage, divorce, separation and/or cohabitation and, in all likelihood, childbirth and child-rearing. Thus my own experiences as an academic and especially as a 'working mother' have been mirrored for most of my class of 66 studying sociology. These lived experiences however may have been more traditionally conventional for the women with whom I was at school; a relatively working-class girls' grammar school in Keighley. Rather than going to university or what was then a teachers' training college, many of them left school at 16, and in all likelihood, worked for a short time, then married and raised a family but have been working throughout much of their adult lives. Yet they may also have experienced family changes. They may also have returned to education at some later stages, combined with child-rearing. These patterns have become more the norm for women of my generation and subsequent generations than for those who were born either within or before the Second World War. And we have been part of the generation, albeit middle class and white, that has taken up feminist political activities and thought as a way to understanding and interpreting our lives in family, education and work.

Over thirty-five years ago the framework for my thinking was set by two parallel concerns – the desire to develop a Marxist or socialist approach, and a feminist perspective. A summer spent in Israel as a volunteer immediately after the Six Day War in 1967, and a year after graduation, confirmed in me the desire to pursue an academic life, laced with fervent political activities. The feminist perspective was developed slowly and through the topics I chose to pursue in collaboration with others, somewhat at a distance from the academy. My initial involvement with feminism, or rather then the women's liberation movement, was as a political activist, rather than as a form of study and it was 'extra-mural' to the university. It would have been, for instance, unthinkable for my grand-mothers – one born in Russia and the other in Germany in the last third of the nineteenth century – to have contemplated or, perhaps, been privileged to have a family and working life such as mine. I have become a member of what Bernstein (1990), Savage and Witz (1992) called 'the new middle classes' and these theories will become relevant to my subsequent discussions about becoming a 'public intellectual' (Sennett, 1996). My working life has been involved in the academy and public and political activities such as feminism in a range of aspects of educa-tion and with the opportunities for international travel and involvement, but increasingly, at virtual arms length via the world wide web and Internet. Never-theless, my family life has also been rich in experiences and relationships. How-ever, my grandmothers – perhaps typical of women of their class, culture, generation and religion – concentrated their efforts on their families and worked, organised and fought for opportunities for their children and subsequent generations. This is despite the fact that work became an economic necessity for my maternal grandmother. In this respect, I have been a beneficiary of their efforts. My maternal grandmother came to England with her family as a rela-tively young immigrant from Russia. She married a man almost ten years her senior and was widowed at an early age. From a modest educational and social class background, she succeeded in getting all three of her children into forms of higher education. Her eldest daughter, born in 1899, studied pharmacy, her son, born in 1901, gained a place at Cambridge University and her youngest, my mother, born in 1909, became an undergraduate student at Manchester Uni-versity in the late 1920s and early 1930s. Her family life, with an ailing and sickly husband and widowhood in 1920, forced her into work as a shopkeeper (of a furniture business in her home) to sustain her family, and was perhaps not as unusual as has previously been thought.

'*Life above the shop*' is how Margaret Thatcher (1995) characterised her child-hood in her autobiography. But her phrase was a way to argue that she therefore had more dealings with her father than would be thought typical of her genera-tion, born in the first two or three decades of the twentieth century. She was born a decade or so after my mother. However, for Thatcher it was also an explanation for her fixation on her father rather than her mother. My mother also described her family life as the daughter of a shopkeeper, influenced by the extensive hours of work but for her, in contrast to Margaret Thatcher, by lack of sustained family contact. My grandmother, as the single parent shopkeeper, might be seen to be more like the generations of mothers nowadays who are in such positions more by force of circumstance, through divorce and/or separation than 'choice' (Riley, 1983).

Both my grandmothers found themselves, as have successive generations in the twentieth century, forced into international travel as a one-way street (and migration) rather than the pleasures that such travel may have since become for some of us more quintessentially and firmly middle-class families. For successive generations, one aspect of developments in the global economy has been the ease and necessity of international travel and yet another aspect has been enforced migrations of people fleeing political and economic oppressions. My maternal grandmother arrived in Britain as a young girl, the eldest daughter in a family of five children in the penultimate decade of the nineteenth century. She came as a result of pogroms in Russia and married here before the turn of the century, producing her first child, a daughter, in late 1899. My paternal grandmother was altogether more privileged in her childhood (also growing up in a family of seven children and one of the older daughters) and young adulthood, and marrying in a wealthy medieval town, Friedberg, on the outskirts of Frankfurt am Main in Germany (and now seen as a commuter suburban town). Her young married life was dominated by the German family credo of *kinde, küche and kirche* (albeit that this latter was the synagogue) in Frankfurt itself in the years before the First World War. Nevertheless her 'family of procreation' was much smaller than that of her family of origin; two as opposed to seven. Her experiences of major upheavals in her family life only began to take their toll a quarter of a century later. Then they were even more dramatic. With her husband, mother-in-law and sister-in-law, she fled to Britain as a refugee from Nazi Germany, and was forced to live in difficult circumstances. Her husband (my paternal grandfather) and her two sons were interned as enemy aliens on the Isle of Man soon after they arrived in Britain. Both grandmothers had family lives circumscribed by economic and major political and social change but both were also confined to their families for their sustenance, both economic and emotional.

Both women passed on to their children their strong sense of women's rights and roles, albeit circumscribed by the circumstances of the times and not especially feminist. Both were relatively modern women, restricting their family size to three and two respectively. Interestingly my maternal grandmother only had three grandchildren, my two sisters and me. Her son never married, perhaps because of the strictures of traditional Jewish family life and his desire, and yet inability, to break out. His elder sister married but never produced children and spent her life divided between running the family chemist's shop and succumbing to mental illness at the menopause. After her husband's death she spent her life in and out of various mental hospitals.

My paternal grandmother only had one other grandchild, the only daughter of her elder son. My uncle too suffered since he became a long term victim of Nazism, having been sent to a concentration camp (Buchenwald) after *Krystal-*

nacht in November 1938 and only managing to escape to England with his parents and paternal grandmother (my paternal great grandmother) with my father's help in early 1939. He too was interned for about a year on the Isle of Man and died early of a nervous illness.

My mother developed a keen sense of her rights and role, having been relatively unusual for a woman of her social class and generation in attending university in the late 1920s and early 1930s. After graduation she trained to be a secondary school teacher but then decided to transfer to primary school. She worked as a teacher in a Jewish primary school throughout the 1930s. At the same time she became involved in helping to rescue Jews from Nazi Germany. She continued to teach until marriage in 1941 put a stop to it, given the then marriage bar in teaching which existed despite wartime strictures and teacher shortages. She had met my father in the mid-1930s as a result of her political activities. After a long courtship, the result of economic hardship and his work to bring his parents, paternal grandparents, aunt and elder brother out of Germany they married. Even then my father was not able to guarantee his family's financial security, and nor was my mother. Her mother, as a shopkeeper, had to act as financial guarantor for my father's family to enter Britain. Even this financial security was short-lived. My father's family arrived in England in early 1939 and settled in Manchester where my father already had a job. Shortly after the outbreak of war, ironically, as with all German Jewish refugees at that time, the men in the family – my father, his father and his brother – were seen as enemy aliens and interned. My father was arrested from his place of work in the spring of 1940 and taken to the Isle of Man where Jewish refugees were interned (see Medawar and Pike, 2001: 191–211). My mother eventually found my father a new job and they were then able to marry in 1941. However, her enforced migration to my father's involuntary place of work in Ware put a stop to her teaching, also given the marriage bar. Moreover, on marriage to someone who had not yet been naturalised she lost her British citizenship. She was able to regain it when my father became a British citizen just before the birth of her first daughter in 1942. By this time my father had found another position back in the north of England, this time east of the Pennines in the West Riding of Yorkshire.

It has been argued that each generation is relatively unique and the experiences of those living through the war would be different from those of subsequent generations. What has happened, as we shall see, is that these common and mutual experiences have had a collective rather than merely personal and individual influence, hastening the changes that began to occur in the aftermath of the second world war and with the national/international desire for economic growth. I, in common with those born over the next few years at the end of the war was indeed part of the *baby-boom*, known especially to players of Trivial Pursuit as 'the baby-boomers', and our experiences may also be said to be relatively unique. However, we have come to be seen as the first of succeeding generations to be privileged and challenged to create and recreate the conditions for our own family and working lives. It is from this generation that my account begins.

We remain influenced by our own experiences of family life. For instance, my mother, as someone steeped in education, was an enormous influence as many middle-class mothers of her generation must have been. An intellectual and firm believer in bookish approaches to life and, especially child-rearing, according to Truby King, I am indelibly marked with this early upbringing. Contrary to popular rhetoric today, I believe that several generations of middle-class families have sought to develop skills and learning in parenting from books and other forms of what are now considered to be 'parent education'. This approach is a new experience only to the extent that it is now recommended for other groups and classes in society. The same may be the case for parental involvement in education at home or at school. My mother read to us throughout our childhood, including reading Enid Blyton whilst we ate our lunches at home, coming back from primary school and returning for the afternoon sessions. She also involved herself in the PTA and, when we were at the grammar school, in a parents' reading group. She was an example of what Puttnam called civic engagement leading to 'social capital' (Puttman, 2000). She took up her career again as a 'married woman returner' in the late 1950s. However, at this point she saw herself as returning to work to earn 'pin money' and contribute for family extras rather than an equal share in the household finances. She continued to teach and act as a tutor until well into her retirement. She retained a strong sense of the traditional family and was resistant to wider changes for herself or her children. For instance, she never considered a career on a par with her husband, also university-educated. Both my parents, being Jewish, were fully committed to education, including higher education, for their daughters, and I never considered not going to university. In other words, my expectations were what Du Bois-Reymond (1998) called a 'normal biography'. My mother also did not reflect upon the wider transformations that have been wrought, and was less forced than her mother and mother-in-law to adjust to enforced migrations on a global scale. Rather she had to adjust to internal migrations, common to many married women, married to their husband's job but not necessarily 'the job' as Finch put it so well (Finch, 1983).

Changing contexts of family lives

Perhaps most importantly from the point of view of families and women's position with respect to them, a key influence over the period since the second world war has been changing labour markets, and women's gradual but more formal involvement in a labour market. Thus women's lives have been changed irrevocably both within and outside families and in the wider public arena and labour markets. These changes have also had an impact upon education and social life such that women have begun to recognise these changes and work together to identify and challenge them. Therefore the women's movement, or second wave feminism as it has become known, has been a part and parcel of these developments and changes, influencing our understandings, interpretations, actions and experiences. Inevitably of course feminists have become an influential part of the sociological endeavour, developing a particular and crucial perspective on our understandings of these wider social economic and political changes. Feminist pedagogy in particular has been influential in developing materials for teaching and learning.

In other words, I argue that the social and educational transformations since the Second World War can only be understood as part of the particular changes in our lives. The changes are embedded inextricably in our lives and can only be understood through our particular lenses. We, as feminists, as social actors, as political beings, are inevitably bound up with the changes and cannot distance ourselves from them. Differently from our mothers and grandmothers, we have played a part in trying to steer the changes in ways that largely would have been unthinkable, except for the very privileged few. These shifts are part of what has become known as reflexivity, along with the interpretation of such changes as leading to post-modernity. The whole of my academic life or rather career has been devoted to studying aspects of family life and their associations with or links to education broadly viewed. Originally I was interested in compulsory schooling, but increasing reflecting a feminist perspective, higher education and life in the academy has captured my interest. Much of the initial interest stems from my parents' commitments to education and yet their expressed wish that my sisters and I would not follow my mother into being a schoolteacher but that we would develop broader interests.' My daughter, the teacher' was not an epithet that my parents readily wanted since that had been the one proudly used for my mother. This chimes in with a most illuminating study of Jewish teachers in the New York city schools (Markowitz, 1993). As it so happens we have all, in our different ways, become teachers and fascinated by the relations between education and families. Perhaps my abiding interest in pursuing first my and then my children's life course stems from the ways in which Jewish family life, whether secular or religious, is regulated by rituals associated with both the annual life events and the life course overall.

Over my academic life sociology has also changed, just as I and other members of my generation have changed and become part of the processes of transformation. The sociology of the family and of family life is therefore now an integral part of sociology whereas thirty years or so ago it was marginal to the mainstream. This is evident from the vast array of books on aspects of these themes and it also includes a feminist perspective as noted above (Morgan, 1996; Bernardes, 1997; Allan, 1999). Indeed as an undergraduate in the 1960s we were not taught a course specifically on the family, but learnt about it more through sociological theory and a course on the social structure of modern Britain. Inevitably for the time, this latter course was taught by the only woman member of staff in the department of sociology (Griselda Rowntree). Her course was what might now be considered more about social policy than sociology. It was rooted in the British tradition of empirical approaches, whereas the bulk of our courses took, as the core, sociological theory as it was developing in the USA, with a sustained critique from a British left wing perspective. For example, Alan Dawe was work-ing on his now famous classic *Two Sociologies* (1970) when we were under-graduates and, as students and tutees of his, we were privileged to be a part of his developing discussions on this new Marxist perspective. His was mainly an attempt to criticise American structural-functionalism, as developed by Talcott Parsons, and to reinsert a theory of social action from a Marxist perspective. Although Parsons' structural-functionalism included a theoretical approach to the family this was not deemed to be of central and crucial importance in the critique. The family was taken to be unproblematic by both sociological theorists and their detractors, all operating within a gender-blind and what would, sub-sequently, be considered patriarchal mould. There were other courses that were equally implicitly sexist, racist and ethnocentric, where 'sociology of the family' was alluded to. They were a course on demography referring largely to the Indian subcontinent; a course on Africa and various African 'tribes' and their cultures, from an anthropological point of view and a social psychology course on cross-cultural developments.

Nowadays courses in sociology are very different, having been subject to waves of development and as part of the wider changing contexts and the expansions of educational opportunities. In particular, the move from elite to mass higher edu-cation, as at least one part of these processes, has been accompanied by moves towards forms of quality assurance and control, including processes and pro-cedures of quality assessments and specific criteria for quality assurance, includ-ing forms of self-assessment. These processes of self-assessment mirror the processes of reflexivity and re-considerations of self-identity which have played their crucial part in the global social transformations that have been taking place. They have meant that sociology – and sociology of education as a particu-lar aspect – as a form of learning and research in Britain has been subject to assessment and evaluation, particularly through Teaching Quality Assessment and the various Research Assessment exercises. Now sociology is diverse and values reflexivity, critical of traditional structures and processes; feminist methodologies are at the forefront of such developments. Sociology has also been transformed from within as well as from without – the wider changing socioeconomic and political context. Sociologists have been involved in developing the theories and methodologies to understand and interpret the transformations. Particularly critical here has been the role and involvement of feminist sociologists. Their theoretical and methodological developments on family, sex and gender, will be crucial to this narrative or life history of sociology from a family life perspective.

The content and structure of the book

This book is therefore unusual as a text, exploring the transformations and changes from both a methodological and theoretical point of view, since it is an original attempt to explore the changes from a feminist perspective that draws on academic theorising in sociology and related disciplines or of schools of thought. Understandings from the point of view of the influences of the transformations on women's lives and their relationships to the family or, more properly, families, which are themselves becoming diverse and distinctive will be the central focus. I consider issues in which women's lives have been especially important and feminist analyses particularly revealing; especially as now presented within the academy.

As mentioned earlier, I initially considered a developmental approach from infancy through to old age, but then abandoned that as I found it constraining and descriptive. However, increasingly this kind of approach has been taken up from a more psychoanalytic perspective and not only has it influenced the material to be reviewed but also the methodological approach, including that of reflexivity and changing social identities. Notions of auto/biography also infused methodological approaches; and indeed, thinking about our biographies is another way of thinking about our families and the influences on our lives and reflecting upon our identities. Some feminists from both within and outside sociology, but within the social sciences, are themselves either fascinated by, or steeped in, psychoanalytic approaches. This book will draw upon these and the evidence that they have to offer. It will also review the work of psychoanalysts who work on issues to do with the family and gender identities, paying particular attention to material around the social and gendered construction of parenthood and childhood and how these may be transformed by wider social and political processes. Most intriguingly most texts on the sociology of the family pay little attention to early gender identities and formation through early childhood and child-care or education. Similarly there is a noticeable lack of interest in the intersections between families and education and/or work in studies in the sociology of family life. Nor has there been much attention to the more didactic and policy-oriented perspectives. This book also tries to redress that lacuna.

I explore the ways in which the sociology of family life has itself developed and taken up particular urgent concerns at certain junctures in terms of phases of liberal political ideologies. I consider the ways in which the wider social and political contexts have influenced both methodological and substantive approaches for feminists studying family. I also consider the ways in which this has been a two-way process, with successive generations having some influence on the ways in which we understand and influence these changes. I weave my own intellectual biography into this, as a way of structuring my interests in family, education, feminist sociology and the understandings of family life that I 'choose' to present. In other words, I aim to present a self-assessment or a reflection on my intellectual life history, situating myself in the various social and political transformations that have taken place over the period of my life course to date. I consider these various methodological approaches in more detail to contextualize my life history and review developments in feminist research methodologies from ethnographic and qualitative methods to a search for under-standing voices, narratives and life histories, to auto/biographies, memoirs and their situated contexts. I look to the key concerns about reflexivity and the refashioning of social and gendered identities through these issues and the ways in which the context influences these notions. Family memoirs show how ideas about self-identity and reflexivity are now part of a more popular and general genre.

The question of social contexts, political changes and global transformations on families and family life from a more general sociological perspective is central to this account. I argue that there have been three phases of political and policy development, which influence, and are influenced by, these changes and I will interweave these with my own intellectual biography. These three phases of liberalism, from social to economic to neo-liberalism, provide a broad framework for my analysis of the shifts and changes in theories and methodologies of under-standing within the academy. The first is social liberalism, linked to social democracy and socialism in the post-war period which allowed for the emer-gence of political and social movements for liberation and change in countries of the western world, most particularly in western Europe, north America and sub-sequently taken up in Australasia. These occurred despite the parallel develop-ments in what became known as the cold war, and the political contestations between the communist (and socialist) countries of Eastern Europe and China and the western countries. From my personal perspective this wave can best be dated from the early 1960s in both Britain and the USA. As I mentioned earlier, Kennedy's assassination on November 22nd 1963 provides a useful point of departure for considering the ways in which social democracy and social liberal-ism framed the political ideas and movements of my generation of young women. My narrative concentrates on these social/socialist movements in Britain and the USA, but paying attention to some developments especially in

France. I am particularly interested in giving consideration to how the concepts and ideas of social and sexual liberation came to permeate the academy despite the struggles that had to be engaged during the 1970s.

The second phase is that of the re-emergence of the political domination of neo-conservatism and the New Right with a focus on economic liberalism. This involved the inscription of markets and the privatisation of public services in the western world. There is no one date by which to signal this shift, except that in public discourse it may be marked by Thatcher's election to power in Britain in May 1979 and Reagan's election as President of the USA in November 1980. By the start of this phase in the late 1970s/early 1980s we had introduced feminist concepts and theories into the academy, in Britain, the USA, parts of Europe, Canada and Australia. Although they remained contested and challenged, they were no longer excluded from consideration as part of the curriculum and peda-gogy of the academy. Indeed, these complex political transformations in the 1980s led to more complex understandings and theories being developed within the academy, both in terms of critical reflections and analyses of the broader political and policy contexts. Feminist theories and methodologies became far more sophisticated endeavours and were intertwined in complex ways with social, socialist and emergent cultural and linguistic theories. Balancing these different approaches and giving them all due consideration was never an easy process. Some of us clung rather rigidly to traditional approaches, especially those rationalist and socialist or Marxist perspectives with which we were rather more familiar, and increasingly known as critical realism (Walby 2001). The backlash against our perspectives and theories developed apace both within the public sphere and that of the academy (Faludi, 1991; 1999).

The third phase is that which Nancy Fraser (1997) called 'the post-socialist con-dition', the period after 1989 when the communist countries of the east began to break up, the resurgence of neo-liberalism affecting our theories and under-standings of social liberalism and economic change and how to influence them. These broader social and economic transformations led to intense scrutiny with-in the academy of collective and individual understandings and the proliferation of reflexive and varied theories and post-structural accounts. At one and the same time these international and global political and economic transformations have led to far more cultural, economic and social diversity and more discursive attempts to interpret and understand them. Yet on the other hand, they have also led to ways of understanding and interpretation that discount the dominance of political theories and structures and attempt to get at the nuances of political dis-courses and the influences on our personal lives. Indeed, one of the hallmarks of this phase of neo-liberalism can be said to be the re-inscription of notions of personal responsibility in public and in all of our lives. Claims about these per-spectives, associated with non-feminist approaches, have become relatively problematic to deal with, particularly the emergent notions of communitarian-ism and social networks or social capital. In other words, these ideas about the personal and political have come to dominate both political and public policy debates and our more academic and nuanced understandings of how to study them. Again there is no one date to signal these complex transformations in theories, concepts and political ideas in relation to the broader political shifts. As I have noted above, Margaret Thatcher's resignation as British prime minister on November 22nd 1990 signals one notion of that break, except that she was succeeded by a conservative administration. Similarly in the USA there was no radical break with neo-conservatism at one juncture. Indeed, one of the charac-teristics of this period is the ways in which traditional social democratic and liberal ideas have intertwined with neo-conservative ideas, forming what is often now called 'neo-liberalism'. In 1979 Hall and Jacques referred to the shifts from social democracy to conservatism as 'the great moving right show'. There was no turn back to social democracy a decade or more later but rather this latter period has been characterised by Giddens (1997; 1998) as the politics of 'the third way'. This both signals the greater accommodation of sociological ideas and socio-logists in public policy debates and the integration of these political analyses in the academy.

The organisation of the book is as follows. Chapters Two and Three are about the phase of social liberalism from 1963 to 1979, political and policy changes, my own personal and political involvement and I reflect upon how women of my generation took up feminist ideas and began to try to use them in the academy. In Chapter Two, I reflect upon the notion of 'the personal is political' drawn from the women's movement and socialist and liberal politics. I consider both textual analyses and political events such as the first women's liberation conference and recent reflections upon it, thirty years on. I also reflect upon the considerable social changes from the 1960s to the late 1990s through popular sociological analyses. In Chapter Three, I reflect upon my initial involvement in early types of feminism, our attempts to introduce ideas about women's studies and feminism and their initial contestation in the academy. I also review how our feminist theories developed in relation to socialist and sociological studies of state policies, family, work and education, distinguishing these socialist-feminist perspectives from radical and liberal feminism.

Chapters Four and Five are about the second phase of economic liberalism from 1979/80 to 1990. The focus is on transformations in the wider political contexts to neo-conservatism and the New Right internationally, the contradictory pro-cesses of feminist engagement in both the economy and the academy and how they influenced our emerging theories about family lives. In Chapter Four, I reflect upon how my personal circumstances in Bristol, the USA and Canada, altered my intellectual and academic interests towards motherhood, childcare and comparative policy analyses. I also interweave how feminist theories became incorporated into academia and were no longer as heavily contested. Similarly in Chapter Five, I reflect upon my move to become a 'femocrat' or 'feminist manager' in an expanding higher education context influenced the studies that I found critically important. Notions of social class, ethnicity and gender influenced our theories and gender analysis of family policies and practices rather than studies of sexual divisions became paramount.

Chapters Six and Seven are about the third phase of neo-liberalism – 1990 to 2000 – and political transformations influencing more complex social and feminist theories and analyses. These drew variously on post-structuralism, psychoanalysis, critical philosophy and notions of risk and reflexivity, drawn from feminist theories but not always acknowledged. Feminist accounts were interwoven with personal and political biographies in far more complex and diverse ways than in the past. Feminist theories merged, coalesced and diverged from social, political, psychological and psychoanalytic theories in complex and intriguing combinations. Successive generations of women and men having entered the academy had a greater purchase on a diversity and range of theories about aspects of family lives. In Chapter Six I reflect upon how political changes shifted the terrain of policy debates and complex emergent theories about identities, subjectivities, risks in personal and family life. I consider how my own research linked with my changing personal and academic circumstances and the changing and reflexive accounts about studies of mothers and children, and the emergent theories about the sociology of childhood in relation to sociology of family lives. In Chapter Seven I reflect upon how the changing and successive generations of feminists in the academy reflect upon and consider their family lives and the lives of other women entering the academy or different forms of education. I shall also look at the effect notions drawn from post-structuralism and reflexive accounts have had on transforming the academy. The curriculum of subjects in higher education offered a variety of approaches to our understandings of our lives in and out of families and in relation to the construction of our social and sexual identities. Finally I also look at how notions of personal responsibility have infused policy developments, and draw from and influence changing social theories and how public political figures are the very embodiment of these notions.

In the concluding chapter I review the complex ways in which transformations in the changing social context have influenced and been influenced by emergent feminist theories. I also review changing political contexts, including evidence of the entry of women, including married women and mothers, into public and political life and the consequent shift from 'the personal is political' to 'the political is personal'. In the public sphere and in the media, details of family intimacies of major public figures are now made public and personalised in ways in which they were not a generation ago. This chapter explores the ways in which these changing contexts have influenced our approaches, analyses and pedagogies, showing the importance of interweaving our own personal and subjective accounts and interpretations within the broader changing social contexts and transformations. A gendered and feminist analysis of both children's perspectives and those of adults, whether mothers, fathers, or others will also be addressed as will be considerations of ethnic and cultural diversity, illustrating the 'maturity' and yet rich diversity of post-structural approaches to the sociology of family lives. These lead to diverse and yet personal accounts of public and personal matters, transforming our notions of the personal is political to demonstrating just how the political is also infused with the personal, and how our understandings and pedagogies take account of subjectivities and critical reflections on our understandings. A critical feminist theoretical engagement with political activities, taking a postmodernist stance, resurfaced in the aftermath of 9/11 with the prospect of war rather than peace.

Notes

1. In Israel at the Hebrew University (May 1999), at the Roehampton Institute, Surrey University in London, (June 1999) at OISE in the University of Toronto, Canada, (October 1999) at Cheltenham and Gloucester College of Higher Education (December 1999), Aston University (February 2000) and at Keele University (March 2000).
2. In the teaching I selected materials from research on families, mothers and education such as that by Dorothy Smith (1987, 1993, 1998) and with Alison Griffith (1990, 1997, 1998) to compare and contrast with my own (David, 1993, 1998; David *et al*, 1993, 1994, 1997, 1998), that of Lareau (1989) and Luttrell (1998). I also used post-structural approaches to family, gender and education such as that of Walkerdine (1997) in contrast to Brown (1998); and Kenway and Willis (1997). I had also wanted to focus on more on auto/biography as a feminist methodology (Stanley, 1992) as well as substantive material (Stanley, ed 1997).
3. Similar stories to mine can be found in *Fathers Accounts by Daughters* edited by Ursula Owen (1986) and the Jewish Feminist Collective's *Generations of Memories* (1988).
4. Reference to the theory of cosmopolitan not local can be found in Popkewitz (2001).
5. Jean Medawar and David Pyke 2001 *Hitler's Gift: scientists who fled Nazi Germany* discuss similar people to my father in their account of scientists who left Germany.
6. Leigh, 'one of Britain's finest film directors also joined Habonim in the 1950s before 'Zionist' became a dirty word'. Jewish Chronicle March 24th 2000: 41 and *The Guardian*.

CHAPTER TWO

'The Personal is Political'

Political contexts and challenges of second wave feminism

Introduction

In this chapter I reflect upon how feminists developed feminist political activities and theorised sexual relations in the post-war period in the context of social democracy in Britain and France and social liberalism in the USA. I consider how the theories that were adopted related to political activities as we, as the first generation of second wave feminists, slowly began to develop 'academic' courses, initially outside the academy, and especially in relation to changing wider social/political/economic contexts. I focus on the origins of feminist concerns with aspects of the family, mainly marriage and children/motherhood and the ways in which these issues gradually developed into an intellectual and academic endeavour. I also explore how I came to develop my interests in feminism, and the ways in which feminists began to reflect upon the issues. Since the 1960s there have been many reflections on these early developments, too many to summarise here, and I shall only consider those that related to the changing policy context and the developing theories of the family. The question is how we pick things out for such a biography/life history/memoir but this one is critically about 'my' generation of young women and especially in relation to issues of sex, marriage and family. It was only later, as the first generation of second wave feminists began to mature, or grow older, that questions about relations to our older mothers and to our children as mothers began to concern feminists.

The 1960s framed these liberal-social democratic developments and social movements, such that we were often seen as 'Kennedy's children' or part of the radical movements of Britain associated with the Beatles. As noted in Chapter One, Kennedy's assassination at the end of 1963 is often associated with the beginnings of the emergence of liberal and social democratic movements in North America. Around the same time in Britain and other countries of Europe social movements for liberation and emancipation were beginning to emerge

from the post-war generations of young people. Thus 1968 is often depicted as a
key moment for these international social movements since it is associated with
student unrest in France, Britain, the USA, and eral other countries. Although
there had been the glimmerings of such developments before, the early writings
of women's liberation linked to social and socialist movements can best be associated with these political developments. They also linked with critiques of both
domestic social and welfare policies in those key countries and international
policies, particularly the ongoing American war in Vietnam. There was a curious
disjuncture between social liberalism in the USA, the social democracies of
France and Britain and their foreign and international militaristic policies. In all
these advanced industrial societies it was during the 1960s that a social welfare
and liberal agenda began to develop, although at a different pace and in relation
to different social issues in each country.

In Britain, under Labour governments from 1964 to 1970, there were various
developments in social welfare policies that were of some importance in relation
to women's welfare. Key changes were the Abortion Act of 1967, introduced by a
Liberal (not Labour) Member of Parliament, and the development of policies for
equal opportunities in work, employment and public services, passed as the
Equal Pay Act 1970 by the Labour government. There were other modest shifts
in social services and social security in relation to women in families, as wives and
mothers. These built upon the kinds of social and educational changes set in
train by the introduction of the welfare state in the aftermath of the Second
World War (Arnot, David and Weiner, 1999). In France, Germany, Sweden and
the USA, there were parallel developments and glimmerings of a more liberal
approach to some women's involvement in public life, rather than their confinement to the privacy of the family, caring for children. It was in this
context of social liberalism that the women's movement, initially as political
campaigning, developed.

The original credo 'the personal is political' of second wave feminism was of
crucial significance since it transformed personal family matters into power relations and broader political, rather than individual, issues. The changes that
feminists originally began to campaign for were part of a much wider social
movement for sexual liberation and social transformation and became an even
more embedded part of the processes of social change, such that it has become
increasingly difficult to disentangle origins and effects. There are different
strands of the story. One strand is the move from a political campaign into a
more complex set of ideas, theories and notions that gradually became part of
social and cultural processes, academic understandings and feminist pedagogies.
They have gradually been incorporated and become acceptable in the academy,
although, of course, not without major controversy and challenge. At the same
time these notions have also begun to gain credence and even acceptance in the

political sphere. The term 'personal is political' has gradually assumed larger political implications and has slowly begun to percolate down into the political system. Now the 'turn' is towards feminist credo being turned upside down and 'the political being personal' (see Butler and Scott, 1992; Morgan, 1998; Giddens, 1998 in his Reith lectures).

My interest in sociology and socialist politics led me down particular avenues, and to a growing fascination with the politics of the family. Most importantly, with the benefit of hindsight, I was influenced by being part of the first post-war generation to come of age in the 1960s. In recent times, it has become an important challenge to think back to how these ideas were formed and framed in relation to family, education and politics. Carolyn Steedman's (1986) study was part of a growing genre of memoirs, reflections and attempts at interpretations of a personal kind. Steedman's work was especially important as it was about the influences in and of childhood, not about the role of intellectual auto/biography, to use the phrase as did Liz Stanley (1992). However, Stanley used Steedman's book as an exemplar of this kind of reflexive writing, considering biography and autobiography as two sides of the coin.

This kind of writing of intellectual biography from a feminist perspective has now become both fashionable and respectable. Nancy Hartstock, reproducing and republishing her key critical essays over a twenty-five year period, also edited them in an autobiographical vein entitled *The Feminist Standpoint Revisited and other essays* (1998). She opened with the comment:

> As I reflect upon these essays, which span a period of twenty years, I am struck with the extent to which they are autobiographical in that they respond to issues I found urgent at different times. In this regard, my work is no different than that of other political theorists: Every social context poses questions for those who inhabit it, construct it, and are in turn constructed by it . . . These essays were written in the context of a series of feminist communities concerned with both reading and writing about issues such as these and using what we were learning to bring about change – in fact, massive social change . . . As a result, I see feminist theory as a collective political practice . . . For example, as feminist theory moved solidly into the academy, questions rooted in academic disciplines became more prominent. (Hartsock, 1998: 1)

I explore the kinds of concerns that I, like Nancy Hartsock, along with other feminists, found urgent at various junctures, locating my collective political practice in relation to both political and academic developments. I construct a narrative about how feminists viewed and analysed the family from the 1960s as well as how they lived it. I insert some of my intellectual development from the kinds of work with which I initially engaged and, from the 1970s, the essays and books that I began to write. I reflect upon the kinds of issues that I amongst others considered 'urgent' at particular junctures. Back in the 1960s, formulating, but not writing, about feminist ideas, theories and critiques of the family were the paramount activity. In those times, there were but a few feminists who were writing theories or even formulating key concepts, and only fragments towards an analysis or understandings. These ephemeral notes and papers gradually began to accumulate. Strands and writings of the early women's movement are now far too numerous just to cite; it is more important to cite how it touched our thinking at various moments. Autobiography is about family and family influences on one's developing social and political identity. It is precisely this conjuncture between the personal and political that has made the campaigns for massive social change so challenging. How this conjuncture has been transformed is itself a fascinating question.

For the post-war generation who became students in the 1960s, political activity was important as a part of our lives as young adults. It could be argued that political involvement was the stamp of my generation of students, in ways completely different from current generations of students. Searching for meaning amongst various political and social movements was a significant process, although there were a number of different, often conflicting, left political groups within the broader movement for social change. Nevertheless, another significant hallmark was the extent to which most of the groupings were to the left, and were about the growing politics of liberation. Although the term 'globalisation' has only recently entered popular and political discourse as a concept about particular kinds of immediate political and economic domination from the west, an instance of how it was foreshadowed may be the world-wide student movement for social change, commenced in the late 1960s. In Paris, across the United States and in London in 1968 students began to stir and demand change.[1]

However, feminism, or what then became known as women's liberation, was not the first of the social and student movements to capture imaginations of our post-war generation. Early developments of left and liberationist politics developed, for instance the anti-war movement, especially in the USA opposed to the Vietnam War, and other peace movements, such as Students for a Democratic Society (SDS). Sheila Rowbotham's (2000) – *Promise of A Dream* – reflections on the 1960s are about her initial involvement as an undergraduate in socialist politics and her subsequent activities in left-wing politics in London. Indeed she barely mentions her formative role in the women's movement in this autobiographical account of the 1960s. But, equally, these movements were about the role of American capitalism and imperialism. Contradictory tendencies began to emerge with, for instance, critiques of American imperialism in the Middle East, including of Zionism, and yet some support for the left movements in Israel, including socialist Zionism and particularly the kibbutz movement as a form of alternative to the traditional nuclear family. Similarly, there were movements against traditional health practices, and the developments of the anti-psychiatry movement. In Britain, Laing's (1963) critiques of psychiatry and the role of the family in mental illness was one such strand. Other forms of critique and developments of psychotherapy were also gaining ground.

A personal and political odyssey

My own intellectual and professional journey has been rather circuitous, and feminist activities have not always been in the foreground of either my political or academic work. In reflecting upon this I am now acutely aware of how constrained by political and social circumstances and ideological constructions we all have been, whilst our intellectual ideas may have developed apace. Moreover, beginning to write about feminism as part of my academic activities was a long and slow process although teaching as a feminist was an earlier and easier one. Feminist ideas have often had to be only part of my personal and political rather than professional life, except that such ideas have influenced the ways in which material was chosen in the academic context. Throughout the late sixties and early 1970s, I struggled to find my own voice and place as a social scientist. I spent six years as a researcher (assistant and 'officer') in three different schools of the University of London. First I arrived in London, fresh as a graduate in sociology from Leeds University to take up a post as a statistical research assistant at the postgraduate Institute of Psychiatry. This post on a comparative Anglo-American study of mental illness was chosen more for the opportunity to live in London than its intrinsic value, except that I only wanted to pursue social scientific research rather than become involved in the ostensible world of competitive capitalism. We had been well schooled at Leeds to be critical of capitalism in its public and business face. No criticisms were then offered of the competitiveness of education and especially not within the academy. My desire then was to be in London, in a metropolitan and cosmopolitan world, with a substantial Jewish community. Meeting Mr Right was also part of my personal agenda whilst my 'career' was ill formulated. I was not fully convinced that I would spend most of my adult life in employment, since at that time, social expectations of women marrying and having a family, returning to work possibly after a career break, were still dominant. However, I was also ambivalent about that and as a young woman wanted to explore various avenues and possible adventures. I was employed on an international project funded by the World Health Organisation (WHO) to conduct a comparative study of mental illness in New York and London, as indicators of American and British differences. (It was subsequently published as Cooper, Kendall and Sartorius (1972) *Psychiatric Diagnosis in New York and London*.) Thus I began to develop an interest in comparative material, often culled from the American literature. Gender differences in mental illness and the role of the family in mental illness began to emerge from the study and to capture my interest, but the overall project did not challenge traditional psychiatric ideas which remained patriarchal and yet gender-blind (a term not yet then coined).

I found it relatively easy to move positions during my six years in London, inter-spersed as it also was with a long spell as a volunteer in Israel immediately after the Six Day war in the summer of 1967. This was the summer of the increasingly loud cacophony of voices of student unrest across northern Europe and the USA. Whilst in Israel I seriously considered becoming a graduate student in sociology at the Hebrew University, having spent some of the time there engaged as an interviewer upon a research project conducted by the Israel Institute for Social Research about American women settlers to Israel. Intriguingly, and with the benefit of hindsight, I recall how many of them told me of their marriages, often of convenience, to aid the process of settlement. I found myself, however, ambivalent about spending what would have amounted to three years study on an MA and excused this by being too afraid to leave home fully at that juncture. Instead I returned to London and found myself a new post as a research assistant at the London School of Economics (LSE). I left the intriguingly bizarre if not 'mad' world of psychiatry, where I had been learning about conflicting theories and approaches to mental illness, including early views of gender and family differences.

The research with which I engaged in the Department of Social Administration at LSE also had embryonic features of a critical engagement with subsequent feminist ideas. It was a study of gambling funded by the Churches Council on Gambling. The ways in which the study was finally conceived and constructed was about how 'ordinary families' engaged with leisure and the possible role of gambling within that. The three male researchers with whom I worked were all young family men and concerned about the care and upbringing of young children. Thus we found ourselves considering family lives of young couples with young children rather more than other kinds of family lives and with an intriguing and somewhat naïve focus on fatherhood. It was only about a decade later that I became aware of this particular male and budding patriarchal bias and yet personal or subjective standpoint to the study, as we eventually wrote up the research material, somewhat at a distance from previous predilections (Downes *et al*, 1976).

I entered a new world of student and university politics at the LSE, which offered a range of socialist and trade union activities, and the glimmerings of some early women's liberation. In particular our concerns focused on employment opportunities and power relations in the workplace, including the academic workplace. We did not, however, focus specifically on employment opportunities for women, although many of those involved were relatively young graduate women. Throughout that time, we campaigned in various groups for social and economic changes in our lives, including at LSE itself. In the summer of 1968 there were yet more battles within LSE, as part of the much wider student movement. During this time I became intrigued and later involved in the burgeoning women's liberation movement. But this initial involvement in the women's movement was very much in my spare time rather than as part of my 'work' whether the research studies or the extra-mural teaching on sociology that I was offered as part of my extra-curricular activities at LSE. Indeed, this was the case for our generation, since few jobs offered or allowed for the expression of our politics: indeed, it is still difficult in Britain to find evidence of 'femocracy' (Yeatman, 1990); that is, posts that allow for the explicit expression of political values of feminism in their content. I had remained in close contact with friends made whilst I was an undergraduate and we began to share and swap ideas about reading, including the growing new genre of women's literature – fiction and non-fiction. I read avidly. This kind of political education became very important to what could be called 'the feminist project' which was also being influenced by ideas drawing on different types of psychology, largely the more psycho-dynamic. Using these ideas we began to consider alternative ways of living to the traditional family and forms of work. Simone de Beauvoir became an especial favourite, particularly her several volumes of autobiography, starting with *Memoirs of a Dutiful Daughter*, followed by *Prime of Life* and *Force of Circumstance*. *The Second Sex*, Beauvoir's critically acclaimed text about women's subordination, and Betty Friedan's (1963) *The Feminine Mystique* were part of our collective readings and literature. Reflecting on these early readings and the uses to which we put them then and subsequently is both interesting and important to our understandings of the specific developments of feminist theories and their uses as ways of living. Intriguingly, the late Jill Forbes made a crucial point about de Beauvoir's memoirs being written quite late in life as a 'construction' of her earlier life, rather than as a contemporaneous memory. This is similar to the process that many feminists, myself included, are now engaged upon.

Critical feminist reflections on early feminist writings

Ann Curthoys addressed the influence of early feminist writings on the feminist project over the last thirty years in an exciting autobiographical essay from Australia to celebrate the millennium: 'Twentieth century feminism was many things: a set of ideas, a political and social movement, a cultural renaissance. It was a force for change and a guide for living . . .' (2000: 3). Her essay is emblematic of all the changing ways of thinking and writing in the academy and how the wider social context influenced our ways of living inside and outside families. She expressed what might be collective reflections: 'Now, at the turn of the century, after thirty years of involvement in feminism in all these aspects, I

ponder the meaning and future of feminism that has helped to shape my life'
(2000: 3). Her essay is also important for her re-reading of Beauvoir and her
influence on feminist theories. She argued that, although *The Second Sex* was
vitally important theoretically, it was Beauvoir's autobiographies and novels that
provided more immediacy to the project of changing family lives and how
women tried to refashion their identities in relation to men and in the rejection of
conventional marriage and children. Her personal views resonate with my feelings about Beauvoir:

> As a young woman in Australia in the 1960s and 1970s, de Beauvoir's *The Second
> Sex* meant very little to me, while the autobiographies, and indeed, some of the
> novels, meant everything. Where *The Second Sex* had intimated that a significant
> aspect of human liberation lay in women reclaiming their subjectivity, it was the
> autobiographies which suggested and demonstrated how this might be done . . . In
> them, the details of a life – as an intellectual, a writer and a woman – were spelt out
> in painstaking and fascinating detail. For us, the young women in the 1960s who
> became the Women's Liberationists of the 1970s, her life was truly exemplary, to
> be pondered and explored for clues as to how we might live differently from our
> parents' generation and from most of society around us. She demonstrated to us an
> art of living . . . the autobiographies helped lay the groundwork for second-wave
> feminism. (Curthoys, 2000: 4)

Curthoys reminisced about the books, how differently she read them with the
benefit of hindsight and how Beauvoir's life has been written by various biographers, the similarities and contrasts with her own reading, and how many of
the accounts were perhaps fictionalised memories. She also made the methodological point about the difficulties of providing fully accurate details of a
life rather than evoking the authentic feelings of lived experiences. Curthoys
surveyed the kinds of literature and novels that her generation read from childhood through to young adulthood.

> Once we reached our twenties, new books took the place of [these] beloved teenage
> novels. In different ways these texts identified and articulated middle-class
> women's rising discontent. We saw our own nightmares in Betty Friedan's evoca-
> tion of American suburbia in *The Feminine Mystique* and Hannah Gavron's exami-
> nation of the loss of freedom entailed in marriage and motherhood in modern
> Britain in *The Captive Wife* (Curthoys, 1998). De Beauvoir's *The Second Sex* pro-
> vided a sweeping interdisciplinary analysis of women's status as secondary . . . and
> many women have since written . . . about the devastating impact the book had on
> them when they first read it. (Friedan, 1985; Wenzel, 1986; Forster and Sutton,
> 1989) (Curthoys, 2000: 12)

Curthoys showed how her own reading accorded with a whole generation of
women across countries and continents and how historically specific it was,
although not mentioning how racially and socially homogeneous it was:

. . . the autobiographies appear to be not nearly so well read today. In Australia they seem to be virtually unknown to young women. This is not surprising. I don't think books such as *The Prime of Life* . . . can have the same meaning now . . . for so much has changed. What was new and scarcely imaginable then is being lived every day in all its messy detail by a multitude of women. The successes of the women's movement have, perhaps, made these texts obsolete . . . In this context of epochal *ennui*, a re-reading of de Beauvoir with a more sympathetic eye may suggest some new lines of enquiry. With her emphasis on women's complicity in their own fate and history, even while recognising the force of sexual inequality, she returns us . . . to problems of individual responsibility and historical agency . . . (Curthoys, 2000: 15)

Curthoys demonstrated in her own autobiographical narrative how several early feminist writers influenced, through their writings, the social changes that began to occur and how women in particular sought to change their lives in similar ways to each other. But she does not demonstrate precisely how these changes occurred except by assertion and by acknowledging how social and familial changes have influenced the next generations of women. In the final analysis she was most interested in considering how these ideas might contribute to new theoretical insights for the twenty-first century. What Curthoys also mentioned was the complex ways in which women, influenced by feminist writings, sought to rethink their lives. Many feminists were concerned about creating new lives in relation to children as much as to men. At the same time others tried to find new ways of living in relation to each other. Their theories developed from a politics into more academically articulated theories. For instance there were also early developments in lesbian politics as part of what was then known as radical feminism.

To return to my own narrative story, groups were beginning to emerge from the more psychotherapeutic consciousness-raising to the more academic or intellectual. We also started giving and attending evening courses and classes. The two texts by de Beauvoir and Friedan were on the reading lists of an evening course on *Psychoanalysis and Women* that I attended at this point, taught by a former student friend. As part of my own extra-mural teaching for London University's Diploma in Sociology I taught a course *The Social Structure of Modern Britain* for four years in which issues about changing family structures were a vital element. Most of the material prescribed for the course was traditional sociological books on family structures and processes, and anthropological work such as that by Edmund Leach (1967), rather than any of this more critically engaged new work. A key text, however, was associated with the ideas of newly forming women's liberation, namely Hannah Gavron's (1968) *The Captive Wife*. This account of the lives of young and newly married women as housewives and mothers was particularly poignant as Gavron died shortly after publication. Literature on women in the family and work was included; for instance Alva Myrdal and Viola

Klein's (1956) *Women's Two Roles*. Stina Lyon, using the methods of biography and sociological narrative, reflected on this in trying to reach a broader understanding of the early developments in feminist thought through the life of Alva Myrdal. She attempted a biographical reconstruction of Myrdal's life and reached far more pessimistic conclusions than Curthoys by contrasting a critique of the life of Myrdal, with that of Simone de Beauvoir. Lyon argued that:

> . . . amongst sociologists [Alva Myrdal] is probably best known . . . for *Women's Two Roles* . . . The latter has often been seen as one of the books that put feminism back on the political agenda for women of the postwar generation. [. . .] During the 1980s and 90s, her contributions became the subject of a great deal of critical re-evaluation by social theorists in search of the complex intellectual origins of modernity and welfare state social engineering, as well as personally in the biographical writings by her own children. These . . . have tried to address the relationship in her own life between high personal, professional and intellectual ambitions and the domestic performance as wife and mother . . . the contradictory constructions of Alva presented in . . . the biographically relevant material written by members of the Myrdal family. (Lyon, 2000: 408)

What Lyon pointed to so vividly is the apparent dissonance between Myrdal's political liberal values, in association with her internationally renowned economist husband Gunnar Myrdal, 'of a uniquely family and woman-friendly welfare state' (p. 407) and their family practices as recounted by their children:

> From within a feminist perspective the article will attempt to show the extent to which judgements of the public contribution of women continue to be framed by socially and intellectually shifting conceptions of their role in the public domain. It also aims to show the value of contrasting different textual interpretations of events in a single person's life as a tool laying bare the powerful gender ideologies that underlie them (Graham, 1992). (Lyon, 2000: 409)

She concluded that 'the 'story' of Alva, like . . . Simone de Beauvoir, provides us with yet another vivid example of what Evans describes as the 'impact of unresolved family dramas on individuals, and consequently on intellectual life and social ideas' . . . (1993: 12) . . . I have attempted to argue that . . . engagement [with masculinity] is also at the heart of biographical writings about women and the continuing complexity of the relationship between their contributions to public and domestic life' (2000: 426). Lyon's account is very much part of the recent usage of biographical methods of inquiry in feminist theory, looking at the contradictions between women's lived experiences in two spheres, namely the public domains of work and politics and those of personal and private family lives. These contradictions were not theorised during the 1960s and only recognised much later. My account can only elucidate these contradictions with the benefit of thirty years of feminist theorising.

However, one of Beauvoir's main innovative biographers and textual analyst,

Toril Moi (1990; 1994; 1999) took a more optimistic view of Beauvoir's life and the continuing influence of her work on feminist theories. Moi considered Beauvoir's own 'lifelong project' namely 'to break down the distinction between philosophy and life so as to endow life with the truth and necessity of philosophy and philosophy with the excitement and passion of life' (1994, p. 147). She argued that it was the writing of *The Second Sex* that turned Beauvoir into a feminist (*ibid* p. 185). Although it may have turned her into a feminist, it took her very much longer to see her way to joining the women's movement, which she only did in 1971 (Moi, 1994, p. 211) when she came 'to realize the necessity of independent feminist mobilization of women *as* women . . . and . . . such separatism remained wholly strategic (1994, p. 212). Writing the book was partly because of her earlier experiences during and immediately before the Second World War; the transformation to feminism was in large measure a consequence of the social context in which the book came to be written, namely between 1946 and 1949 and in the turbulent aftermath of the war in France (*ibid*, p. 186). Moreover, part of the impulse came from Beauvoir's growing realisation of how she herself had been 'shaped by patriarchal mythology' and yet had failed to recognise it (1994, p. 190). Moi also asserted the initial influence of Beauvoir on the first generation of second wave feminists:

> Precisely because she occupied a unique position in relation to the intellectual discourses of her time, she also became the greatest feminist theorist of our century (*sic*). Long before the emergence of the women's movement *The Second Sex* posed every one of the problems that feminists today are still working to solve. The book literally changed thousands of women's lives'. (Moi, 1994: 1–3)

But she also argued that *The Second Sex* is deeply ambiguous about sexual politics:

> Nowhere in *The Second Sex* are the tensions between the personal and the philosophical stronger than in Beauvoir's representation of masculinity . . . If Beauvoir argues that women under patriarchy are torn by conflict and inner strife, the very texture of the book reveals this to be no less true for herself than for other women . . . The deepest paradox of all is that the most powerful anti-patriarchal text of the twentieth century reads as if it is written by a dutiful daughter only too eager to please the father . . . but . . . to read Beauvoir for a theory of female subjectivity is to read her on premises drawn up by feminist theories of the 1970s . . . Judging by the available evidence, however, the hundreds of thousands of women who found inspiration, comfort and the will to fight in *The Second Sex* in the 1950s and 1960s did not pay much attention to Beauvoir's account of sexuality; what they found was a scorching critique of bourgeois marriage, a blistering attack on repressive laws concerning contraception and abortion, and the best analysis of housework ever written. They also found a breathtaking vision of freedom . . . The opposite of freedom is oppression: her problematics is one of *power*, not one of identity and / or difference. (Moi, 1994: 178; 184)

In *What is a Woman and other essays*, published in 1999 for the fiftieth anniversary

of the publication of *The Second Sex*, Moi addressed theoretical and philosophical issues about personal life and writing, drawing on Beauvoir. Moi
remained of the view that 'the reception of the work of one of the greatest intellectual women of this century (*sic*) is a chronicle of sexism, careless reading, and a
desperate failure to take her philosophically seriously. The Simone de Beauvoir
we know today was shaped by that reception, one that I do not wish on any intellectual woman today. I hope that these essays . . . will help change this situation'.
(1999: ix) Moi's own project was about the ways in which Beauvoir's theories
and philosophies arose from her own situation, but it is also an attempt to render
it understandable to contemporary feminists. In particular, Moi grappled with
the concepts and theories that beset early feminist thinkers, namely whether the
distinctions between sex and gender are theoretically necessary. As she put it, it
'is an attempt to liberate the word 'woman' from the binary straitjacket that contemporary sex and gender theory imprisons it in' (1999: ix). The two new essays
produced in 1999 return to a much more theoretical and philosophical reading of
Beauvoir than the accounts in her previous studies but they also accord her a
continuing place in current academic feminist theories of personal and political
life.

Much of the early writing of the women's movement was not undertaken by
academics but intellectuals, as can be seen from this consideration of Beauvoir.
The works came to be regarded as the early academic texts, and as Hartsock
mentioned most feminist theory was critically linked to feminist political
activity. The early texts came directly out of women's experiences and involvement in the women's movement, particularly in the USA. This is the case with
Betty Friedan, a freelance journalist and the author of *The Feminine Mystique*
(1963). She recounts in her autobiography (2001):

> I never set out to write a book to change women's lives, to change history. With
> three little kids and that big Victorian house, still writing 'housewife' on the census
> blank, each magazine article a traumatic chore . . . The book I actually wrote,
> though objective in its technique and search for evidence, came from my personal
> truth, my personal objective-subjective participant observation of my own and
> others' experience and from my repudiation of so-called accepted truth, social
> scientists' truth, psychiatric truth, when it didn't ring true to my own observa-
> tions, my own following of clues to a new, larger truth about women . . . Before the
> Smith questionnaire and my later interviews of . . . women I had virtually decided
> to stop magazine writing altogether. I was going to be a housewife, yes suburban
> housewife, period'. (Friedan, 2001: 107–8)

The Feminine Mystique, published in February 1963 in the USA, quickly became
a best-seller and contributed to the beginnings of the women's movement in the
USA. Horowitz (1998: 5–15) wrote an unauthorised biography of Friedan to
acknowledge the influence of *The Feminine Mystique* on the creation of second

wave feminism and its entry into academia in the USA in the twentieth century. Although he acknowledged the critical influence of this text on both women's lives and academic feminism, he was not at all sympathetic to its author. As a historian he aimed to provide *the* intellectual history of the American women's movement but this kind of biographical writing could demean and destroy as well as celebrate feminist political action and writing. In her own autobiography Friedan wrote that: 'I had no idea that my book would start a revolution. Until that revolution came – the women's movement – new possibilities for women's lives weren't visible. But I did understand that what I had figured out – that the feminine mystique was no longer a valid guide to women's lives, that it was *obsolete* (*sic*) – implied monumental social change . . .' (2001: 135).

By 1966 there were moves to found a national popular women's organisation in the USA and Friedan was at the forefront:

> The name of the modern women's movement we decided would be the National Organization for Women, NOW. It wasn't going to be women against men; men had to be included, though women must take the lead. I wrote the first sentence of NOW's Statement of Purpose on a paper napkin: 'to take the actions needed to bring women into the mainstream of American society now, exercising all the privileges and responsibilities thereof, in truly equal partnership with men.' Actions, not just talk . . . NOW officially began on October 29th, 1966, with some three hundred charter members . . . There was this *sense of history* we all shared as we began to make it happen. Here women, for all these years, had done volunteer work and helped organise and support causes of anti-fascism, of the plight of the poor, organising for everything but women themselves. But now, finally, we were doing it for ourselves – for women . . . The timing was indicative of the way move-ments happen in America . . . Just as the first women's movement came on the heels of the black movement to abolish slavery, so did the modern movement we were starting come soon after the March on Washington for the blacks and passage of the Civil Rights Act of 1964. Liberation was in the air . . . (Friedan, 2001: 174–6)

The popular movement developed, through NOW and the subsequent founding of *Ms* magazine, a regular glossy magazine linked to the *New York Times* but arguing explicitly for women's liberation from traditional family ties and for employment opportunities, edited by Gloria Steinem. *Ms* became an 'official' voice. The term *Ms* signalled the demand and desire for autonomy and inde-pendence from traditional marital ties. It eventually became acceptable as a public and quasi-official term in the USA (but not Britain), partly influenced by Steinem's campaigning (Heilbrun, 1993).

Key women's writings gradually entered the academic sociological agenda in the 1960s and various courses in sociology began to find a place for some embryonic work on women and their roles within families and the relation with the world of employment. The more self-consciously feminist or women's liberation literature was not included here. For instance, in the extra-mural course that I taught, we did not cover Beauvoir or use Friedan, despite the fact that they both dealt in their different ways with women's roles inside and outside the family. Moreover, these courses were not firmly within the academy, but being developed in extra-mural settings, by political and social activists. However, the more liberal and progressive mood of the sixties was marked by both political events and by the social commentaries of academic social scientists, which influenced the intellectual aspirations of our post-war generation and which we in turn attempted to influence.[2] Other critiques of the traditional family, from both feminist and more conventional routes, began to appear with increasing regularity.

The changing family as critical to 'A Runaway World?'

Some liberal social scientists were also beginning to popularise critiques of social changes. At the same time social and liberal campaigns were emerging within the political and policy sphere (see Marwick, 1999, especially Chapter Six). An instance of this emergent public recognition in Britain of family changes and social transformations might be dated to the BBC's Reith lectures on the radio in 1967. Professor Sir Edmund Leach, a renowned social anthropologist at King's College, Cambridge University, was invited to present an analysis of social change and family life in the post-war period. The Reith lectures have been seen to represent the apotheosis of middle to high brow culture available to a wide if not mass audience, especially with the advent of such means of mass communication, and before the enormous popularity of television as a key medium rather than the radio. Entitling his lectures '*A Runaway World?*' Leach was perturbed by the pace of change and how the family was being transformed by other social and economic factors and was spiralling out of control. He argued against the prevailing support for the 'nuclear family' in that 'far from being the basis of the good society, the family, with its narrow privacy and tawdry secrets, is the source of all discontents.' He also suggested that we, in Britain, no longer had what he called the Kellogs Cornflake nuclear family of breadwinner father and stay-at-home housewife and mother, a term that he also introduced into more popular culture. He noted with concern the increase in the proportion of 'working mothers' of young and/or dependent children. As a social anthropologist accustomed to the analysis of societies other than his own which had not developed such a highly diversified social and political system, he was perhaps more keenly attuned to note the differences rather than similarities. He argued for an alternative and more caring kind of family, in which children would be treated more sympathetically. By a curious quirk of fate, his daughter was one of the students on my extra-mural course, the following year. This was one of the sparks of my enduring interest in these issues.

Thirty two years later, the BBC invited another former King's College Cambridge social scientist to deliver the Reith lectures; Antony Giddens, by then Director of the London School of Economics, chose an almost identical title for his 1999 Reith lectures *'Runaway World'*. During the thirty years from Leach to Giddens' Reith lectures, sociological analyses of the family had been transformed, especially using feminist concepts and theories and building upon the relations between the personal and political. In his lectures, Giddens demonstrated these transformations but did not attend to feminist contributions. Rather, he emphasised transformations in what he called the 'personal' linked to his key theoretical ideas of identity, reflexivity and reflexive modernisation which are of quintessential importance in the sociological developments that frame this narrative of the life history of feminist ideas within the social sciences. A crucial element of the global social transformations was the sociology of emotions and the family. His theme was not dissimilar to that of Leach's but he asserted as a fact that we were at the start of a runaway world demonstrating the range of social and economic changes and transformations in the family that had occurred. However, only one of the five lectures was devoted to the family in which[3] he argued that:

> Among all the changes going on today, none are more important than those happening in our personal lives – in sexuality, emotional life, marriage and the family. There is a global revolution going on in how we think of ourselves and how we form ties and connections with others. It is a revolution advancing unevenly in different regions and cultures with many resistances. As with other aspects of the runaway world, we don't know what the ratio of advantages and anxieties will turn out to be. In some ways these are the most difficult and disturbing transformations of all . . . We can't opt out, however, from the swirl of change reaching right into the heart of our emotional lives . . . (Giddens, 1999)

Giddens addressed questions of the family and 'personal' in ways that many social scientists had chosen not to do before, foregrounding an agenda set by feminists. Ostensibly the most famous British professor of sociology, (Webster, 1999) who had become director of the London School of Economics less than six months before the general election of 1997, he was also invited to provide advice to the New Labour government. He was billed as 'the Prime Minister's favourite intellectual' or 'guru' (Giddens, 1998). It was only during the 1990s that he began to engage with policy debates; prior to that his work was theoretical. His first engagement was through a text entitled *Beyond Left and Right* (1993) where he began to consider policies situated in the context of global transformations and their implications for social and sexual relations, including what he styled 'lifestyle politics'. His more recent text spelt out a specific policy agenda for New Labour entitled *The Third Way* (1998; 2000).

It is one measure of the extent of social change that Britain's most famous sociologist pinpointed changes in family life as of critical significance to a political and a sociological analysis as we entered the new millennium. Leach's lectures had pointed to how family lives were being transformed in the last half of the twentieth century. Giddens confirmed this by arguing in *The Trans-formation of Intimacy* (1992) that the changes as a result of globalisation had so affected the family and marriage that these had become 'shell institutions' rather than economic institutions. He pointed to a shift to relationships based upon love, trust and commitment rather than contractual obligation and emphasised the role of education, political and social transformations in making possible these global changes. He argued that family changes, equality of women in families and social democracy, were interdependent. Thus he argued that the world had runaway from traditional institutions, including fundamentalist religions and that globalisation had wrought new social and economic relations characterised by risk and trust or commitment rather than stability. He also inserted psycho-dynamic approaches and notions of emotionality, through trust and commitment into his powerful analysis. Although he emphasised notions of reflexivity, he did not reflect personally except by reference to changes between the generations and personal anecdotes about his grandmother. However, his analysis went beyond the glimmerings of a new world Leach had been cautiously optimistic about back in the 1960s.

Early feminist writers in Britain and contributions from abroad

During the late 1960s women themselves were beginning to organise and demand political and social changes in their personal lives, including organising more formally in the women's movement. These all occurred rapidly as the 1960s shaded into the 1970s. There were then several publications which attempted to theorise the politics of the women's movement and contributed to the growing scholarly debates, albeit that they were seen as challenging and controversial accounts. In Britain a number of writers wrote important critiques of aspects of women's lives. For instance Lee Comer (1974) wrote *Wedlocked Women* which spoke to many ordinary working class women's lives; Juliet Mitchell and Sheila Rowbotham also contributed early critical studies. However, Germaine Greer's *Female Eunuch* (1970) received a huge amount of media attention but was not used particularly in the development of academic scholarship. Greer became identified with the quasi-official voice of women's liberation, despite the fact that the various women's liberation meetings and national conferences argued for a different kind of political activity in which no-one individual was separately identified. *The Female Eunuch* became identified as one of the key texts and she became a very public face of feminism in Britain, despite her Australian origins. Greer wrote a quasi-autobiography – *The Whole Woman* – despite her best intentions (1999; 2000 March in paperback) since she claimed to be opposed to biographies. She had refused to authorise a biography written by an avowed feminist of the younger generation in that it did not contribute to more academic and intellectual analysis. As Greer's Australian feminist biographer wrote:

> This book is not a conventional biography; it does not pretend to be an exhaustive account of Germaine Greer's life. Rather it focuses on why she was different from other second-wave feminists, why she could be so contradictory and why, despite this, the net impact of her influence has been generally positive . . . Greer opposed the book from the outset, and went to some lengths to sabotage what was always an honest and well-intentioned project. Her attack included personal threats and vilification, and the warning off of sources by letter, in print and through speeches.

> This was part of her long-expressed hostility towards literary biography, in particular that concerned with living writers . . . The issue of authorised versus unauthorised biography was canvassed widely in the media during the writing and publication . . . where authorised biography is concerned, there is a serious risk that 'authorised' will mean 'compromised', that some of the trimming of the sails will be required by the subject. This can jeopardise the ethical obligations incumbent on all writers dealing with the real world . . . (Wallace, 1997/2000: x–xi)

Juliet Mitchell and Sheila Rowbotham were two of the first feminists in Britain to provide more scholarly and less popular versions of writing on women's liberation and feminism, albeit that their writings were more oriented to a political than an academic audience. Penguin published both their first works in paperback and as part of the publisher's serious but popular works, known as Pelicans. Both Mitchell and Rowbotham were very significant to the founding of the first women's liberation annual meetings and conferences. Originating on the left, and as part of *The New Left Review* co-operative group, Mitchell's first seminal essay, which came to influence women's writing and thinking, first outside, and later within the academy, was published in *New Left Review* in 1969, entitled *Women: The Longest Revolution*. About this time she also began teaching women's studies at a distance from the university, in what was probably the first course of its kind in England (Humm, 1989). This was subsequently transformed and extended into a book entitled *Woman's Estate* (1971). This book addressed two key concerns – one was the politics of women's liberation and the second and complementary issue was women's oppression. Mitchell spent a considerable portion of her analysis on aspects of women's oppression, through on the one hand what she called 'the ideology of the family' relying on a Marxist analysis and on the other psychoanalysis and the family, derivative of Freud. She concluded:

> Women's position in society is in the home – and outside it, in production . . . Within the family, the reproduction and socialisation of children are made to balance each other . . . Marriage is a 'life-long union' . . . These, then, are some of

the contradictions in the position of women within their world – the family; and within – 'it's a man's world'; – the economy. These factors doubtless caused the resurgence of feminism. But its specific timing and particular characteristics (in revolutionary potential) are also the result of a second force: the preceding and concurrent political movements of the sixties. (Mitchell, 1971: 174–5)

Later she wrote a set of essays entitled *Women: the Longest Revolution: Feminism, Literature and Psychoanalysis* (Virago, 1984). Mitchell became increasingly fascinated with psychoanalytic ideas and began to apply them to her writing, publishing *Psychoanalysis and Feminism* in 1974, and moving to train as a psychoanalyst by the end of the 1970s. She continued to write and publish but mainly on psychoanalytic ideas and with an account of Kleinian theories. A number of edited essays also brought French psychoanalytic ideas and feminist psychoanalytic concepts to our attention. Mitchell and Jacqueline Rose showed the value of psychoanalytic ideas to feminist theorising, especially on family issues, sexuality and emotions. Although steeped in theories about feelings and emotions, Mitchell did not venture into more personal forms of reflection but rather her writings, especially with Rose, became increasingly abstruse. Towards the end of the 1990s, Mitchell returned to academic life as a lecturer then professor of women's studies at Cambridge University, highlighting how feminist ideas had eventually become acceptable, even within elite academic institutions.

Mitchell co-authored or co-edited three books with Ann Oakley, (*The Rights and Wrongs of Women* 1976; *What is Feminism?* 1986; *Who's Afraid of Feminism? Seeing through the backlash* 1997). This last edited book was on the history, origins and influences of feminism and feminist thought in academia, the aim of which has been 'to reflect on three decades of change, stabilization or regression' (1997 p. 1). Juliet Mitchell, however, has a very different but complementary perspective and approach to Ann Oakley. Together they wrote:

> We both see ourselves as feminists yet our theoretical approaches to feminism are in many ways discrepant. Ann Oakley is a socialist and sociologist; Juliet Mitchell is a Marxist, and after a career teaching English literature is now training to be a psychoanalyst. Ann Oakley takes her distance from theoretical Marxism and is more than a little sceptical of psychoanalysis; Juliet Mitchell has her doubts (and prejudices) about the type of 'empiricism' on which much sociology and non-Marxist socialism are based. (Mitchell and Oakley, 1976: 10)

By the third volume of their collaboration they were able to reflect back over the 20–30 year period and write:

> This . . . focuses on the struggles of feminism in a period of backlash. When we edited *The Rights and Wrongs of Women* in 1976, we saw the book as a response to the gap between the revolutionary practices of the women's liberation movement and the existence of academic texts from which women's voices were missing. There was little empirical evidence, then, on which to base 'the case for or against

feminism'. Ten years later when we edited *What is Feminism?* a substantial literature had accumulated both mapping the statistics of women's position and demonstrating the ways in which the voices of women have been systematically silenced in the study of human culture. But feminism itself had by then begun a period of discreditation as a political identity. Young women, in particular, doubted its relevance to them. Looking back, we can now see this moment hovering on the edge of time, to borrow Marge Piercy's phrase: could feminism be resuscitated . . . or were we doomed to enter a phase of unreconstructed reaction in which the moral right cast feminism as the evil responsible for (almost) all social ills? The case against feminism is clearly more complex than that . . . the backlash is itself a cultural construction – a moment in the long history of the relationship between personal identity and civil rights – the interwoven fabric of economic production and social reproduction. It is not peculiar to women's place . . . (Mitchell and Oakley, 1997: 2)

Sheila Rowbotham also played a major part in developing the historical material and analysis of women's movements and revolutionary practices in Britain before second wave feminism, and the politics and practices of the second wave women's movement, through her involvement in organising the first women's liberation conference at Ruskin in 1970. Her work on the history of women's activities, associations and involvement in labour movements and her biographical work on Stella Browne who developed the birth control movement provided some of the early texts and materials for a background in looking at the history of family lives from a feminist perspective.[4] Throughout the early period of feminist activism she wrote a number of autobiographical essays[5] but later produced a popular study of the 1960s in which her feminist activism did not feature strongly (2001). During the development of more academic feminism, she, with Lynne Segal, an academic psychologist, and Hilary Wainwright, a political campaigner, remained central to the intellectual developments of the women's movement, rather than becoming academic feminists *per se*.[6]

Many writers, especially American feminists, began to popularise women's personal accounts, similar to Lee Comer's *Wedlocked Women*. In the United States, in the early 1970s, there were major debates about feminism as a popular versus academic movement and, as in Britain, about the academic status of women's studies and feminism. For instance some of the early writings such as Kate Millett's *Sexual Politics* (1970) and Shulamith Firestone's *The Dialectic of Sex: The Case for Feminist Revolution* (1970) came to occupy the same centre stage, except that it is their politics rather than the basis in personal experience that has been seen as so critical.[7] Millett wrote, at the end of the 1990s, a biography of her mother, reflecting upon the differences in generations as well as between mothers and daughters. It was widely criticised and her life came under the spotlight for her apparent eccentricities, continuing the way her original feminism had been remarked upon. When Millett's first text, which was in fact based upon a doctoral thesis, was published in England it was rather over-whelmingly and critically received. Mary Stott wrote in *The Guardian*:

> Kate Millett, author of 'Sexual Politics' came, was interviewed almost non-stop for radio, television and the newspapers, departed for Paris, and is now back in New York, leaving behind her an explosion of argument. It is astonishing that the author of a book with such a repellent title, written as a PhD thesis, should have had a mass coverage that the sexiest film star or novelist might envy; astonishing that a book written as an academic treatise, typically academic in its language, work method, its selection of illustrations from literature, sociology, and political history, and its terrific bibliography, should have become an international best seller. Sales in the United States are about 85,000, it has been translated into French and German, and is delighting her publishers here . . . 'Women's Lib' is currently a hot topic for the media but not therefore ephemeral. It is a continuing ferment, created in part by exceptional women like Kate Millett, but so widespread that it is forcing a wider recognition that attitudes to sex roles need to be examined . . . You do not have to go along with Kate Millett – as I certainly do not – in her revolutionary (and inadequately argued) revolutionary (*sic*) view about the institutions of marriage and the nuclear family, to feel grateful for the shake-up she has given to our thinking. (*The Guardian*, March 31 1971 p. 11)

Similarly, American novelists such as Erica Jong, whose *Fear of Flying* published in the early 1970s to major critical acclaim, have been dubbed quintessential American feminists, setting the parameters of feminist thinking. According to the publishers of her numerous novels and her autobiography, *Fear of Flying* made Erica Jong an icon of feminist liberation. Her mid-life memoir, *Fear of Fifty*, was a passionate look at marriage and motherhood, fame, creativity, men and sex.

My personal involvement in the politics of women's liberation

During 1969, still struggling to find a voice for my ideas, I changed positions again and went to work as a researcher on a project on the politics of education at Queen Mary College, University of London. This topic and the associated teaching was somewhat more to my satisfaction, given the opportunity to learn more about the political processes of government, especially with respect to education. I remember well being asked, at interview, by Maurice, now Lord, Peston whether I might get married and leave, abandoning the project. This kind of personal question confirmed the assumption with which I had been operating about women's role in the family. Given my radical personal life-style in London, involved in various political and social groups, this was a highly sensitive question, which seemed impertinent to ask. It was the kind of issue that the growing women's movement was beginning to question. The specific question in relation to employment issues has, as a result of feminist and other equal opportunities campaigning now been deemed illegitimate, if not illegal, through legislation in the 1970s and 1980s. These issues also were put on the public and political agenda and were theorised in the 1990s. The more personal rendering of our lives has also become part of our writing of personal experiences and narratives, which were at that time still seen as private matters. It is only with these political changes brought about by feminist activism and theories that these kinds of personal accounts can now be written. The research began my lifelong academic interest but not as intended. However, it was through this research project, funded by the then Department of Education and Science, that I ended up in the USA and continued the association with educational issues. It also was the occasion to allow me to become more interested in women's issues, if not the women's movement. Peston did also try to get me to think about women, rather than gender, and education. Initially I was reluctant and could not see quite how; hoping to retain that interest for my personal rather than professional politics. Ironically this is not how things have transpired. It was here that I began to see how to formulate academic concerns but remained distanced from women's issues, which continued to be pursued as an extra-mural and political activity, [separate from 'work' so to speak]. With the benefit of hindsight it is fascinating to note how our campaigning for employment and educational opportunities still left a separation between form and content. However, the research also spoke to other political interests.

After a visit to Leeds with old student friends when I attended one of the first women's liberation political meetings which was not then single sex, and after much soul searching, I finally decided to join a consciousness-raising group in 1969 in London. Our group was made up of women of my age and generation, white, middle class and graduates, who were mainly single women although we also had a couple of married women with children amongst our number. We met for over three years, and we became involved in a range of political activities, including political writing. In particular we were part of the generation of women who founded the women's movement in England, paralleling the work that had begun in the USA five or so years earlier. For instance, as part of the London Women's Workshop, where Mitchell was a frequent speaker, we agreed to write an edition of a newspaper, entitled *Shrew*, dedicated to women's liberation. Our various contributions to this were largely autobiographical and included photographs of ourselves in the processes of putting together the paper. We also attended a range of local meetings and national demonstrations including the first ever women's march in March 1971. We had missed the first national meeting of women's liberation held at Ruskin College, the trade union and working men's college, in Oxford in 1970. We were determined to attend the second national women's liberation conference in Skegness in 1971. It was held in a Butlin's holiday camp where Trade Union Congress meetings were routinely held.

The fragmentary nature of these early political activities was symptomatic of the way the political movement developed. I well recall driving to Skegness with my elder sister, Judy and an old friend of mine, Viv, from our days growing up near Bradford. At this time women's liberation or the women's movement was about our personal and political lives and had little to do with our professional or working lives. However, Judy and Viv came together from their consciousness-raising group that was one for mothers of very small children; unusual then and also later. One of the keynote speakers at this national meeting, representing Wages for Housework, was Suzie Fleming, another member of that same small Jewish community – based largely on refugee Jewish families from Nazi Germany, Austria and Czechoslovakia – in Bradford. Given the smallness of that community and the relative smallness of the national meeting (about 250 women attended) it provides an insight and illustration of the social class and ethnic composition of these early women's liberation meetings. Many of these women, including Suzie Fleming, have remained loyal to feminist activities and she was present at the thirtieth anniversary meeting in March 2000.

Personal reflections on feminism and women's liberation 1970 to 2000

The thirtieth anniversary meeting of the first national meeting of the women's movement was held at Ruskin College, Oxford in March 2000 confirming how political and academic feminism had mushroomed informally and in a reflexive way. Given the importance of the inaugural women's conference in establishing feminist principles and demands, reflections thirty years on was critical to understanding the continuities and changes in feminist theories, methodologies and influences. However, the conference was organised by, and for, historians of the women's movement and the proportion of academic feminists and sociologists in attendance was quite limited. The absence of some of the founders and key writers on feminist theory was quite notable and yet many of these women remained wedded to academic feminism. Entitled *Reflections on Ruskin: Celebrating the Women's Liberation Movement Thirty Years On* the introductory pamphlet and programme claimed:

Ruskin 1970 – Ruskin 2000

In 1970 a small group of women organised a women's weekend to be held from February 28th to March 1st at Ruskin College, Oxford. The response was enormous, and over 500 people turned up on the first day. As a result, the conference had to be moved from Ruskin to the larger venue of the Oxford Union. The Ruskin conference became the official founding moment of the Women's Liberation Movement in Britain. Over the weekend, all sorts of issues were raised including women, home and family, equal pay, and women and history. The conference ended by drawing up the four original demands of the women's liberation movement: for equal pay; for equal education and opportunity; for 24 hour nurseries; and for free contraception and abortion on demand.

The conference on March 18th 2000, has been called to mark the anniversary of the original conference on February 28th–March 1st 1970 and the first international women's day of the new millennium. Around a hundred and fifty women will be travelling from all over Britain and from the United States to mark the anniversary, share memories of Ruskin and attend workshops on lots of different aspects of the women's liberation movement. They will be drawn from different generations of women ranging from some who attended the original conference to young women just beginning to get involved in politics today. This will be more than just another history conference. It will provide an opportunity to look back over the last thirty years, to draw links between then and now, and to discuss what the future is for women's liberation.

The first women's liberation national meetings in Oxford and Skegness had indeed organised around four campaigning strategies that were formulated as 'demands' on the state, and developed in association with international women's liberation campaigns. They were all challenges to women's traditional roles within the family. First of all, the demand for free contraception and abortion to enable women to decide when and if to have children coincided with changes in the law in relation to abortion rights, which had occurred in 1967. Although extremely liberal as a piece of legislation, it did not provide for free or unfettered abortion rights but linked them to medical opinion. Contraception was not made freely available, although clinics and health centres were developing to allow for more accessible information. Thus a notable campaign in the early 1970s was for the extension of these rights. *Not the Church and not the State, Women Must Decide their Fate* was the campaign slogan as we marched through the streets of London in March 1971.

Secondly, the demand for childcare for babies and young children, formulated to illustrate the essentially private nature of early child-care, was thus entitled 'Twenty-four hour day nurseries'. Women in the women's liberation groups who already had young children were to the forefront of this campaign. In the late 1960s, this was not seen as intellectually a problematic issue but rather one for immediate action. One of the other activities with which our consciousness-raising group was associated in London was the campaign for childcare and in particular we focused on the setting up of a community creche in a house in north London.[8] This later became the Dartmouth Park Hill community child-care centre and then the children's community centre.

The campaigning for this community creche formed part of the basis for what subsequently mushroomed into the National Childcare Campaign in the early 1980s. This campaigning group was somewhat distant from other forms of feminist campaigning since it had a very specific policy to be implemented, namely the public provision of nursery and facilities for the under fives and especially pre-school provision aimed chiefly at mothers in employment. It was particularly influential in developing policy proposals and action plans around childcare, including obtaining funding from government departments for childcare projects often run by voluntary organisations. Together with Caroline New, I later explored the more vexed and intellectually challenging issues about families, children and the public and private issues that were here entailed (New and David, 1985). We invited several members of the National Childcare Campaign to contribute accounts of their innovative projects that had been developed, as part of the story that we wished to tell about the developments in childcare provision. We wrote:

> We look at a few of the many projects which effectively contradict widely accepted notions about children's needs and capacities. Pre-school children, especially under-threes, are supposed to be cared for with others of the same age and away from their mothers. We turn this assumption on its head and argue that young children need to be together, as much as they need to be with adults . . . we . . . show that there is plenty of evidence that day care can enrich children's lives. Yet much of this evidence is ignored in the conventional view that the most we can hope for from non-maternal care is that it does no harm. Community nurseries go even further and challenge the philosophy and practices that have grown up in the nursery world itself. They begin to question the divisions between parents and professionals, between trained and untrained workers, and open up possibilities for the sharing of care and commitment between parents and others. (New and David, 1985: 241–2)

The National Child Care Campaign continued to develop proposals and action plans for forms of nursery and childcare throughout the 1980s and 1990s, although much of its work was voluntary funded, and pressure group politics, drawing on the experiences of developments in Europe. Indeed a strongly European based network also emerged. Most recently the work done for and by the National Child Care Campaign was re-invoked and renamed as the National Child Care strategy under the New Labour government in 1997. This provides one of the few instances of the ways in which early feminist campaigning eventually became a significant activity in the Labour party, and later the government. However, this was not a central part of the women's movement then and was mainly due to the persistence of some key campaigners.[9] Harriet Harman, who became Labour's first Secretary of State for Social Security and minister for women was a member of this campaign in the 1980s.

The other two demands were for equality of opportunity in relation to education and women's employment rights in terms especially of pay. They were 'equal pay for equal work' and 'equal educational opportunities'. These two were often linked, since it was seen that women could not enjoy employment opportunities without the education and training as a background. However, the women's liberation campaigns were largely waged by students and university-educated women at that juncture in the 1960s. The links were also made, possibly more importantly, with the difficulties of women with children being able to benefit from employment without childcare support and help. On the whole, however, these early campaigning activities were seen as essentially by and for educated middle class white women.

In the 1970s the four demands became known as 'the working women's charter' and at least three further demands were added, namely women's legal and financial independence, women's freedom from violence and intimidation and women's rights to determine their sexual orientation. At the same time, the complexity of the issues that women from various different backgrounds faced was becoming an important issue, and various new strands and groupings began to emerge, such as the socialist women's national meetings, of which one was held in Birmingham in 1975. It was at this stage that the campaigns and the issues began to assume more complexity, with attempts to link what was becoming identified as either women's 'oppression' or discrimination against women in the public sphere with economic, legal and social questions. Class and race questions were raised, as were relations between and within different groups of women, with different socio-economic and financial circumstances but they had not previously been theorised.

I was determined to attend the thirtieth anniversary of feminist activism as I had not been at the first and because I wanted to reflect upon issues of continuity and change in respect of feminist ideas, theories and perspectives on women and the family. However, the event was relatively small by comparison with the social and political resonances of feminism and feminist politics in academic life nowadays. There were about two hundred participants, mainly drawn from either participants from 30 years ago and a particular generation of women or women who have been interested in researching the history of the women's movement in Britain. The celebration was quite specific to the first conference although there were also reminders of other events around that time. The first national demonstration for women's rights had been held in London composed of 3000 women on March 6th 1971. An innovative film was made to cover a number of these events, from Ruskin to the national demonstration and to survey attitudes and perspectives to women's liberation and women's rights. Entitled *A Woman's Place* and made by Sue Crockford this film was shown again at the Ruskin anniversary. It was evocative of a particular generation, signified by education, dress and style and yet it laid the foundation for myriad subsequent media and academic developments.

Two of the keynote speakers at the Ruskin anniversary meeting had been speakers at the first conference – Sheila Rowbotham and Sally Alexander, both of whom remained involved as feminists in academic life; both also still feminist historians. Their reflections on that first women's conference were rather different, with Sheila Rowbotham in her presentation entitled 'Before Women's Liberation' talking about the political and social changes of the sixties which, in her view, led up to the founding of the movement. She emphasised both the liberationist and liberal atmosphere in social, media and political issues and the influences of civil rights and other movements from the USA. Her focus was on sexual politics or the changes affecting the generation of women and women students in the sixties and as seen through film, television as well as the growing political movements for wider changes for women. She also emphasised the importance of changing techniques of family planning and birth control, in particular, the contraceptive pill, to women's initial sexual liberation. However, changing family mores and state policies or regulations, about marriage and motherhood were more hard won. Sally Alexander talked specifically about the organisation of the 1970 Ruskin conference and the particularities of the relations between men and women within the organisation and the event itself. What was particularly notable about these reflections was the emphasis on the wider changes influencing a particular generation of women, and their involvement in movements for wider social and political changes. Sally Alexander pointed to her recollection of the difficulties men had of being involved. This was not the recollection of her male partner. Both drew attention to the sea changes in attitudes and approaches to women's lives, such as from the dominance of marriage and dependence on a male breadwinner for the majority of women. In the general discussion mention was frequently made of the difficulties for women in terms of sexual relations until the availability of the pill in the late sixties, and the enduring shame of becoming an unmarried mother. Mention was also made of the subordination of women in terms of employment and access to public services, in particular when married. These issues were also raised most powerfully in discussions and in workshops, providing salutory reminders of the importance of the ways in which the women's movement had opened up private family issues to wider public scrutiny.

The third speaker had not attended Ruskin 1970 but was invited to reflect upon the future. Lynne Segal, an Australian by origin, had also been involved in feminist politics for about thirty years and became a major chronicler of feminist ideas as an academic feminist social scientist (Segal, 1975; 1983; 1996; 1999). Her talk entitled *Feminist Futures* provided a theoretical overview of a revival of right-wing politics, social Darwinism and women's roles within the family covering an array of academic and journalistic writers, on issues about rape to how women's evolutionary psychology affected their biological destiny as wives and mothers.[10] She addressed issues of continuity and change about women's oppression within the family indicating just how far feminism had succeeded in opening up matters about women both politically and academically. She showed both in terms of political strategies and ideas how far feminism had gone in freeing women from the constrictions of family, and particularly dependence on men rather than autonomy as independent workers and participants in the public sphere. On the other hand, the resurgence of a new right quasi-academic literature which presented an ostensibly intellectual approach to women's renewed confinement to the privacy of the family illustrated how tenuous that progress may have been. It could also be argued that it has been the very success of feminism in putting these issues of women's position in the family and the economy on the public agenda that has created its own backlash. It had led to the revival of a politics, justified intellectually, that seeks the return of women to the family.

I had agreed to present a workshop and was coupled with my former colleague and friend Hilary Land in a workshop entitled *The personal and the political*. It was an absolute pleasure to be able to present our complementary reflections on the developments in feminist activism and analysis over the last twenty to thirty years. Working together with Hilary Land again provided an overview for us both of the continuities and changes with respect to feminist perspectives on the family. Entitling my talk *The personal is political: feminist campaigns about the family*, I provided my personal reflections on the women's movement and the demands that addressed two interrelated themes about women and the power relations within the family, namely sexual liberation and women's liberation. The first two demands – equal pay and equal education and opportunity – were more to do with women's rights as women, and the power relations with men but not necessarily having to do with intimate sexual relations. The second two were more directly to do with the family and were to do with women's relation to men and reproductive rights. First was free conception and abortion on demand, enabling women to choose where and when to have children; and second 24 hour nurseries as a way to open up discussion about children being more than the property of their parents and mothers. Both of these demands, however, were about women's sexual relation to men. I then questioned how these had developed into a more theoretical analysis and perspective on women's lives inside and outside the family and whether women's family lives themselves had been transformed over the last thirty years. Hilary Land provided her reflections, twenty years on, on the fifth demand that was for women's financial and legal independence, originally formulated 5 years after the first demands in November 1975. She also mentioned her involvement in the *Why be a wife?* campaign which developed out of the fifth demand in 1977. She produced the campaigning leaflet and talked of the issues raised there about the needs for change in government policies for married women. Interestingly, many of these policy questions remain unresolved, covering tax and social security laws, the right to go out to work for all married women, the provision of adequate child-care and support for women caring for 'the old and the sick'. The campaign also raised the question of changing 'public attitudes towards the role of marriage in our society' and asked girls and young women to 'look at alternatives to marrying and that married women will look at how they can make their own marriages more fair to themselves'. Here she mentioned how there had been a shift in public attitudes but no commensurate change in social policies. Indeed, in some respects, she argued that there had been a reversal in women's fortunes through New Labour's neo-liberal perspectives on social welfare and their financial plans.

The lively discussion that ensued demonstrated precisely our changed perspectives and understandings about the extent of shifts over the last twenty to thirty years in family and attitudes to particular aspects. On the one hand, many contributors pointed to the ways in which consciousness-raising and in particular thinking through how 'the personal is political' had led many of us to a wider understanding about our private family lives. We had learnt that our growing up in the intimacy of particular kinds of families had enabled us to see how general rather than particular our situations as young women were. Suzy Fleming, a key contributor to the first Ruskin conference, and subsequent national conferences and this workshop, articulated her own revelations about how her continental and refugee Jewish family was not unique but mapped on to other family lives. This had been a complete revelation to her and had thus made her involvement in feminist activities the greater. To that extent these issues of personal family matters no longer being seen as entirely unique and private has been one of the key sea changes in perspectives and attitudes, leading some social and political commentators to believe that this is post-feminist society. Similarly, others raised the question of the traditional views of lone mothers and women having children illegitimately as having helped to shift and change through feminist perspectives. The burden of guilt and the humiliation of pregnancy out-of-wedlock no longer held the stigma that surrounded it just thirty years ago. Indeed, the shifts through changes in the legal institution of marriage and divorce towards cohabitation rather than marriage, and reconstituted families through remarriage and step-parenthood, have taken place at an enormous rate over the last 30 years. Thus single or lone parenthood is no longer socially stigmatised as it was 30 years ago, although it may not be socially and morally acceptable at the level of government policies. Many noted the contradictions in New Labour's developments of educational policies on the importance of marriage as the basis for family life, attempting to steer away from publicly acknowledging homosexual relations. Moreover many referred to New Labour's limited attempts to address the conservative backlash to progressive approaches to marriage and family matters through the abolition of Section 28, which banned the promotion of homosexuality in schools. The government response had been to develop a very traditional approach in curriculum matters for schools by specifying marriage as the crucial approach to sexual relationships, illustrating the enduring traditional principles. Nevertheless, as others commented, this has become the subject for social and political debate in ways which were socially not accepted thirty years ago. Yet others addressed the campaigns for abortion and contraception, especially WACC (women's abortion and contraceptive campaigns) as of singular importance to the changes brought about. And yet others to the working women's charter group that tried to develop strategies for women to be involved in employment and have support for their caring work. Others addressed the question of the origins of these campaigns and claimed the importance of thinking about how girls' particular kinds of post-war education – in single sex schools either girls' grammar schools or public schools had influenced the rise of feminism in that particular era. And at the same time acknowledgement was made to the diversity and change of family lives that is now addressed by policy makers. Here it was also acknowledged just how unchanged, however, government responses have been to some of these shifts. Others pointed to how little had been made of the wider principles of involvement in running public and social services as one of the issues that feminists had tried to address.

This workshop alerted us to both the extent of change and the involvement of academics in being able to theorise more clearly and cogently than hitherto the ways in which feminist ideas and politics had been subject to both continuity and change. What was also alluded to was the ways in which out of these early beginnings and feminist acorns an oak tree of feminist academic theories and methodologies had emerged. It was only slowly that these ideas were put into courses, first outside the academy, but later by this generation of feminist academics who achieved positions, albeit, for many, initially tenuous ones that led to the burgeoning of this more academic scholarship, remaining reliant on particular political analyses.

Given that the majority of attendees had remained involved in academic life the consideration of the ways feminist ideas had entered and were firmly within the academy was important. At another workshop entitled *Into the academy* another former colleague and friend, Liz Bird and June Purvis addressed how these notions were introduced into academic sociology. Liz Bird's talk entitled 'The academic arm of the WLM: women's studies 1969–1999' addressed the growth and development of academic women's studies and the study she had conducted on feminists involved in developing women's studies within the academy. June Purvis entitled her talk 'From women's history to gender history? Reflections on our past'. She spoke to the shifts and changes in academic concepts and analysis within academic life. Yet another workshop looked at types of theory that were applied and in particular the uses of psychotherapy.

In so far as there were 'disputes' at the Ruskin anniversary conference they were about the women's own memories as to whether or not the inaugural conference had been more or less oppressive to women with or without children. There had been different campaigns over the family: a campaigning group which argued 'to smash the family', meaning the traditional patriarchal nuclear family; altering the traditional power relations between men and women and opening up possibilities of more liberal sexual relations, especially through free contraception and abortion on demand. Another early campaigning was around children and collective childcare, encapsulated in the demand for 24 hour nurseries. Although it could be argued that early feminists belonged to one post-war generation in terms of their political socialisation, their political concerns about the family were rather diffuse. There were at least two groups of women, both young and in their 20s and early 30s. One campaigned for sexual liberation (and later radical, in terms of gay and lesbians) and the other who were or about to be mothers made demands about women as mothers and the sharing of childcare. Fundamentally the early issues for the women of the women's movement were about how a generation of women, largely brought up in the post-war period and coming of age in the liberalising era of the sixties, wanted to break out of traditional families. The desire to create new opportunities and perspectives on their own lives as adult women, free from the constraints of power relations within the traditional family was evident in their original campaigning. This reflective conference addressed how far changes had been introduced into both the academy and into our understandings and interpretations of the shifts and changes over the last twenty to thirty years. As I have argued the origins of WLM lay in socialist and civil rights movements including from the USA. Thus the early theoretical developments lay in socialism and liberal theories about civil and other rights, and these were slowly but clearly introduced into the academy and feminist sociology.

Returning to my personal and professional odyssey

Even a year in the USA at Harvard Graduate School of Education as an interlude did not provide for more academic and professional engagement with women's issues. It did however give me the opportunity to meet with other political feminists and I joined a Jewish feminist group where I met Nira Yuval Davis who became a long-term friend and professional feminist and sociological colleague. Her early work (1978) about 'Jewish mothers' entitled 'Women: the bearers of the collective' has been of great importance in developing culturally specific theories about family lives. It also gave me at least two critical academic issues to frame and develop my thinking; one being the ability to link educational policy-making with issues of family; and the other to link education to wider social policy issues. Both allowed me a way to develop academically whilst also maintaining my personal interests and predilections. They also built upon the process, begun in London, of long-term engagement with issues of education at all ages and stages, since I had studied the politics of local education policy-making in some communities of the greater metropolitan Boston. In England, I had concentrated on the professional aspects of the policy-making processes, by conducting case studies, through interviews and documentary analyses, and that study was subsequently published (David, 1977). Once firmly based in the USA I was encouraged to look at both professional and political aspects. I found myself taking advice from a wide range of colleagues and became far more familiar with political, as much as more technical and economic, issues to do with decision-making. In particular I became a close associate of colleagues in the Centre for Educational Policy Research and more involved directly with issues to do with educational policy and social inequalities.[11] The year I spent there was the time that *Inequality: a reassessment of family and schooling in the USA* was published, and subsequently Bowles and Gintis who were involved in the former published a more Marxian analysis of schooling (1976). These two publications aided the development of a critical Marxist, and subsequently feminist, analysis of family and education, albeit from a schooling rather than more academic perspective.

Whilst in the USA I adopted a different approach to research, looking at how families, especially women as mothers, in certain upper middle class communities such as Wellesley and Weston by contrast with Quincy and Melrose, engaged with decision-making (David, 1975). This began my now long-term interests in, and fascination with, the very broad topic of family and education. However none of the advice came from women who then saw themselves as feminists, but rather were interested in the politics of education. The study highlighted the role of upper class housewives in the politics of education at local school board level; and reflecting back on this study, it revealed the continuation of the issues for such women within the parameters set by Betty Friedan's by then classic study *The Feminine Mystique*. With Amy Stambach (2003) I have recently reflected upon how these innovative notions have been hijacked from current policy analysis and discourse. In the USA I learnt a great deal about how the politics of women's liberation and more generally, single issue politics, were developed and applied there, in a culture altogether more individualistic than England, or other countries of Europe. My year in the USA was a year in which federal politics reached its nadir, with the re-election of Richard Nixon and his subsequent impeachment (which actually occurred in 1974 when I had returned to England). I also learnt a great deal about the construction of social policies at the time in the USA, since I was appointed as a teaching assistant to Nathan Glazer, a renowned commentator on American politics, on a course in American social policy and he became one of my many mentors for my research. This enabled my immersion in social and educational policies and policy-making in the USA and also helped me to think more clearly about a long-term career and fascination with these topics. However, the intellectual ideas current at the time were about liberal politics and policies, including issues to do with mirroring British welfare policies, just as Britain tried to 'borrow' from the USA. Glazer was a close colleague and friend of Moynihan.[12] He was, at the time, a famous and controversial academic turned government advisor, based at Harvard, having written a book entitled *The Negro Family* which set up distinctions between white and black patterns of child-rearing and mothering. This led to his interest and involvement in policy-making and the development of proposals for a family assistance plan for the Nixon administration. These 'welfare plans' were also at that time the subject of much popular and political dispute, although feminist debates were certainly not foregrounded. Nevertheless, the racial and gender implications of such policies led to challenge and critique, subsequently formulated in more academic terms.

Conclusions and reflections

In this chapter I have reflected upon the contexts and challenges of women's liberation as a social campaigning movement and how it developed into more academic and theoretical notions about women's personal and professional lives. The first generation of second wave feminists tended to be highly educated, white and middle class. A major contrast for women's campaigning that had occurred in the years from the first to the second wave feminism was over educa-tion, and particularly in the academy. Although for middle class women in the nineteenth century education had been a major prerequisite the emphasis was largely about involvement in the polity. The second wave was more wide-ranging but the education demanded and successfully achieved meant the slow process of including women in the academy in increasing numbers as academics rather than just as students. As Toril Moi pointed out in 1994:

> Simone de Beauvoir is the emblematic intellectual woman of the twentieth century . . . [she] belonged to the first generation of European women to be educated on a par with men . . . Precisely because of that unique position her experiences gain in intensity and sharpness of focus: in her texts, the conflicts and contradictions experienced by intellectual women in a patriarchal world emerge with unusual clarity. Born in 1908, Beauvoir belongs to the generation of intellectual women who came of age in the 1920s and 1930s . . . they tended not to be conscious of the social significance of their own femaleness . . . it was only in 1946, if we are to believe her memoirs, that Beauvoir realized that to be an educated woman is not, after all, the same as to be an educated man. With a rare sense of moral and political integrity she faced the consequences of that insight: the very moment she realized that she was an intellectual woman, she started to write *The Second Sex* . . . (Moi, 1994 p. 17)

Thus Beauvoir in France, Friedan (amongst others) in the USA, Myrdal in

Sweden, were all highly educated women who chose to reflect upon their positioning as women in families and argue for political campaigns to transform
women's lives. They became the precursors of second wave feminism in the
form of women's liberation and their diverse ideas were taken up by women,
mainly highly educated middle class women initially in the wake of more socially
liberal political agendas. However, the processes of transformation and adoption
of these ideas in the polity and the academy was slow and highly contested. Yet
thirty years on from the first 'formal' event of women's liberation in Britain, set
at an elite academic institution, such ideas have mushroomed and become more
diverse and theorised differently in various cultural contexts. Some women's
lives have been transformed dramatically and academic agendas have integrated
a multitude of feminist ideas about family and personal life, whereas political
agendas may remain more cautious and conservative. I turn now to how these
ideas were adopted and adapted in the academy.

Notes

1. For example, see, for France: Reader (1999) Personal Voices, Personal Experiences *French Cultural Studies* 10 (3) no 30: 265–275; Reader and Khursheed (1993) *The May 1968 Events in France;* Duchen (1986/7) Feminism in France: From May 68 to Mitterand *French Studies* 61 (4): for USA and GB: Blackstone, T *et al* (1968) *Students in Revolt:* for UK: Williams' inaugural (2000) where she referred to Daniel Cohn-Bendit influencing her in 1968.

2. Carolyn Heilbrun. (1993). This has also been used as an expression by many other writers. (e.g. Young-Bruehl, 1998, *Subject to Biography: Psychoanalysis, Feminism, and Writing Women's Lives;* Middleton and Weiler, 1998, *Telling Women's Lives*).

3. Broadcast on April 28th, and repeated on May 1st 1999, this was personally significant since my mother would have been 90 on May 1st 1999. Giddens claimed that family life changes were the shift in attitudes of women towards family relationships and he cited the example of his great-aunt who had been married for fifty years and admitted never to having been happy at the end of her life. Although my mother pined for my father after his death in 1980 until hers in 1996, she never presented a picture of marital bliss. Never-theless, quite contrary to Giddens' comments she would never have conceived of breaking up with my father, and she imbued in us a strong sense of commitment and fidelity.

4. *Women, Resistance and Revolution* (The Penguin Press 1972; Penguin Books 1974) *Woman's Consciousness, Man's World* (Pelican Books 1973) *Hidden from History 300 years of Women's Oppression and the fight against it* (Pluto Press 1973) and *A New World for Women: Stella Browne – Socialist Feminist* (Pluto Press, 1977); *Dreams and Dilemmas: collected writings* (Virago 1983).

5. One in Ursula Owen's book on *Fathers by Daughters* Virago 1980? and one in Liz Heron's *Truth, Dare or Promise: Girls Growing up in the fifties* Virago 1978?; 2001.

6. Beyond the Fragments, 1979.

7. Shulamith Firestone's *The Dialectic of Sex* (1970) was originally published in the USA and as a paperback in Britain in 1971. She was a self-styled founder of the women's liberation movement in the USA, although originating from Canada and from an orthodox Jewish family. Like Millett she was also an artist and writer.

8. Sue Crockford whom I had met through the Theatre Group at Leeds University was a founder of this action and went on to become a film-maker making the first film of the first

women's liberation march through the streets of London and footage of the first national conference in Oxford at Ruskin revived for the anniversary.

9. Helen Penn was a major campaigner and writer on behalf of the National Childcare Campaign (1997).

10. Many of these writers, as women, see themselves as liberal feminists, women such as journalist Melanie Phillips in her book *The Sex Change Society* and Helena Cronin, an academic researcher who founded the Centre for Darwinism and evolutionary psychology at the London School of Economics.

11. Mary Jo Bane, Sandy Jencks and David Cohen were contributors to *Inequality: a reassessment of family and schooling in America* published the year that I was there, that is early in 1973.

12. Glazer and Moynihan, *Beyond the Melting Pot, 1967*. Moynihan was Democratic senator for New York who resigned in the summer of 1999 and whose seat Hilary Clinton won in 2000.

CHAPTER THREE

Feminists move into the academy

Introduction

This chapter traces the ways in which changes in my personal and professional life as a woman becoming a tenured academic were interwoven with those of other women of my generation of second wave feminists, set in the broader social and political canvas of the 1970s. I reflect upon my perspective on the introduction of feminist ideas into the academy in Britain in the 1970s, also drawing on evidence and feminist theories from Europe, the USA, Australia and Canada. Initially we developed substantive agendas about women and the family and focused on historical material and critiques of the emerging social policy agendas in the political arena. As noted previously our political activities resonated with the socially liberal era. One indication, however, of how these also chimed in with developments in academic life was that the *Times Higher Education Supplement* began life as an independent weekly newspaper in 1971 and its circulation has grown. By the early 1970s in Britain that liberal agenda had produced a number of policy measures aimed at modifying public positions for women, namely the Equal Pay Act of 1970 which was later tied in with the Sex Discrimination Act 1975. Together with the Abortion Act 1967 these measures seemed to augur well for changes in many women's lives but there were moves to tighten these with the return of Tories in the early 1970s. However, the Tories implemented a number of measures relating to women's lives as wives and mothers that, whilst contradictory, modified family lives and women's financial independence in the family. For instance, family allowances introduced in 1942 (Land, 1975) were transformed into child benefits and there were moves to extend nursery education for pre-school age children in 1973.

Margaret Thatcher was the Tory Secretary of State for Education during this brief period of Conservative administration and implemented contradictory proposals which earned her the nickname 'Thatcher: the Milk snatcher'. The Conservative administrations from 1970 to 1974 were dogged by political problems and with the successful re-election of the Labour party in 1974, the Conservatives sought a new leader. Mrs Thatcher became the first woman leader of a political party in Britain from 1975. In 1979 she successfully won the election and became Prime Minister, the first woman leader of a British government. These political events framed our thinking and teaching and enabled us to develop both new substantive agendas about women's involvement in public life and new pedagogies around personal experience. The chapter covers the embedding in the academy of feminist ideas from the early to the late 1970s and the start of Thatcherism. During this period we were attuned to the implementation of more liberal ideas, but we were also wary of the re-inscription of a more conservative agenda.

My own political and professional awakening was much in line with that of other women of my generation of 1960s graduates, a slow process of continuous professional engagement, and employment, but with an equally slow process of adopting and, more importantly, applying, in my academic endeavours, a specifically feminist perspective. There was also a generation of women who had reached maturity during or in the immediate aftermath of the Second World War and were professionally engaged. Thatcher was an example of the social and educational transformations of women's lives. She herself was initially someone who could be called a liberal feminist, given her own writings on the importance of women remaining in professional employment – an article entitled *Wake Up Women,* published in 1952 (Arnot David and Weiner, 1999). There were others who were more theoretical and critical and provided the materials and basis for our feminist politics, thoughts and theories, many referred to in the previous chapter, Friedan and Beauvoir most especially. Materials from Europe, the USA and Britain were published in profusion during the 1970s and we began to contribute to that endeavour, slowly and haltingly in relation to our own family backgrounds and lives.

Our lives also became more complex personally and professionally. During the 1970s a number of women who had become second wave feminists were appointed to tenured positions in academic life and even more were engaged in more tenuous contractual positions. During this same period some of us also developed more settled family lives, including marrying or cohabiting and having children, whilst continuing to be involved in paid employment. I married in 1974 and had children in 1978 and 1979, whilst continuing to work as an academic. At the time I felt myself to be unusual in these family processes and was called an elderly prima gravida at the maternity hospital. Subsequently I realised that I was also part of a new wave of professional women having children late having established a career first. These family processes are now commonplace but then they seemed relatively new and daring. I will thread these issues through this account of changing feminist perspectives and family and professional lives.

My personal and professional engagements

I returned to England from the USA in the summer of 1973, to a tenured academic post in the Department of Social Administration at Bristol University that later became the School of Applied Social Studies. This allowed me to pursue my interests developed in the USA in policy, education and family. Thus my first real engagement with what was later to become known as academic feminism was when I arrived in Bristol. Yet here again the process was somewhat slow and tortuous because of academic resistance to the involvement of what were deemed to be political ideas in academic subjects and disciplines. However, the reception to our emergent notions of thinking about and theorising women's lives was enthusiastic by our students both within and outside of the academy. A majority of the undergraduate students in the social sciences whom we taught were young women and our initial attempts at teaching women's studies were to women of our generation, outside of the academy who were equally enthusiastic to share personal experiences and develop ideas. As I had done in the USA, when I arrived in Bristol I looked for the women's movement. To my now more accomplished eyes, I was able to find it back in England, whereas I had had tremendous difficulty in the USA locating a brand of the women's movement that suited my interests and politics. The women's centre in Bristol was at that time located in the basement of a house of an Australian academic couple – Ellen Malos and John Malos – renowned for their political involvement in a host of left and liberationist issues. Numerous groups and activities were taking place and I quickly got involved. This time we managed to fuse our teaching of women's issues with the more overt political activities and campaigning and it gradually began 'to change my life' in terms of my professional academic interests. This phrase was one that Betty Friedan (1982) had acknowledged and taken up with reference to the impact of her book and politics on generations of women in the USA.

A colleague from Bristol days, Liz Bird, conducted a study of how feminist academics in the UK and North America reflected upon the introduction of interdisciplinary women's studies into the academy as degrees over a thirty-year period from 1970. Reflecting on her research, she stated (2001, p. 468): 'My research involved interviewing more than 60 women (and one man) who had all been involved in introducing named degrees in Women's Studies into their academic institutions, in the period from 1970 to 1995. All of the women were still in the academy or had recently retired, and they were therefore, by definition, women who had survived within its walls. Most had been involved in the women's movement in the 1960s and 1970s, and can thus be described as radi[c]al (*sic*) activists.' The research as conducted is part memoir/auto-biography and can be placed alongside a growing literature that draws on women's memories of the 1960s and 1970s (Duplessis and Snitow, 1998; Howe,

2000; Rowbotham, 2000).[1] Bird also wrote in a reflective vein remarking on the difficulties of breaking down traditional disciplinary boundaries to incorporate new 'knowledge' and argued that for the most part the boundaries were redrawn rather than demolished:

> In about 1977, Miriam David and I were drawing up a curriculum for a new Certificate in Social Sciences, to be offered by the Dept of Extra-Mural Studies at the University of Bristol, for part-time evening study by local mature students. Sociology was to be one of the 'core' subjects of the certificate, and five of the 15 first year lectures were on the sociology of education. The first of these lectures was entitled 'What is taught and Why?' It seems appropriate to open this paper with a personal reminiscence, as the research on which it draws involved over 60 feminist academics being invited to reflect on their own engagement in the curriculum, in a period beginning about 30 years ago . . .' (Bird, 2001: 463–78)

Thus it was a slow and contested process to develop not only a curriculum and a pedagogy which involved personal experiences but also to challenge traditional academic notions about the disciplines or subjects in relation to our own subjectivity. We had all been schooled in the traditional disciplines and had to consider how to adapt them to the emergent new ideas and theories, taking account of women's positioning and experiences.

Emergent feminist theories within sociology and the wider social sciences

Many of my colleagues and postgraduate students had an interest in the challenging and growing ideas about the women's movement, and its close association not only with personal (including family) politics but also academic ideas. In that exciting academic environment, I became involved in numerous activities, political groups and reading groups on feminism, socialist-feminism, Marxism, and Marxism and psychoanalysis, including a *Capital* reading group organised by Martin Jacques, then a lecturer in Economic History at the University, later to become editor of *Marxism Today*. We all read voraciously and discussed incessantly,; in particular French intellectuals were as much in vogue as Marx and his successors. I personally became enamoured of Althusser, and some of his students such as Foucault, but this was somewhat in advance of the popular academic interest in post-modernism and post-structuralism. We were eclectic and read widely: Bourdieu and the French psychoanalyst, Lacan and his influence on feminists and female psychoanalysts, such as Kristeva, Cixous and Irigaray. These various theoretical notions were variously adopted and adapted for both teaching and research in the heady climate of the 1970s. However, during that period the main emphasis in critical and feminist thinking was drawn from socialism and Marxism. It was only a decade later that the more theoretically 'daring' ideas about post-modernism and post-structuralism became influential in the curriculum of sociology, social policy and cultural studies.

Slowly these various political and intellectual ideas entered the academy in various forms, but as regards feminism, it was through political ideas and forms of organisation. A measure of the swift processes of change, from this vantage point, was that the first sustained attempt to bring together early feminist work within sociology was at an annual conference of the British Sociological Association, that was devoted to considering relations between the sexes, or sexual divisions. This conference, organised by Diana Leonard Barker and Sheila Allen, was held in April 1974. The conference was critical in the development of what now might be called the sociology of family life from a feminist perspective and especially with a concern to make explicit sexual divisions or relations. It had been attended by a balance of men and women, reflected in the contributors to the publications from the conference. (I missed it – in order to get married! This shows something of the ambivalence that many of us had to the ideas in practice whilst we were extremely enthusiastic to propound them in theory.) The papers were subsequently published in two volumes, one entitled *Sexual Divisions: Process and Change* (1976a) and the other *Dependence and Exploitation in Work and Marriage* (1976b). They illustrated initial feminist concerns within traditional sociology and attempted to open up questions about gender and the relation between men and women. One was about sexual relations, sexuality and the regulation of marriage, divorce and reproduction. The thrust of most of the papers was a textual and structural analysis of public policies and ideologies. Allen and Barker wrote:

> The sociology of the family is a case in point. It might be expected that work on gender relationships would be most advanced and the theory the most critical. However, it suffers from a marked lack of status in British sociology, deriving from its lack of 'theory' – except for Parsonian functionalism, its concern with the so-called non-work/non-market area of social activity, and its attention to women and children. In consequence it is frequently not taught at all, or given to the woman in the department, and rarely specified as a preferred specialism in job advertisements. It has certainly not shown the expansion in research or teaching experienced in many areas of sociology.

> There is an even more marked lack of sociological interest in sexuality (human sexual conduct) . . . The sociology of social movements has similarly ignored the feminist movements of the nineteenth and early twentieth century (Banks and Banks 1964; McGregor 1955) and the contemporary liberation movements. (Freeman 1973).

> The papers in this volume thus deal with aspects of social relationships consistently neglected by sociologists, and ridiculed or denigrated by some. But in so far as sexism constitutes unproblematic, commonsense behaviour in contemporary British culture, it should not surprise us that it appears thus in sociology. (Barker and Allen, 1976a: 2)

The other conference volume was about the interdependence of work and marriage; drawing attention to the lack of such an analysis in traditional sociology. Allen and Barker wrote:

> We hope that this volume will contribute to changing the way in which questions are posed about the divisions between the sexes in our society. We began by pointing to the cultural values which stress the separation of 'the home' and the 'world' and to the way in which the dichotomy between loving home life and rational, aggressive, urban industrial capitalism has become elided with the dichotomy between femininity and masculinity . . . women have been occluded time and again by encapsulating them within their fathers' or husbands' social persons. The papers . . . stress that women live, move, and have their being outside as well as inside the family; that the household is a group of individuals, having economic as well as emotional relationships . . . and that the relations between the sexes outside and within the family are inter-related. (Barker and Allen, 1976b: 16–17)

These ideas about women, sex and the family and how they should be theorised were the subject of debate both nationally and locally. We attended numerous groups and conferences and drew ideas from a variety of sources. At the time the concept of gender was not used as much as that of sexual divisions; the shift towards 'gender' began to occur in the 1980s. In Bristol, a loosely-knit group of women composed of relatively young and junior academic social scientists, drawn across sociology, social policy, psychology, education and the humanities, together with postgraduate researchers, began to meet together and organise politically in the women's movement and also to work together academically. We organised a group for the BSA, called the South-West women's caucus, and campaigned for women's better conditions within the BSA, as well as within the academy. At the same time we met together to discuss intellectual ideas and develop together our knowledge of theories about sexual divisions and women. Some of us also met in a consciousness-raising group. Parallel with this we were involved in the WLM and wider political campaigns about working women's lives in association with the local community. Our work and ideas were closely linked with our political activities and it was hard to separate emerging views that were based on both personal experiences and practical politics.

Early feminist teaching in Bristol

In 1974 a group of us were engaged to teach about women's issues for the extra-mural department of Bristol University. Over the next four to five years we worked together to develop what became the first reader of women's studies in the UK. We eventually entitled this *Half the Sky*, drawing on the old Chinese proverb that women hold up half the sky. Ten women, including an artist, formed the group that we eventually agreed somewhat reluctantly to name the Bristol Women's Studies Group, having had far more fanciful ideas about our collective identity, such as matrix. As we said in the introduction to the book:

> One apparently glaring omission is that there is no chapter on the Family. We
> started out with one but had to abandon it in that form since it really comes into
> every topic on women and so is, in effect, the substance of the whole book. (1979: 7)

Our family lives during the course of the book's production were relatively
typical of our generation of women. Again this group was largely made up of
relatively young white and middle class women. Over half of us were married.
During the course of the period several of us divorced and/or changed partners
and sexual orientation. Four of us were mothers at the start (with seven children
amongst us) but during the course of the book project another three of us produced four children. My two children were born in 1978 and 1979. Another
three children were born subsequently. The book had been one of my (and our
collective) first attempts to grapple with what were only then just becoming
known as feminist ideas and trying to put together these ideas in an intellectually
coherent fashion. We had all been part of the growing women's movement in
England, some of us starting out by seeing ourselves as part of women's liberation, as a political movement outside the academy. Most of us had been and continued to be involved in consciousness-raising groups. Indeed, it is a matter of
some note that although most of the nine of us had academic positions, with the
rest in more insecure research or teaching posts, we did not then see our main
work as university teachers as doing feminist research or even women's studies.
However, three of us did not have what were then 'proper' tenured positions but
were either research students or former graduate students, active politically in
both the women's movement and left wing or socialist politics. The courses that
formed the basis of the material we used to put together the book were largely
taught in the interstices of our main 'jobs', in the evenings and at weekends.
They were aimed at extra-mural groups of women who were themselves outside
the mainstream of academia rather than undergraduates or postgraduates and
usually housewives and mothers. The courses were often early forms of
consciousness-raising and initial developments in feminist pedagogy based on
personal experiences.

Looking back on *Half the Sky: an introduction to Women's Studies* (1979) it is
interesting to note the issues that we had found urgent and important. The
twentieth anniversary of our first collaborative feminist endeavour was celebrated in the summer of 1999. At this anniversary party we ten women of the
Bristol Women's Studies Group spent much of our time reminiscing and
reviewing our involvement in feminist activities. We indulged in creating our
'collective memoirs' to use the term that one of us, Liz Bird, (2001) had picked
up from a research visit to the USA. We had developed the text around a number
of potential courses to be taught, largely about a woman's life or women and
the family. Thus we constructed the text around the notion of the traditional
'family life course', starting with infancy and childhood, through education and

schooling, and developing female bodies and minds. The chapters were about how girls learn to become women and in what their lives as adult women mainly consist, namely marriage (and possible divorce), motherhood, work and what we called 'creativity'. We were, however, reliant upon the materials available for use at that stage that were largely ephemeral and not generally highly theoretical. However, we considered ourselves innovative in particular in our use of notions about the construction of females through childhood, and especially over issues to do with the body, and in our broad use of literary, artistic and creative materials as well as the more social and economic contexts. We also talked through the processes of developing and applying these ideas to our teaching and research practices. We all acknowledged both the pleasures and pain of having been involved in these burgeoning women's activities and their slow and difficult or contested introduction into the academy. Most importantly, we recognised our own key roles in creating this collective endeavour, including the naming of this as feminism, rather than its initial naming as women's liberation as a social movement, closely associated with other liberation movements of the 1960s and 1970s. As we developed women's studies for extra-mural students initially and later for undergraduates, closely followed by postgraduates, we began to revise our terms and our approaches. Nevertheless, feminism as a term for scholarly activities was not initially acceptable in the academy, without an enormous and collective struggle. It is hard from this vantage point, where feminist scholarship is now 'allowed', if not securely, in the academy, to recall all those difficult struggles, although our individual and collective paths had been marked by our prominent involvement in many of the struggles to get the ideas into the academy. In most respects we worked together collaboratively rather than individually. This also became a matter of some concern to the university authorities when trying to identify our individual academic contributions. This task became increasingly urgent in the 1980s with the advent of forms of quality assurance or control through research and the official policies on research selectivity exercises, as the first ones were known.

The wider social and economic transformations resulted in more reflective accounts theorising change in women's lives, and deeper political projects. As part of this there were various approaches such as narratives, life histories, auto/biographies and memoirs. A most innovative and creative approach to family memoirs is one creative collaboration by a mother-daughter duo, using the notion of voices, and mixing this with narrative and conversation. This most inspiring personal account came from reflecting upon their shared and yet different experiences over two generations in the women's movement. The mother, Marilyn Porter, was a close friend and colleague in the early women's movement in Bristol and a member of *Half the Sky* collective. As part of the second generation of post-war women her biographical path fits with mine. Her daughter, Fenella, was a very young child (and one of the seven referred to above) when this text was written. As a mature young woman and a feminist she and her mother wrote together about their diverse experiences of coming to feminism. This unusual reflection considered the role of feminism in their growing and developing relationship. I quote extensively from Marilyn and Fenella Porter's conversation since it also illustrates some of the themes explored here. In this instance the Porters take up a more intellectual approach and demonstrate the wider social changes that have impacted upon their lives and relationship:

> While we were exploring the contrasts and continuity in the experience of one mother/daughter dyad, we also became increasingly interested in how and whether having feminism as a guiding principle in our lives as feminist mother/ feminist daughter made any difference to our relationship or to our feminist analysis of that relationship . . . In focussing on 'learning and resistance', we want to identify the processes that have occurred in exchanges between ourselves; the different contexts in which our own learning happens, and what sometimes prevents it; and the patterns of resistance that we develop against learning from other feminists, feminists who may differ from us in generation, racial or ethnic background, sexuality, class or ability or any of the other myriad ways in which we differ and, all too often, divide ourselves. We see these processes of learning and resistance as crucial to the growth and development of the women's movement. And we see them closely connected with the use and misuse of *power and authority* (authors' emphasis) in feminist organisations around the world . . . Because this paper is rooted in our own lives, we felt that we should introduce ourselves more explicitly . . . We have chosen to use two 'methods' to present this. The first is to proceed from 'key text' to 'key text' . . . by breaking into our different 'voices' to present our different points of view. As we discussed the texts, we found ourselves checking them against the reality of our experience . . . small case studies . . . We are addressing our work to all mothers and daughters, and all feminists concerned about the development and enrichment of the Women's Movement, whether they are activists, academics, practitioners – or all three . . . we hope that 'academic' readers will be able to relate their thinking to their work as activists as well. We do not really see a clear distinction between the two identities . . . (Porter, M and Porter, F, 1999: 3–5)

Back in the 1970s women's questions and studies about women were urgent matters and to the forefront of my students' and my personal interests. They also linked with changing political debates and the policy initiatives of the Labour government in office during the second half of the 1970s.

A feminist introduction to family and social policy

Teaching and research around feminist matters became our priority. Together with a colleague in the Department, Hilary Land, and with Jackie West from Sociology, we started a feminist course on 'family and social policy' for undergraduate students in 1974. Again, looking back it is important to note the centrality of how our ideas about women's issues linked with the family and both historical material on changing family lives and critiques of social and educational policies. At her retirement seminar held at the Nuffield Foundation to consider family changes and family policies, Hilary Land (2002) acknowledged both how innovative and how enduring these ideas that we developed were. She had kept copies of our examination papers that illustrated our historical and policy foci. Albeit that we had to invent an approach to the issues, foregrounding women, their lives and personal experiences in relation to family, economic context and social policies.

The course explored the ways in which the notion of the family was both implicit and explicit in the construction, historically of women's lives in relation to education, employment and legal and social regulation of women's lives. The material that we had available was very sketchy and drawn from the emerging work by Rowbotham amongst others that I referred to in Chapter Two and will discuss below. There were some significant contemporary studies such as Comer's *Wedlocked Women* as well as growing historical material. It was from this course that my ideas for *The State, The Family and Education* (1980) were initially sketched. I also developed a similar and parallel course on Social Policy in the USA, which developed a critical feminist analysis of welfare and social policies around notions of the feminisation of poverty and through a focus on AFDC. This enabled us to draw out international comparisons, although we also reflected upon the problems of such studies. I was also closely associated with the forming of the first Centre for the Study of Women and Education by Sandra Acker, closely paralleling the first centre for research on gender and education, initiated by Diana Leonard at the London University Institute of Education. Many of our students became deeply engaged in this kind of work and have gone on to become well-known feminist academics, including, amongst others, Claire Callender and Naomi Fulop. My first three doctoral research students[2] all, in their different ways, taught me a great deal about the idea of women's struggles to release themselves from the legal and social constraints of particular aspects of family life and how to theorise these notions. In particular the naming of our activities as 'feminist' was a political struggle in itself, and particularly difficult to find acceptance in the academic environment.

Linda Ward was singularly important in persuading me, much against what I thought was my better judgement, to take up the word feminism for my scholarly activities rather than continuing to use women's studies or sex and sexual divisions. She was studying the origins of the movement for birth control in the 1920s in England and became familiar with the regular use of the term in relation not only to family planning but also other family matters. Indeed, in reviewing the historical development of women's issues, it became increasingly clear to us that the first wave of the women's movement adopted the term and wore it proudly. Although many of us were slowly beginning to use the term feminist rather than women's movement or women's liberation, since the latter term signalled a particular perspective and ideology with respect to women, it was in itself a struggle. However, Linda Ward decided boldly to use the notions in her study and indeed eventually insisted on using it in her doctoral thesis title. This then sparked an intellectual and academic battle within the social sciences at the University. At that time, supervisors of doctoral research students had to defend their students' titles at a meeting of the relevant Faculty Board. I was therefore closely questioned on why the term 'feminist' was in the title. This was compared with what might be considered the illegitimate use of the term socialist (but not conservative) in a thesis title. Fortunately, two other respectable studies used the term. Olive and Jo Banks, eminent sociologists had written a study entitled *Feminism and Family Planning* (1965) about birth control at the turn of the century. Linda Gordon's parallel study of birth control in the USA from a feminist perspective had recently been published and I was able to make the association. Linda Gordon's subsequent academic studies followed a similar path in developing a critical feminist edge to her work from her initial historical materials. She too moved to a broader study of welfare policies in the USA and, twenty years later, in association with Nancy Fraser (1996), wrote an important essay on the construction of female dependency through welfare policies in the USA. Their work also reflects a growing concern with the marginalisation of feminist ideas within the political arena and the difficulty of continuing to address traditional concepts and theories. (I return to this in Chapter Seven.)

Feminism married to Marxism, liberalism or radicalism

Back in the 1970s it seemed appropriate for those of us who had started with a version of a radical politics to associate our emergent theories about women and family with other controversial social theories. However, there were a range to choose between from the liberal notions associated with political theories about the state, equality and women's rights, to more radical questioning of political rights and a more thorough-going desire for social and political equality, associated with socialist or Marxist ideas, or to a more fundamental questioning of the relations between the sexes on the grounds of women's difference from men. These different strands of political thought were all linked to feminist ideas and theories and were identified as differing liberal theories. A usual classification was to demarcate three differing strands, namely liberal-feminism, socialist or Marxist-feminism and radical or lesbian feminism (Banks, 1976).

My own intellectual struggles remained about the balance between a socialist and feminist perspective, one shared by many at that time, and appropriately evoked by Heidi Hartman's article entitled 'The unhappy marriage of feminism and Marxism'. In trying to develop a socialist analysis, I also became intrigued and fascinated by what the French Marxist intellectual, Althusser (1971) called the *family-education couple,* which he considered to be the major ideological state apparatus. Having previously pursued documentary analysis and qualitative research in the form of interviews of parents, education professionals and politicians (David, 1975; 1976; 1977) I set about applying his notions to documentary, textual and other historical material. In developing this and other political ideas I used it initially for a study of what became a major dispute in education and the teaching profession: the debacle over the William Tyndale school in London. It was a dispute that reached legal controversy and was settled in court and focused on the differing roles of parents, teachers and schools in the provision of education (Littlejohn *et al*, 1978).

So, at this time I was developing a feminist perspective, and putting that together with Althusser's Marxian concepts, wrote *The State, The Family and Education,* which came out in 1980. This was a socialist-feminist analysis of social policies on family and education. The ordering of the twin terms was then apposite since socialism was seen as the senior or elder perspective. Feminism, however, was the term which led to the choice of studying family matters, since the then prevalent political debates centred on women's confinement and constriction within families, their responsibilities for caring for husbands and dependent children. What I was concerned to understand and explain were the ways in which the state had developed policies about the provision of education for different social classes and groups in society, especially here with a view to considering different developments for boys and girls. At the same time, I was fascinated by the links with families and the expectations developed about mothers' and fathers' different roles with respect to education. It could also be shown how these expectations underlay teachers' roles, especially for young children. The book therefore provided detailed accounts of the historic developments of education in Britain, drawing out gender differences at several levels. The book's themes linked with my personal and familial concerns, since my parents had always been involved with education and my mother was a teacher. Similarly, the approach also allowed me to think about wider family matters and was linked with my changing family concerns. It was published after the birth of both my children but allowed me to develop my educational concerns as a mother.

My colleague Hilary Land was especially influential in initiating an analysis of state policies, especially the origins of the welfare state with respect to the balance between men and women's work and 'home' responsibilities (Land, 1976). Her work was critical and seminal in carefully documenting, through textual policy analysis, despite the lack of naming it as such, the ways in which the state and its policies create contexts and constraints for family lives, in particular in terms of women's two roles as housewife and mother. A major contribution that Land made was to present a feminist analysis of the framing of the

post-war welfare state through a key document – the Beveridge report of 1942.
In 'Women: supporters or supported?' (1976) Land developed this analysis,
which she had first presented at the first conference of the British Sociological
Association on sexual divisions, referred to above. She wrote by way of a conclusion:

> Women then are regarded either as workers or as dependants. Their role and con-
> tribution to society as mothers caring for young children or looking after elderly or
> disabled relatives is totally ignored. No distinction is made between the woman
> without children who works and the working mother. Neither is there a distinction
> made between the wife who stays at home because she has her children or relatives
> to care for and the wife without dependants who stays at home by choice. Each
> situation is different, and questions which need to be raised and answered are
> whether or not marriage *per se* should continue to be subsidized by the state and in
> what ways should the needs of the responsibilities arising from parenthood be met.
> (Land, 1976: 128)

Land then went on to review aspects of welfare state policies and the evidence in
relation to women's work, developing contemporary analyses of the government's policies and comparisons with France and the USA. A key publication
was 'the myth of the male breadwinner' in which Land (1977) showed wives'
essential economic and social contributions to the household and to household
income. Hilary and I were also closely involved with our personal as well as professional lives, later sharing childcare.

Elizabeth Wilson was also an early essayist, giving consideration to the ways in
which women were and are framed and formed not only by family life but also
by public and social policies. In this respect, her *Women and the Welfare State*
(1977) was critical in commencing an early analysis of the origins of women's
oppression not only through the family, but through the ways in which the state
reinforced the rules and regulations about family life. She constructed an ideological picture and wrote:

> Feminism and socialism meet in the arena of the Welfare State, and in the manipu-
> lations of the Welfare State offer a unique demonstration of how the State can pre-
> scribe what women's consciousness should be . . . Only feminism has made it
> possible for us to see how the state defines femininity and that this definition is not
> marginal but is central to the purposes of welfarism. Woman is above all Mother,
> and with this vocation go all the virtues of femininity; submission, nurturance,
> passivity. The 'feminine' client of the social services waits patiently at clinics,
> social security offices, and housing departments, to be administered to sometimes
> by the paternal authority figure, doctor or civil servant, sometimes by the nurtu-
> rant yet firm model of femininity provided by nurse or social worker; in either
> case she goes away to do as she has been told – to take the pills, to love the baby.
> (Wilson, 1977: 7–8)

Developments of a critique of the role of the welfare state were founded upon more overt political campaigning. Elizabeth Wilson developed a range and diversity of thinking and writing within sociology or social policy and cultural studies and the relation between the welfare state and families. In particular, her strength was to meld together political work and writing with more academic approaches within the social sciences. She also wrote an early autobiography, perfecting that tradition of thinking and writing reflexively; *Mirror Writing* (1983) drew on the twin traditions of psychoanalytic thought and her interests in cultural and policy studies.

British feminism was born in a particular generation, of women who were to become the founders and sisters, rather than mothers of academic sociological feminism. It is important to note how the women's movement was built upon generations of feminists such that feminism and feminist theories developed analyses which linked and related to women's lives to their lives especially as mothers or as others (e.g. Adrienne Rich, 1980). By the end of the 1970s, I had become thoroughly imbued with a feminist perspective and aimed to use it in all my academic endeavours, however difficult the process might be. Yet this was largely seen as a collective struggle both in the public world and that of the academy, where such notions and ideas still did not find ready acceptance. Our abilities to provide rounded theories were thus somewhat constrained by our involvement in academic life and the struggles in the forming and framing of feminist theories and ideas in the academy. Our working lives as women and mothers were relatively unfettered compared with those of working class women who had to take paid employment to maintain their families – husbands and/or children.

Feminist theoretical notions about women and work

In the early 1970s, very little specific attention was paid, by either feminists or sociologists, to children and their care or upbringing, at least in Britain. Stevi Jackson (1982) and Denise Riley (1984) were relatively unusual in developing this approach. As I noted in Chapter Two, the women's movement in England had drawn up four initial 'demands' in 1970 (Coote and Campbell, 1977). The one on childcare argued for 24 hour nurseries as an impossible 'demand'; whilst the other three were all more within reach – equal pay for equal work, equal educational opportunities and free contraception and abortion on demand – and framed within the political and liberal feminist framework. At that time however within the burgeoning women's movement there was considerable debate on housework rather than childcare, perhaps reflecting the ages and concerns of the majority of women who were becoming involved with women's liberation, seen as freedom from the family and household rather than men and children. Indeed a major slogan that developed was 'Smash the Family' (Coote and Campbell, 1982). Moreover, 'Wages for Housework' was one strand of campaigning within the women's movement and it drew on international campaigning; particularly from the USA (Selma James with Susie Fleming) and Italy (Maria Della Costa). As Suzie Fleming was active in the Bristol women's movement, we had highly charged debates about how to understand and campaign about women's work, housework and paid employment.

Feminists thus introduced the debate about the nature of work, and the comparisons and contrasts between work and housework, into sociology. In this they drew on feminist economics and contributed a strand to women's studies, separately and jointly. (Jean Gardiner, 1974; Irene Bruegel, 1979 and Wally Seccombe, 1974). Increasingly the debates and theories drew on Marxist and Marxian theories about labour as contrasted with work. Some of this was subsequently published in a collected form entitled *The Politics of Housework* by Ellen Malos (1980); a text more inspired by the writings by and for the women's movement than feminist sociology although the two were relatively contiguous. This debate was inaugurated somewhere in the interstices between academia (especially sociology and the wider social sciences) and the women's movement, with academics, becoming feminists, and academics manqué, involved in developing the women's liberation movement equally and intimately involved. It was but one of the many ways in which we as feminists attempted to make 'the personal is political' a reality by implementing the slogan. This term, at the time, drew more on political work in the women's movement outside the academy rather than within it.

Out of this arose the notion of sisterhood to enable women to work together more collaboratively, and use the language of family to attempt to subvert sexual and social relations of domination and submission. However, over time, it was increasingly brought into the academy and into academic sociology, at least. Ann Oakley was probably a pioneer, although she did not use the phrase, and indeed later wrote a robust defence of its inappropriateness with Juliet Mitchell:

> When the present phase of the women's movement established itself in the second part of the sixties, there was a need for a unifying ideology while ideas were being worked out or rediscovered. 'Sisterhood' served a rhetorical purpose of political under-development; it was a useful rallying-cry. But its implications were not thought out and it seems to us to mask both an absence of any real unity beneath it and to ignore the highly problematic relationships that in itself it implies. We do live in a hierarchical world; the women's movement does not just combat structures of dominance, it is also surrounded by them and embedded in them. The ideological argument for sisterhood is that sisters must be exempt from the pernicious influence of the nuclear family; they constitute a horizontal alliance within a hierarchical structure. Potentially they have a double bond, for as girls they are socialized into positions inferior to those of their brothers, and they are the children against the domination of parents. Sisterhood can undoubtedly be a relationship of solidarity and support. On the other hand, literature and mythology,

replete with misogynistic jokes against women's family roles (such as mothers-in-law, stepmothers, and so on) has some nasty things to say about sisters too . . . we should remember that ideology not only reflects but also influences social reality. The sisterhood of feminism cannot, in other words, be an instant and transcendent unification of women; it must to some extent repeat the terms of women's social relationships with one another – relationships that, as with all relationships in a family-oriented society, are based upon a family situation. The unity of sisterhood may have magic as a political slogan, but we do not have the ability to conjure it up at will . . . (Mitchell and Oakley (eds.), 1976: 12–13)

Oakley also wrote three key texts in the early 1970s that were highly controversial and contested as contributions to feminist sociology. The first, *Sex, Gender and Society*, (1972) presented both a polemical critique of traditional sociological concepts and set out new approaches to considering differences between men and women. She provided an innovative approach in her distinction between sex and gender. A number of feminist writers have hailed this as innovative in introducing the term 'gender' into social sciences (Segal, 1987, p. 119; Komarovsky, 1988, p. 592; Oudshoorn 1994, p. 152; Hood-Williams, 1999). Oakley's book drew on the work of many international social scientists and women who were trying to develop a critique of traditional approaches to studying men and women. She wrote:

'Sex' is a biological term: 'gender' a psychological and cultural one. Common sense suggests that they are merely two ways of looking at the same division and that someone who belongs to, say, the female sex will automatically belong to the corresponding (feminine) gender. In reality this is not so. To be a man or a woman, a boy or a girl, is as much a function of dress, gesture, occupation, social network and personality, as it is of possessing a particular set of genitals . . . (1972: 158)

She also elaborated the ways in which these terms operated culturally and in specific contexts:

At the present time, society is becoming oriented around the nuclear family, and this means that gender identity has to be acquired more and more narrowly within the family . . . the bias of our culture is still patriarchal; it is women who are claiming the rights of men and who need to be defended against charges of inferiority. Perhaps there is only one area in which attempts are made to prove the reverse – that men are not inferior to women – and that is the home. But even the most participatory father is not shamed by either real or imputed failure, since he retains the prestige of his masculinity . . . (1972: 207–9)

Moreover, it was the first time that such a clear and concise perspective had been presented that allowed for manifold developments in sociological understanding of sex and gender differences and their associations with traditional family and ideological stereotypes. As Toril Moi (1999), amongst others, has argued, these concepts became highly contested within post-modern and post-structural accounts in the 1980s and 1990s as feminists developed more complex theories interweaving biological and social accounts and giving greater consideration to homosexuality, bisexuality and heterosexuality.

Oakley's first text was quickly followed by two complementary texts *The Sociology of Housework* (1974) and *Housewife* (1976) that drew on her material for her PhD on the lives of mothers with pre-school children. However, as Oakley noted, the emphasis was not on motherhood but rather on 'women's household work' (Oakley, personal communication, March 2000). The two perspectives on her studies were well positioned within the conventions of sociology at the time of careful empirical quantitative research with a mix of qualitative supplementary material. Indeed, the two books were published almost to illustrate the two approaches, with *Housewife* (1976) containing the qualitative, discursive and anecdotal material from the interviews with the mothers. *The Sociology of Housework* (1974) provided the clear empirical, quantitative and statistical material about the various women's lives as housewives with young children with only the most cursory of supplementary commentary. These two studies and their particular focus were, interestingly, very much products of their time and the key conceptual notions about women's lives in families in the 1960s and early 1970s. They may also have been influenced by American approaches, in particular that of Betty Friedan's (1963) notion of the 'problem without a name' addressed about the concerns of American middle class housewives. They focused not on women's roles as *mothers* so much as on women's lives as *wives*, and drew on the traditional or then conventional sociological views about work and how to understand and analyse work as an economic activity. Feminists at the time were particularly concerned to debate the economic basis of women's household work in order to try to transform it.

Oakley also wrote about feminist research methods on interviewing and urged women researchers to provide a sympathetic ear and empathy for their subjects. 'Interviewing: a contradiction in terms' discussed the relative positioning of women as researchers and research subjects and suggested reconsideration of the two positions and subjectivity and was published in Helen Roberts' edited collection *Doing Feminist Research* (1981). Her extended argument was produced in *Subject Women* (1982) where she raised strongly the questions of subjectivity in terms of both the researcher and the researched. Here, she extended the arguments that she had initially made almost a decade previously and also began to consider in more depth the nature of the research process. These arguments were not of her own making; she was drawing on an array of arguments being developed both within sociology and in the women's movement. She wrote:

> Feminism can be defined in many ways and just how to define it is one task of the women's movement at the moment . . . Ultimately any feminism is about putting women first; it is about judging women's interests (however defined) to be important and to be insufficiently represented and accommodated within mainstream

> politics/academia. However, this position allows a very wide range of stances,
> theories, practices and recommendations to be selected . . . The main division is
> between socialist feminists and radical feminists. While the former implicate
> capitalism as the perpetrator of women's oppression, the latter accuse men of being
> its prime movers and beneficiaries . . . These varieties of feminism are distin-
> guished from each other on the basis of different theories about why women con-
> stitute the second sex. The question 'what are the origins of women's oppression?'
> cannot, then, be separated from the question, 'what is feminism?' . . . Not the
> smallest of our difficulties is that there is no way of directly examining the evidence
> . . . I have also argued (see pp 331–4) that we are in unfathomable water in deduc-
> ing from sociological data a patriarchal model of society and then further pre-
> suming that this model bears a true correspondence to the cultural maps possessed
> and operated by women . . . The rise of the second sex demands a new language
> and new structures of thought to gestate a completely different society . . . to
> describe it is an act of fiction. (Oakley, 1982: 335–340)

She was seen as emblematic of the new approach of emphasising subjectivity and
qualitative perspectives. Before the 1970s sociology had tended to spurn strong
subjectivity in favour of objectivity and a structural approach. This was even
more the case with respect to sociology in the USA. More importantly, perhaps,
she was a key person amongst second wave feminists in Britain at least to start to
develop a feminist approach to research and to think reflexively. Again, she was a
critical influence on different styles of research and writing, whilst continuing to
pursue research on women. This latter work was increasingly in terms of various
aspects of women in families, as housewives and then about women in childbirth
(*Women Confined*, 1980) and motherhood (*Becoming a Mother*, 1979). She also
began to write in different styles, and produced autobiographical writing in
Taking it like a Woman, published in 1984 although it could be said that her
novels stand in some particular relation to more clearly personal and subjective
accounts. She too has reflected upon her early feminist writing and revised
her perspectives in a book entitled *Experiments in Knowing* (2000) which was in
part an attempt to reflect upon and qualify earlier attributions (personal
communication with Ann Oakley, April 2000). She did not fully acknowledge
her influence on the growing genre of feminist scholarship and wanted to
separate her principles from her methods:

> When I embarked on a randomised controlled trial of social support and pregnancy
> in 1985 . . . it was certainly with the purpose of trying to put into practice some of
> the recommendations about integrating 'qualitative' and 'quantitative'/experi-
> mental methods . . . In my own view, feminism is as much a part of the 'new'
> Oakley as the 'old' one, and so is the belief in ways of knowing that allow the voices
> of research participants to be heard above the (generally) louder noise of the
> researcher's own. Self-labelling as a feminist means only that one declares one's
> values, whereas the dominant tradition is not to do so. (Oakley, 2000: 20–21)

Oakley's methodological journey was to try to integrate so-called 'qualitative' and 'quantitative' approaches, but feminist sociology was, early on, aligned with qualitative approaches and Oakley was identified as a pioneer of those methods. Thus she took a path which ultimately ended up by being both self critical and antithetical to the academic or intellectual sociological movement that she helped to inaugurate. She wrote rather disarmingly on reflection:

> One difficulty . . . is that I myself have a certain involvement in, and even complicity with, the problem . . . To put it in terms of the paradigm argument, I began by singing the praises of 'qualitative' research, of in-depth interviewing and observation as ultimately more truthful ways of knowing, and I have ended up advocating the use of 'quantitative' and experimental methods as providing what is often a sounder basis for claiming that we know anything . . . In the late 1960s and early 1970s I interviewed women about housework, and analysed what they said as providing a basis for a conceptual and political shift – towards including domestic labour in definitions of what work means and how it affects workers in modern society. The book I published about the housework study (Oakley, 1974) opened with a chapter entitled 'The invisible woman: sexism in sociology', which was written as an afterthought at the request of the publisher. The publisher was quite right: it was important to see sociological neglect of housework within the framework of a misogynist social science that had ignored, or distorted, critical aspects of women's situation. The housework research, in the course of which I became a feminist, was followed by another project on women's transition to motherhood (Oakley 1979, 1980) . . . I describe the feminist critique of 'quantitative' methods and 'malestream' social science as though I were outside it; but in fact this is not the case, I was (am) very much inside it. I am proud to own up to having made a certain kind of contribution to academic women's studies through my work on housework, motherhood, research methods and a sort of stubborn insistence on the difference between biological sex and social gender. My contributions to feminist social science have been much-quoted and much-criticized . . . It is as a 'qualitative' feminist sociologist that my work is most often referenced . . . One of the volumes which reported the transition to motherhood study (Oakley 1980) also made much use of statistical tests as a way of arriving at a model of childbirth as a human experience . . . I suggested that women's reactions to childbirth could best be understood by seeing them as people rather than as women. As this is my most neglected book, I have often speculated that my use of the 'quantitative' mode was what put people off. (Oakley, 2000: 13–17)

The work of Michèle Barrett made a most significant contribution to the early writings on feminism in sociology. In *Women's Oppression Today* (1980) Barrett provided the theoretical framework for a feminist sociological analysis. She built upon the work that other feminists and Marxists had begun, particularly within sociology and provided a critique of the various approaches. This was not dissimilar to Ann Oakley's *Subject Women* published at about the same time, but Barrett, rather than reviewing and presenting evidence under a number of themes as Oakley had done, provided a more overt theoretical approach within one of the two traditions that Oakley attempted to explain and explicate. Thus she took a socialist feminist perspective in presenting her material about the various aspects of women's oppression. Her second major contribution, with Mary McIntosh, *The Anti-Social Family* (1982) went further in developing a socialist–feminist analysis of aspects of family life. Here, however, the authors are concerned to develop an analysis that drew on the work of French social theorists (but not necessarily feminist, yet a part of that same intellectual tradition) and especially the work of Donzelot (1979) entitled *The Policing of Families*. Taking the notion of social regulation of families, the authors demonstrated their theoretical perspective through the evidence that they presented about aspects of family life, from childhood through to old age.

Thus developments in feminist sociology from their early beginnings relied heavily on the personal and political activities of the women who were involved in both. Feminist sociology as this historical or biographical account of the birth of an academic, and political endeavour, has shown, relied upon the exploration of personal experience and feelings in establishing new ways of looking at ideas through female rather than male or non-gendered eyes. It did this specifically to establish new ways of thinking and using personal lives and experience to enrich sociological understandings with feminist methodologies and perspectives. These ideas did not come to British women alone but drew on the concepts, theories and experiences of both French and American women. The origins of feminist sociology in the USA and Canada are altogether far more complex than the ways in which feminism eventually began to enter academic life and sociology in Britain. The moves from feminist political and public campaigning to a more academic approach cannot be easily condensed in the ways it can, albeit polemically, for Britain; the movements were altogether more diffuse and related across the range of disciplines. However, there are a few texts that have come to be associated with, and influential upon, the early writings of the women's movement and then academic feminism and have come especially to influence developments in Britain. As we have already noted Betty Friedan's *The Feminine Mystique*, published in 1963 has been widely acknowledged as a critical influence on the developments in second wave feminism, both as a political campaign and as a more scholarly activity (see especially Horowitz, 1999; Friedan, 2001).

The rather sober *The Politics of Women's Liberation* written by the feminist sociologist Jo Freeman and published in 1973 received relatively little media attention but was taken up by many academic feminists in debates about strategy and campaigning. In particular Freeman's argument against early women's liberation forms of unstructured organisation, based upon a theory of sisterhood, which she dubbed 'the tyranny of structurelessness' received widespread debate and, ultimately, support. This study was developed in the context of growing development of sociological work on women. Much sociological work on women as housewives and mothers began to appear in the early 1970s. This was largely developed by the older generation of women sociologists. A particular influence was the work of Jessie Bernard in which she wrote first about what she called 'the future of marriage' and secondly 'the future of motherhood'. Her work brought together numerous previous studies and she reviewed aspects of the development of different perspectives from the points of view of men and women. She was quickly followed by many other researchers developing collections of work around women, marriage, its darker side divorce, and motherhood. Arlene Skolnick became a major editor of volumes on these issues largely for what the Americans considered a textbook. By contrast, Adrienne Rich's work as a poet and writer, especially *Of Woman Born* (1976), was a huge influence on the development of a history of women's role in families and their vital place as mothers but her work did not receive a media fanfare in the way in which more popular novels did. It did however have a significant influence on the development of feminist sociological scholarship in Britain.

Nancy Chodorow's sociological and psychoanalytic account of mothering practices in the USA, published in 1978 as *The Reproduction of Mothering* was one of the first attempts to provide a more complex and overarching feminist theory in sociology. However, this theoretical account became the basis for major theoretical debates about women and the family and it became highly influential as a relatively new and innovative approach to the study of mothers in the social sciences. By the end of the 1970s, there had been a massive outpouring of literature both popular and scholarly and academic which had become the theoretical and substantive material for courses in higher education. A good deal of this work focused upon historical and contemporary approaches to women's subordination and oppression, seen as residing in the structures of family life in contemporary America. For example Ehrenreich and English's *For Her Own Good: 150 years of the experts' advice to women* (1979) reviewed the ways in which women as mothers and carers had been treated within the health care services.

Further reflections on early feminist experiences

Reflecting on how all of this diverse feminist scholarship and endeavour on women and family in relation to education has become integrated into the academy only serves to show the unevenness of the social transformations. On the one hand, feminist scholarship is no longer only taught and taking place outside the academy and only influencing political activities. It is now seen as a somewhat acceptable form of scholarly activity; with women's studies as an area of acceptable research pursuit; albeit as a sub-set of sociology and usually still subordinate to other scholarly disciplines (Morley, 1999). Indeed perhaps feminism is now more acceptable as a form of scholarly activity than political pursuit as social and economic transformations, along with political ideologies varying around forms of liberal political theories, have wrought changes in women's lives.

My work, also with numerous colleagues, has paralleled and developed alongside that of Land, West, Bird, Porter and many others. Over the last twenty-five years I too have shifted my methodological concerns from statistical to Marxist to more substantive and yet still theoretically informed studies of mothers in diverse family contexts in relation to children, childcare and education. Whilst initially fascinated with the more detailed policy debates about mothers as parents and in relation to wider policy analysis pursued by Hilary Land, my interests have shifted as both sociological analysis has shifted, and in relation to wider policy transformations. For a time, my interests involved importing of materials from USA and especially being influenced by Nancy Chodorow's *Reproduction of Mothering*. My concern was then to understand how women continued to accept their role as mothers and in relation to girls' development. However, as my own life course and my children's social and educational development changed I became more fascinated by more immediate issues of concern to me. I was initially fascinated by the debates that arose from Chodorow's work about work, children and forms of parenting called shared parenting from USA rather than the more sophisticated attempts to rewrite psychoanalytic theories from the point of view of feminism. I turn now to consider my early work on mothers and childcare in historical, political and socio-economic contexts.

Notes

1. Duplessis R and Snitow A 1998 *The Feminist Memoir Project: voices from women's liberation* NY Three Rivers Press; Howe, F (ed) 2000 *The Politics of Women's Studies: testimony from thirty founding mothers* NY The Feminist Press; Rowbotham 2000 *Promise of a Dream* (London Allen Lane The Penguin Press).
2. Both Gill Blunden and Myna Trustram also pursued feminist interests, and involved me in new areas of scholarship and feminist activities. Gill worked on issues to do with the history of further education for women, (Blunden, 1983) whilst Myna studied married women's relation to the army in the nineteenth century. (Trustram, 1985) Myna also became more closely involved with psychotherapeutic ideas and the development of co-counselling. This later led to more close associations with Caroline New and the development of our work on childcare.

CHAPTER FOUR

New right turn and feminism in the academy

'Bristol Fashion'

Introduction

In this chapter I consider whether and how the changing social and political context towards Conservatism of the early 1980s influenced our feminist ways of working and women's ways of knowing (Belenky *et al*, 1986) in the academy and our family lives. As noted in the previous chapter the liberal mood and social policies were important in developing our theoretical perspectives and our activities, although we remained highly sensitive and vigilant to the possible return of a more Conservative and traditional social agenda. By the end of the 1970s, this had indeed happened with Thatcher's election to power in Britain in May 1979, and Reagan's election to office in November 1980 and becoming President of the USA in January 1981. However, these political processes were contradictory as there were a growing number of feminist academics, researchers and theoreticians and women were increasingly involved in the public spheres of work in non-traditional ways.

I consider how we tried to influence and transform those wider social and politi-cal changes and how we tried to theorise and write more academically about these issues as they related to our developing family lives. We were developing what became known as radical political economy or critical social policy. It was a period of intense political and academic activities around feminism and family and it is difficult to do justice to the wealth and scope of activities although many of these are now part of the personal reflections and experiences that also emerged out of these momentous changes. For me, a key issue has been the ways in which family events and processes, including developments in my own and my children's lives, have influenced my academic practices and predilections or interests. In particular, during the first part of the 1980s, my political and policy critiques increasingly became linked to aspects of my personal and family life, both in Britain and on a wider international platform. In Britain I became more involved with both political pressure groups such as the *National Child Care Campaign* and more academically-oriented critical reviews such as the *Critical Social Policy* collective and the *British Journal of the Sociology of Education*. I also spent two long periods in north America – six months in the USA in 1980 and three months in Canada in 1983. I consider how these various moments influenced my feminist theories and family practices.

The death of my father and feminist awakenings about the power of patriarchy

The most significant personal event for me was that my father died as the decade opened, on January 2nd 1980. Emerging from the long shadow of patriarchy has been a very slow intellectual and personal process, punctuated by some dramatic moments, some of which are recounted here. It was a time replete with other personal and professionally linked events; my close friend and colleague Hilary Land gave birth the previous day, telephoning to let me know within seconds of my mother ringing to tell me about my father. I had last seen my father on Christmas Day, and had hoped that he would recuperate sufficiently to visit us on our impending stay in the USA. My daughter was just three months old and her brother only 18 months. They were cared for by a former student of mine, Judith Pliatsky, whose mother died the next day, intimating a difficult time for us all in the USA. Her father Sir Leo Pliatsky had just been appointed by Thatcher to review and transform aspects of the public services, named as Quangos (Quasi-Autonomous Non-governmental Organisations) foreshadowing major changes in what was then called the welfare state.

There were a number of highly significant political transformations surrounding the opening of the new decade and my personal experience of them. Thatcher had just become Prime Minister and there were signs of a more conservative mood in the USA. There was also the failed passage of the controversial Equal Rights Amendment (ERA) in the USA in 1980 which had been fiercely debated throughout the 1970s about women's public and private rights (Eisenstein, 1980). It was a backlash against liberal and social feminism that damned the ERA on the grounds that women would have to become combatants in American wars if it were to succeed on grounds of equal rights for women with men. These rightward shifts were the subject of much comment at the time and have been the topic of much subsequent review, especially in the closing years of the twentieth century (Eisenstein, 1982; Petchesky, 1984).

However, whilst these political events were of seismic significance and I, amongst others, was involved with writing critically about the political shifts and influences upon social and family policies, they were not dramatic in terms of their influence upon the academic labour market. Quite the contrary. By the end of the 1970s, many women of my generation had obtained secure (and tenured) positions within the academy, both in Britain and other advanced industrial societies, such as Australia, Canada and the USA and many parts of Europe. Academic feminism and feminist perspectives on the disciplines were becoming embedded within our practices within the academy as well as in our more external and political activities. (In Chapter Five I consider how this was subsequently theorised within various disciplines.) In this chapter I consider our developing critiques in relation not only to political and social transformations but also our changing family lives and their two-way influences. There are two threads and themes here – the increasing influence of my personal circumstances, including motherhood, on my professional activities, and the growing theorisation of my political and professional activities.

Personal family circumstances and critiques

My decision to marry and have children was contrary to the strictures of the growing and influential women's movement of the time. Unlike many of my contemporaries, I had been fortunate to avoid the problems of unplanned pregnancies and the necessity of an abortion, although by this stage it was no longer the moral dilemma that it had been for us in our early twenties when abortions were still illegal. I was of the generation convinced of the efficacy and effectiveness of the pill (oral contraceptive) and had few qualms about its use and possible long-term negative effects on my health. I had not yet developed a critique of media constructions of health (Graham, 1980; Lewis, 1980). However, having children 'out-of-wedlock' remained a social stigma, or something to be frowned upon during the 1960s and 1970s, as did forms of cohabitation rather than marriage (Kiernan, Land and Lewis, 1998). Most women of my generation married, particularly those from my social, cultural and quasi-religious background, although many more of those marriages resulted in divorce than from previous generations. The evidence for these momentous changes began to be gathered both by feminists and through the backlashes during the 1980s.

Being somewhat tied to my conventional and traditional Jewish family background I was not able to shake off its yoke and be as brave as many of my friends and colleagues in being able to cohabit and bear children. Indeed, some of my closest friends, Hilary Land amongst them, became closely involved politically in the *Why Be A Wife* campaign, aimed at transforming social policies on family life and particularly women's economic dependence upon their husbands. Whilst I might argue forcefully about this both academically and politically my private and personal life remained at odds with it, a contradiction that has only subsequently been frequently observed and which I can now reflect upon. Being a wife and mother were also two sides of the same coin and changes in both proceeded unevenly for many women of this post-war generation. Since the 1970s, social and cultural changes in the conditions attaching to both wifehood and full-time motherhood had been very dramatic through policy changes and the wider social and economic shifts in patterns of employment and paid work (Land, 1977; Kiernan, Land and Lewis ; 1998; Lewis, 1980; Haskey, 1998).

The marriage bar to women's professional employment that had been enforced in many professions, especially education and the law, from the early twentieth century through to the late 1950s, no longer held (Oram, 1989). However, it was an issue that fascinated us, by its extent and effects, in our early studies (David, 1980). We had, for instance, learnt of the continuing and recent use of family allowances for academics, within London University until well into the 1970s, and my first head of department in Bristol – Professor Roy Parker – had been a recipient. So too had both Hilary and Steven Rose (personal communication at Hilary Land's retirement seminar, March 25th 2002). There were some lingering restrictions about marriage within universities, and some continuing conventions that married women should not work in the same department, faculty or institution as their husbands. My marriage to a colleague in a cognate department, although not formally debarred, was occasionally frowned upon. (Similarly there were questions asked about the Vice Chancellor's wife's appointment to an academic department.)

I was able to buck the social convention of being a full-time working mother with pre-school children. Having children and continuing to work full-time whilst they were either pre-schoolers or dependent was something that many women of my generation found difficult to do (including my sisters, literal as well as those in the women's movement *pace* Mitchell and Oakley). This was in part because of social conventions but more especially because of the lack of availability of childcare provisions. However, I was fortunate in my colleagues and work situation and became involved in ensuring this possibility of full-time academic employment. (Commentaries about women even being able to work in academia and be treated equally recently surfaced about women scientists well into the 1960s and 1970s (Rose, 1995). The example of Jocelyn Bell Burnell, a research physicist and scientist, and member of Through the Glass Ceiling, has been cited in making the award of a Franklin prize for women scientists by Patricia Hewitt, Secretary of State for Trade and Industry in the New Labour government, *The Observer,* January 20th 2002, p. 12).

During the 1970s we campaigned nationally for widening maternity rights and leave, including for academic women. British maternity rights had been created in the early part of the twentieth century and extended as part of the provisions of the post-war welfare state, and paralleled in most European countries but not in the United States. Indeed, American social provisions for women as potential and actual mothers, including for childcare, were based upon a male view of political rights, as with the ERA, rather than a more flexible notion of equal rights and opportunities as in Europe. As recently as 1978, the US Supreme Court had continued to uphold the view that it was not discriminatory to deny women social and health disability income compensation since if men were pregnant they would also not be entitled to such rights (Eisenstein, 1982; David, 1984; 1985). In Britain, organisations such as universities were able to augment state-funded schemes. We had success in changing the provisions within academic life for all mothers, whatever their marital status. These topics also became the subject of our academic studies and practices. We were trying to transform our family lives as we lived them and aiming also to transform the lives of women through accumulating the evidence about the impacts of such limitations and restrictions on women's lives, as well as accounting for particular policy initiatives and developments cross-nationally. We also began to campaign for childcare for pre-school children as part of the early second wave women's movement. Hitherto, there were no public or few private provisions for the collective and social care of very young children. The solution that the vast majority of women who had children made was of 'their own choosing' rather than being facilitated by government action and provision (Riley, 1983). Thus, for middle class and professional or educated women, choices were as limited as those for women who needed to work or take paid employment to care for and bring up their children (New and David, 1985). As Land (1976) described, caring for the family was largely women's responsibility. Middle class women had to take either what became known as 'a career break' or work part-time, and/or pay for private childcare with nannies, au pairs and private nurseries. Working class women and mothers without the financial means were forced to use child-minders; women who cared for children in their own homes and were registered by local authorities (New and David, 1985). Most women were not able to do what Margaret Thatcher had done three decades previously, despite her articulate clarion call for this strategy (see Arnot, David and Weiner, 1999).

Thatcher and the rise of Thatcherism

Although Mrs Thatcher had become the first woman leader of the opposition in 1976 and then Prime Minister during our feminist campaigns in the 1970s she was not recognised at the time as someone at all sympathetic to these women's issues. Rather, she was regarded as a person opposed to liberal social policies. It is only more recently that we have begun to recognise the contradictory processes at work, which led both to her achieving political office and power and the changes in many women's lives. The social and political transformations have been such that many women are now, at the time of writing, found in positions of prominence in the polity and in all forms of paid employment. This shift in the sheer numbers of women in such positions within the political system either as elected representatives, or appointees, or as policy advisors and more generally in the economic system as paid workers or professionals has been dramatic. This has also become the subject of much social research into the ways in which shifts in forms of employment, associated with social and economic transformations, have affected the social class systems and processes. In particular, the rise and expansion of the new middle classes has been theorised by many, most interestingly by Bernstein (1996), Bourdieu (1980) and Savage (2000). However, it is only more recently that this has been the subject of feminist analysis and theorisation. Ehrenreich (1989) did begin to draw attention to the concerns of middle class families about their children's educational fates.

During the previous thirty years the shifts were beginning to make themselves felt even in the political processes but women in prominent political positions remained rare and relatively unique. Margaret Thatcher, as Britain's first woman Prime Minister, thus had iconic significance and status but this was not matched by many other women's positions. As I reflected with colleagues, Thatcher was both a conundrum, given her 'Victorian' views on women and the family and her own personal political career and development, and representative of the social transformations that were beginning to be felt around women's changing social and public position (Arnot, David and Weiner, 1999). We wrote:

> Margaret Thatcher's administrations of the 1980s initiated a once-and-for-all break with Victorianism in terms both of greater gender equality in education and of the modernization of family life and associated work practices. Thatcher's life and work embodies a tension between Victorian family rhetoric and the reality of modern family life. Paradoxically, despite her espousal of Victorian political and family values, she has become an icon of female educational and public achievement for the late twentieth century.
>
> Of interest to us at this point are the contradictions (revealed in her own and her husband's biographies, the latter by her daughter) between public espousal of traditional or 'Victorian' political and family values and the ways in which Margaret Thatcher lived her own family life – contradictions that were to inform her political practice in complex ways. This tension is no more clearly illustrated than in her career, leading her to becoming Britain's first woman prime minister. It could be argued that her particular conservative views enabled her to uphold apparently contradictory values. Her belief in liberal or *laissez-faire* conservatism (and the importance of limited government in the context of the free market) is one which could offer her a number of scripts for her own personal life and direction. Her politics, of individualism and liberalism, in the economic sphere in fact also directed her to a kind of 'liberal, individualistic feminism' which she applied to her politics of family life. (Arnot, David and Weiner 1999: 42)

Around that time we were only dimly aware of the contradictions, and far more concerned to criticise her right-wing politics and campaign against these issues than to theorise them from a feminist perspective. Thus our efforts at providing intellectual, political and academic critiques of her family, education and social policies were redoubled. We also continued to develop historical accounts, linked to other social and political theories, of women's family and political lives, locating them in relation to our growing feelings of dissatisfaction with our restricting and restricted horizons and opportunities. But we were not very reflective or even reflexive, although some feminists had begun to write auto-biographically either about their early lives or in relation to particular family issues.

Feminist reflections and autobiographical accounts

Our own family lives, and those of the preceding and succeeding generation, may have begun a process of some subtle change, and the early glimmerings of slight dissatisfactions, leading later to feminist consciousness. These dissatis-factions were to do with our mothers' roles and positions as subordinate, if not totally economically dependent, upon their husbands and as carers of families rather than 'workers' or professionals in their own right. They were also to do with notions of happiness or not which may not have formulated themselves at that point into major forms of marital change. Dissatisfaction certainly did not lead the majority of such women to protest their 'lot' through 'radical' measures such as separation or divorce. It is certainly the case that these feelings can be identified amongst those second wave feminists' writing first in their own books such as Jean McCrindle and Sheila Rowbotham (1977) on themselves as 'dutiful daughters' and later with others in the now widely established collection *Truth, Dare or Promise? Girls Growing up in the fifties* edited by Liz Heron (1985). Steed-man (1986) first developed her own memoir or biography as a contribution to this volume, later extended into her book, *Landscape for a Good Woman.* Swindells (1995), drawing on Sara Maitland's essay in her edited collection, pointed out that this kind of reflection on the early glimmerings of the second wave feminist accounts, by women who might consider themselves in their childhoods as pre-feminists, began to emerge in the early 1970s and was profuse by the 1980s. There were also accounts by emerging feminists of their relation-ships not only with their mothers but also their fathers (see Ursula Owen, 1986). Autobiographical accounts were developed by succeeding generations of women who variously considered themselves as feminists, and at various stages in their lives and/or academic careers. However, for many this was not their only approach and in sociology, for instance, qualitative methods of a more formal kind were also pursued.

As mentioned in the previous chapter, Elizabeth Wilson (1983) was one of the first British feminists to write autobiographically, having already established herself as an academic, writing in the early 1980s in *Mirror Writing* of her life as a dutiful daughter. Her background was not dissimilar to that of Beauvoir.

She attended a well-known girls' public school, and later Oxford University in the immediate aftermath of the Second World War and she painted a picture of a family life of increasing discontent, if not malaise. She emphasised her changing consciousness from that of her own bourgeois family background and in association with other budding feminist academics. Similarly, as part of the same developments, the British sociologist Ann Oakley wrote her first auto-biographical and feminist account *Taking it Like a Woman,* published in 1984. These women were among the first to experiment with this new genre of writing, distanced if not divorced from their more conventional academic work which had already become quite well-established. As Stanley (1992) later wrote, commenting upon them:

> The[se] autobiographies . . . self-consciously and self-confidently mix genres and conventions. Within them fact and fiction, fantasy and reality, biography and autobiography, self and others, individuals and networks, not only co-exist but intermingle in ways that encourage, not merely permit active readership . . . These feminist autobiographies challenge the boundaries of conventional auto-biographical form, indeed play with some of its conventions . . . of confessional truth-telling, a narrative that moves uni-directionally from birth/beginning to maturity/resolution/end, and the insistence on unitary self. (Stanley, 1992: 247)

Reviewing Ann Oakley's autobiography in *Network* the magazine of the BSA in 1985, I praised this new 'form' and her ability to mix conventions and assert a new life as a woman, attempting to break down conventions about family, sex and sexuality. However, I well recall being taken to task by many more tradi-tional feminists for my comments on the life of someone who was seen to be so individualistic and self-indulgent. In particular, her chapters were interspersed with more poetic, personal revelations of her supposed 'adultery' and sexual liaisons and, in the context of attempts to develop more appropriate forms of academic feminism, were seen to be derisory. Indeed, Oakley's account was seen by many to infringe traditional protocol by writing of her parents' and her own intimate and family lives so frankly and yet at another level so fancifully. Since then however she has developed far more 'playful' and fanciful writing and narratives in the form of a series of novels about women's lives, which play with family and sexual lives. Similarly, Wilson and others continued to write in this kind of vein. Other feminists have written accounts that also illustrate these changing family lives and women's ability to build upon their early experiences to challenge conventions in family life. These various accounts include challeng-ing traditional marriage with divorce and the responsibilities of parenthood as well as having a full intellectual and/or working life; or developing alternative sexual life styles through lesbianism combined with parenthood. At the same time however many feminists have developed more traditional autobiographical accounts of how they became feminists, including in academic life as well as in politics.

Liz Stanley, a sociologist, had been moved to develop her methodological work, with Sue Wise, being deeply influenced by personal circumstances. Stanley and Wise's *Breaking Out* (1983) was one of the first attempts to theorise a feminist and qualitative methodology from their personal experiences of abuse as a result of their research methods of seeking information about lesbianism by advertising in the press. Their book became a key text of feminist methodology within sociology and was republished ten years later (Stanley and Wise, 1983; *Breaking out again* 1993). Almost a decade later, reflecting upon the more directly auto/biographical writing Stanley addressed these issues especially in her *The auto/biographical I* (1992) where she concerned herself particularly with the multiple understandings of life, texts and feelings. Interestingly, however, she did not fully address the issues from the point of view of family. (Indeed, family was not a term in her index; neither was mother, parent or daughter, child) but rather 'lives'. Yet she drew on her mother's 'tragedy' of a stroke to make some key points about her own theorising and ontological being. She wrote:

> Understanding and theorising 'the self' is no easy matter. If theoretical accounts do not fit actual biographical selves and the material reality of their lives then there is something wrong with the theory, not the lives. Auto/biographies . . . [give] the primacy of everyday life and its concrete material events, persons, conversations. 'Bio', the narration of the material events of everyday life, is the crucial element in theorising and understanding both 'auto' and 'graph', albeit, written (but not spoken) auto/biography . . . (Stanley, 1992: 246)

She went on to justify a feminist approach:

> . . . some may think that proposing a feminist auto/biography which is reflexively concerned with its own labour process is merely narcissitic. But . . . the aim here is to enable more people than just one, the auto/biographer, to analytically engage with the auto/biographical investigative approach. For instance, Carolyn Steedman's *Landscape for a Good Woman* (1986) points up the severe limitations of most feminist biography for those who are not middle class (and, I would add, not white or heterosexual), and emphasises how interwoven *her autobiography is with her construction of her mother's biography*; it also illuminatingly shows the reader that understanding these links involves a process within which her changing thinking is located . . . Biographies and autobiographies . . . can provide feminist heroes to stand alongside the more usual subjects . . . Nonetheless, we need to develop the means for a more active readerly engagement with such writings, one which does not take them on trust as sources of fact and information, but rather recognises their role in the construction of particular views of the 'self' they represent. (Stanley, 1992: 254–5) (my emphasis)

Liz Stanley was at the forefront of developing this kind of analysis and methodology in the early 1980s both alone and jointly with colleagues. However, we in Bristol remained wedded to a more conventional social analysis, which, whilst taking the Weberian viewpoint seriously, did not then permit us to be so self-consciously reflexive, although it did mean that we began to develop what soon became known as 'standpoint theory'. It was only slowly that we married our more socialist-feminist engagements with this kind of approach to reflexivity. In researching and studying family life, we are in effect studying the context that we live within, that constitutes us as we constitute it. It is like studying the air we breathe whilst we study it. A theoretical notion used for the extent to which we need to be constantly vigilant to this conundrum is the notion of reflexivity – reflecting upon our research and practices, our positionings and our personal perspectives as we study and research them. We are enjoined to express who we are, where we come from and what our interests and perspectives are and reflect upon how they may influence our perspectives and understandings, and increasingly now our emotions. This may however make our understanding and knowledge partial and distinctive.

Another less reflexive approach to personal experiences that many of us were facing in the early 1980s centred on the politics of childcare; a politics, practice and set of theories that led to complexities and arguments within feminism and academic feminism. Indeed, many women have written evocatively of the difficulties of combining work and childcare and Caroline New and I tried to theorise and generalise these accounts (New and David, 1985). A particularly powerful instance of this politics in the early years of more academic feminism was the controversies evoked by Sylvia Ann Hewlett in her best-selling book *A Lesser Life* (1986). She wrote both an academic account of attempts to develop childcare policies in the academy in the USA and how these strategies and campaigns were interwoven with her own personal life, as an émigré from Wales to the USA. Her moving account of her treatment as a pregnant woman and for writing so frankly about her dilemmas and life in an elite academy in the USA when having her children provoked enormous controversy within feminism. Segal (1999) recently wrote that Hewlett was scornful of prior feminist debates and campaigns for equality. Yet she subsequently returned to England and was involved with Labour strategies for childcare in the early 1990s. These debates have become, on the one hand, much more muted and on the other hand more strategic and less personal as the generations of feminists in the academy have altered and shifted. Thus one of the more programmatic areas of feminism is about family life, care of children in comparison and contrast with care of older family members. Yet Hewlett's passionate story of her life as a mother in a strange country and even more strange university setting provides contrasts with our challenging engagements.

Feminism Bristol Fashion

In Bristol, we campaigned for and succeeded in getting a university nursery established in 1980. This campaign was developed initially by the Students' Union for provision for students as part of a national strategy by the National Union of Students (NUS). Locally women members of the academic teachers' union – the Association of University Teachers (AUT) – eventually joined the campaign. Whilst the strategy was initially contentious with male academics voting for car-parking in preference to facilities for their children or those of their colleagues we negotiated successfully with the university authorities for a small-scale provision. However, initially the university insisted on employing a private contractor to manage and run the nursery, a company set up locally to run a number of private nurseries within the city. As a result of mismanagement by this company the university conceded a year later that the parents could run and manage the nursery through a limited company. The University Nursery Parents Association (UNPA) was thus created and I became its first chair. Both my children were born in the twilight of the 1970s and were ostensibly 'Thatcher's children' in that they grew up knowing political life solely under a Conservative administration. My son Toby was born in the summer of 1978, a year before Thatcher came to office whilst my daughter Charlotte was born in the autumn of 1979, in the shadow of Thatcher's election. I continued with my university career, taking only time out through maternity leave and arranging childcare as co-operatively as my husband and I were able to. Many of my colleagues and friends had babies around the same time and we shared and developed forms of childcare and our children's upbringing in both nurseries and nursery education. As a baby, Toby was cared for privately at home by a young woman who lived locally and was between school and university. The following year, for the first six months he shared childcare at home with his friend Graham before we departed for the USA. On our return he went to the university nursery whilst Charlotte was cared for privately at home as she was still too young to attend the nursery. Toby then went to a nursery school part-time with his friend Anna Freeman (Caroline New's daughter) for a year before entering primary school, whilst Charlotte and Dienka (Hilary Land's daughter) became stalwarts of the university nursery, before going to primary school.

It was during this period that Caroline New and I, having joined the embryonic National Child Care Campaign, a national feminist strategic and campaigning group, decided to write about childcare policies and practices more theoretically and develop initiatives and strategies for wider public provision. In the NCCC we met many political activists as well as theoreticians, especially Sheila Rowbotham, Pamela Calder and Helen Penn. This eventually resulted in our book *For the Children's Sake: making child care more than women's business* (Penguin

1985). The book was a long time in the making, for various reasons, not least the one that we were both working and taking the lion's share of responsibility for childcare, despite our partners' active involvement. It is no accident that it was Caroline and I who decided to write the book, not Norman and Robert, also both academics with interests in children, child development and families. We also were very actively engaged in a range of extra-mural political activities both for the women's movement and other socialist campaigns. We also spent periods of time abroad, Caroline in Australia and Canada, and myself in the USA and Canada, working on other related projects and campaigns. We also wanted to draw in other people to share examples of shared parenting and shared childcare, and we sought out other contributors with particular kinds of expertise. Our main argument, however, was to be influenced by the various emergent feminist theoretical and research work on motherhood, childcare policies and practices. In particular, we wanted to build upon the developing theoretical and empirical work about these issues and practices internationally. We were limited in the extent to which we were able to draw on material from European countries, especially France, and Eastern Europe, and concentrated more on the Anglophone countries. We used feminist work from Britain, such as that by Oakley (1978; 1979), Barrett (1980) and MacIntosh (1982), separately and together as well as Land (1976; 1977) as referred to previously. We were also interested to explore the wider sociological studies of motherhood from the USA, such as Jessie Bernard and Arlene Skolnick's seminal work, and that influenced by psychoanalytic perspectives developed by Nancy Chodorow (1978). We also wanted to include the most innovative work by feminists on childhood and sexuality by Stevi Jackson (1982), which had been a relatively taboo subject, and emergent work on childcare by Denise Riley (1984). Moreover, we addressed the rather more limited work on what is now known as but for which there was not really a term 'fatherhood'. Finally we wanted to develop a strategic approach to childcare, by suggesting some programmes that might not be merely utopian. Thus this book drew on two emergent themes – one being broader feminist theories and the other critics of policies and contexts, such as the new right as it was emerging in the USA and Britain.

Feminist friendships and international critiques

My husband and I had been given sabbatical leave for the spring and summer of 1980 and had planned to spend time in the USA as visiting professors at the University of California in Irvine, where we had each been offered some teaching in the 'program of social ecology'. I was to teach an undergraduate course on family policies and to join with the new program across the university in women's studies. We continued with these plans despite our changing personal family circumstances. I was keen to explore various developments in feminism and women's studies and the changing political context. As it happened, the time we were there was highly significant in that we witnessed the beginnings of the right-wing presidential campaigns for Reagan in his home state (although he was not elected as President until six months later). We also were involved in feminist and socialist lobbying against the rising anti-abortion campaigns. A huge rally was held in Anaheim in June at which there was a massive counter-demonstration of radicals, feminists and socialists as well as student activists. Living in Orange County gave us a particular take on the contradictory forces and the rise of the new and moral right during this period. The local airport symbolised some of these contradictions and changes, having recently been renamed John Wayne airport, and that particular area of southern California held a variety of social groups committed to different values and ideologies – from film stars to the new urban poor and radical and emergent environmentalists. Mike Davis (1986) described these graphically in his *City of Quartz*.

I engaged with various social and political groups, although feminism was not uppermost as the women academics I met were politely friendly but distant. Francesca Cancian subsequently published her study on friendships that seemed to encapsulate these problems. Childcare both personally and politically became a concern of mine as Judith Pliatsky unexpectedly left us early and returned to England. Having inspected the various franchised childcare operations we decided to share childcare for the duration of our teaching. Childcare as a business was emerging in California at that time, but it was not at all characterised by liberal, socialist, feminist or child-centred ideas. On the contrary, these centres were extremely regimented and controlled, with children confined to age hierarchies and dormitories, redolent of what nineteenth century baby farms might have been like. Given my interest in family and education, especially parents and schools, and my emerging fascination with motherhood and schooling, as a result of reading about the politics and policies of motherhood in the USA, I decided to pursue some studies of teen pregnancy (Hass, 1980; Zellman, 1981). This was then emerging as a major social issue, linked to problems of poverty and 'race', and being seen as part of what was identified as the feminisation of poverty. I was scorned by some major international family policy scholars for my interest and told that this was merely a 'black' problem, and not one of central and critical social policy concern. Given New Labour's elevation of this to a key issue of social exclusion and poverty through the Social Exclusion Unit's report in 1999, I now realise what I had identified but could not then theorise. My interest centred on school-age mothers and I also visited a number of childcare centres attached to schools. Again I was surprised to find how restrictive and indeed punitive the regimes for both mothers and babies were, here reminiscent of mother and baby homes in Victorian times. However, over the intervening years from 1980 to 2000 there have been numerous studies of the issues of teenage pregnancy cross-culturally (e.g. Burdell, 1995/6; Hudson and Ineichen 1986; Phoenix, 1990; Kelly, 2001).

I also spent time in New York, attending two meetings – the American Sociological Association and the 'triple SP' (that is, the Society for the Study of Social Problems), a more radical and fringe meeting of sociologists. At both of these meetings, together with British colleagues, we explored and learned about developments in socialist feminist theories and practices in the USA, especially through the work of Piven and Cloward, (1970; 1976; 1979) on poverty policies, and Ehrenreich and English (1979), who had already written extensively, problematising the histories of women in relation to medicalisation and health.

Sex and social policy: the backlash

Walking in the streets of New York one day with Diana Leonard, her three children, and my two small children, we overheard a man comment that women breed like rabbits, presumably thinking that all five children belonged to just one of us. A small incident, but his comment seemed emblematic of the growing backlash against women. My stay in the USA alerted me to a series of issues that have been threaded through my subsequent work and link with the themes identified above. I developed my socialist feminist perspectives and work on the moral right in the USA, combining an interest in family, sex and education issues. California had been the home of the American far right and the issues that were then emerging from this sojourn helped to crystallise the ways in which the moral right was beginning to target questions of sex and sexuality and develop an anti-feminist agenda about abortion, women and family poverty. American socialist feminists were writing excellent and extensive critiques of these emergent issues such as abortion and the so-called feminisation of poverty (Eisenstein and Petchesky) and we began to adopt and adapt these ideas for a British audience. We also in particular tried to consider the changing role of the state and the ways in which the new right governments were modifying its operations, despite the social and economic changes that had begun to take place.

This was a time of intense social transformation and our emergent collective work was increasingly reflecting our concerns with the growing assault on our accomplishments both politically and theoretically to date. In particular, we were increasingly invited to comment on social and political and policy shifts and changes. For instance, my colleague Hilary Land and I were invited to contribute to a Fabian society seminar reviewing the effects of the Labour government in office in Britain in the 1970s, held in the summer of 1981. We agreed to look at the various developments in equal opportunities policies for women throughout the 1970s, from changes in social security and welfare policies to childcare and education. In particular we looked at the developments from the perspective of the legislative framework that had been created through the Equal Pay and Sex Discrimination Acts, jointly implemented from 1975 and speculated on the likely effects of the incoming Conservative administration. We considered that the legislation would be watered down by the more lukewarm commitment of the Conservatives, despite the leadership by a woman. We were subsequently invited to write up the paper for publication in an edited volume of papers from the conference and to be entitled *The Future of the Welfare State*. Provocatively and deliberately entitling the piece *Sex and Social Policy* we addressed these questions of the future by citing the resignation of Lady Howe from her post as Deputy Director of the Equal Opportunities Commission (EOC), created through the SDA to monitor developments in equal opportunities. She had resigned on the appointment of her husband, Geoffrey Howe, as Chancellor of the Exchequer by Margaret Thatcher as part of the incoming Tory administration in 1979. When the book was published in 1983 Lady Howe had become a student of social administration at the London School of Economics and the book's editor was one of her teachers. It became required reading and as a result we were sued for libel since we were said to have misrepresented her reasons for her resignation from her post. Many could not understand the furore, in particular my mother and women of her generation felt that it was right and proper that women should defer to their husbands and careers. However, the libel was settled out of court and the offending sentence removed from subsequent publications, with the original book also being recalled by the publishers.

This incident revealed to us the controversial impact of even relatively mild forms of equal opportunities proposals and policies which did not go beyond the liberal perspective on employment rather than the deeper issues of childcare, sex and sexuality. Our intention was to use a particularly public example to demonstrate the difficulties of equalising opportunities for employment between men and women even within the liberal polity. If it were difficult for middle class women and families, however much more so we reasoned for working class and poor households. Whilst it appeared that Lady Howe was arguing that the Conservatives were fully committed to liberal legislation and the equalising of employment opportunities between men and women, under the Conservative administrations from 1980 to the late 1990s, equal opportunities legislation was not strengthened. Indeed, there has been an erosion of policy implementation, whilst, at the same time, there has been a dramatic growth in women's employment, especially for middle class and professional women. What had become clear was the complex relationships between social and economic transformations, political ideologies and public policies and the political involvement of women.

Reflections on comparative research on mothers and education

During this period, we also began to develop studies about not only the impact of policies but also the wider social assumptions about women in their caring roles and capacities, drawing upon comparative literature, and in particular that gleaned from the USA and Canada. Again, however, these notions were not simple but contested and highly complex. For instance many feminists in sociology in the USA especially had abjured looking at women as mothers and had argued for more theoretical and educational perspectives on women's complex social and sexual positioning, related to various different political theories. However, Friedan (1982), for example, argued about liberal and individual theories about how feminism might move into a second stage. This book became very controversial for its arguments about the role of the family drawing as it did on her knowledge accumulated from psychology and sociology. Indeed she began to teach as a sociologist arguing that:

> . . . the concepts of what I came to call the second stage. I started to systematize [these ideas] in the early and mid-seventies when, as a visiting professor of sociology . . . I decided not to teach 'women's studies' but to call my courses 'The Sex Role Revolution-Stage Two' and 'Human Sex and Human Politics' . . . (Friedan, 1982: 5)

> The new frontier where the issues of the second stage will be joined is the, I believe, the family: that same, trampled, bloody ground which the enemies of feminism are now supposedly defending against deathly siege . . .

> It is hardly new for women to be concerned with the family, I realize. But weren't feminists supposed to be liberating themselves *from* the family? (Friedan, 1982: 89–90)

She went on to argue for a feminism that was liberal rather than radical and which incorporated approaches to family life that might be considered quite traditional. She went on:

> The *personhood of women*, that's what it is really all about . . . and real equality, for men and women . . . The right to choose is crucial to the personhood of women (1982: 92) . . . The point is, the movement to equality and the personhood of women isn't finished until motherhood is a fully free choice. (1982: 93)

She also acknowledged her own inabilities to be able fully to conquer her mixed and ambiguous feelings about family life and how they were rooted to some extent in her relationship with her mother:

> We all carry in our personal history the evidence of this heritage. My own feminism somehow began in my mother's discontent, forced to quit as woman's page editor of the Peoria newspaper when she married my father' . . . then why did I, despite a superior education not available to her, give up psychology fellowships

and feel almost relieved when I was fired from a newspaper job during my second pregnancy? I was determined to be 'fulfilled as a woman' as my mother was not. My own conscious feminism began in later outrage at that mistaken either/or choice that the feminine mystique imposed upon my generation. (1982: 99)

Thus her strategies for feminism of the second stage became liberal, individualistic and linked with commitments to human liberation rather than transformations and revolutions in the ways in which relationships between men and women developed. It could be argued that these ideas came from her ageing:

> The second stage is going to be defined by a fluidity, flexibility and pragmatism demanding more individual responsibility and voluntary pooling of community resources than has been demanded of American democracy for many years – though it is the essence of the American tradition. It is what we demanded of ourselves in the women's movement.

> If we can eliminate the false polarities and appreciate the limits and true potential of women's power, we will be able to join with men – follow or lead – in the new human politics that must emerge beyond reaction. And this new human liberation will enable us to . . . affirm new and old family bonds that can evolve and nourish us through all the changes of our lives . . . (1982: 348)

However, most academic feminists and sociologists were developing far more critical theories about mothers and their social condition, not accepting that their political activities and theories had already had a political impact. I remained within a more critical and radical tradition, linking my studies with the work of others such as Dorothy Smith (1978; 1982). I wrote several pieces around these issues (Barton and Walker, 1983; Lewis, 1983), drawing upon the moral and social order and assumptions, and trying to tease out the ways in which conservative agendas bore with them particular moral codes about appropriate cultural behaviour and activities for men and women. Feminists were theorising these questions from a socialist perspective, and developing a form of social and sociological analysis that would accommodate these issues methodologically. Dorothy Smith's work on developing an analysis from the standpoint of women was becoming particularly influential although it did not appear in full publication until 1987 with the title of her early work *The Everyday World as Problematic* (1987). She later reflected on how she came to write in this vein:

> I began thinking through how to develop sociological inquiry from the site of the experiencing and embodied subject as a sociology from the standpoint of women. In the women's movement, we began to discover that we lived in a world put together in ways in which we had very little say . . . We discovered that we had been in various ways silenced, deprived of the authority to speak, and that our experience therefore did not have a voice, lacked indeed a language, for we had taken from the cultural and intellectual world created largely by men the terms, themes, conceptions of the subject and subjectivity, of feeling, emotion, goals, relations and an object world assembled in textually mediated discourses and from

the standpoint of men occupying the apparatuses of ruling. We came to understand this organisation of power as 'patriarchy', a term that identified both the
personal and the public relations of male power . . . Our discoveries of a language,
political, cultural, artistic, philosophic, were grounded in the practice called 'consciousness raising' . . . Speaking from experience was a method of speaking; it was
not a particular kind of knowledge, but a practice of telling wherein the particular
speaker was authority in speaking of her everyday life and the world known to her
as she was active in it . . . Sociology did not know how to develop inquiry from the
standpoint of a subject situated in the actualities of her life. Indeed it abjured such
a standpoint. (Smith, 1990: 1–2)

Smith had also begun to study women as mothers, and the ways in which these
assumptions affected how mothering was conducted, and the relationship to
children's education and care. Smith continued to apply her Marxist analysis to
the studies, developing such substantive analyses alongside her more theoretical
and methodological developments over the last thirty years. She viewed the ways
in which motherhood has been regulated and developed by state policies, including on education, as to do with work rather than emotional activities of care. Her
emphasis was on studying this relation as a work relation. This contrasted with
more recent studies and approaches to mothering such as Arlie Hochschild's
(1990) approach of studying such relations as about emotions and emotional
work for instance. What was particularly significant about Smith's work and
Alison Griffith's, amongst others, was how it emphasised mothers' relations to
children in the context of educational policies. This mapped on to my ways of
thinking and studying mothers. I was very excited to be invited to spend the
summer at the Ontario Institute for Studies in Education (OISE) in Toronto,
Canada working with Dr Smith and teaching a summer course to graduate
students on critical feminist pedagogy.

Dorothy Smith's feminist approach became highly influential. She was invited
to give keynote addresses at the BSA conferences, first in the 1980s and again in
1998. Her methodological approach of studying life from the standpoint of
women as institutional ethnography and grounding the analysis in the everyday
lives of ordinary and working class women was the start of an understanding of
social forces as they operate to confirm and continue inequalities and privileges
of dominant classes. She provided the particular example that if we had started
from the perspective of women doing housework, the then conventional sociological distinction between 'work' and 'leisure' would never have become so conventional. Her ideas have drawn on, and been drawn on by, Sandra Harding
(1993). She too argued to 'start off thought' from the standpoint of women
but not necessarily from those women who are academics and researchers.
Rather she was concerned with the lives of women as marginalised groups, and
especially 'people at the bottom' (1993, p. 54). Nancy Hartstock's work on standpoint theory has also been highly influential and, as noted at the beginning of

Chapter Two, she herself has reviewed the ways in which she began to approach these issues and questions within a changing social and political context. Other feminist sociologists and scholars also developed variants of standpoint theories drawing on feminist notions about personal experience and consciousness, including Donna Haraway's (1989) application of these notions to scientific theories.

Standpoint theory, as it has become known, in feminist research circles, has also led to the burgeoning of autobiographical accounts from a researcher's point of view. Stanley and Wise (1983; 1993) argued that feminist social researchers should start from their personal standpoints whilst others have argued for a more muted approach and a distancing although taking into account personal experience. There is a growing body of autobiographical accounts of being a marginalized researcher as a woman, often also related to sexual orientation, gender, race, or disability. The epistemological and methodological value of these kinds of perspectives have become hotly debated topics and a matter of 'contention' (Reinharz, 1992). Patricia Hill Collins (1991) has taken this further by considering the standpoint of black women sociologists and particular forms of sociological 'knowing' from their unique black perspective and the growing 'disciplinary community'.

Indeed, that summer turned out to be very productive of feminist collegiality, scholarship and friendship. It began a long term partnership with Dorothy Smith and her colleagues, particularly Alison Griffith, studying mothers and their children's schooling or education. It also enabled engagement with other active feminist scholars in Canada, the USA and Britain, since that summer Jane Gaskell, the late Gail Kelly and Madeleine Arnot also taught summer school. We all worked together on developing feminist perspectives and critiques, largely within educational theories, comparatively and theoretically. Gail Kelly's work on comparative studies of Vietnam and Africa were particularly challenging and exciting and I drew increasingly on her work too. Tragically her work was prematurely curtailed by her death. Work with Jane Gaskell had been more sporadic, but recently has gained momentum again with her colleague Deirdre Kelly's studies of pregnant schoolgirls, and the meanings attached to sex and sexuality. Developing into critical feminist ethnography has taken a long time but been particularly productive. These ideas will continue to be threaded through this story.

The beginnings of an intellectual collaboration with Madeleine Arnot were slow to emerge out of this innovative summer event. As noted above, we only began to write together almost a decade later but now are firm partners in a feminist endeavour to understand not only the impacts of historical trends on women and their lives in education, but also to theorise social change and transformation. At this time, it seemed more urgent to unravel the influences and effects of changing political and moral orders on policy developments and changes for women. I continued with a theme that had been commenced in the 1970s of critical policy analysis, writing a series of pieces for *Critical Social Policy* the journal of which I was on the editorial collective. These studies were also enhanced by work with a politically astute colleague Ruth Levitas and her edited collection on studies of the New Right and its morality. Another strand of the policy debate that was maintained was that about women's regulation by the state. Initially there were several groups who wrote both analytically and strategically. A Penguin series was inaugurated in the 1980s, entitled *What is to be done about?*. Lynne Segal edited a series on the family, whilst Elizabeth Wilson provided one on violence against women. With the benefit of hindsight these strategic debates and issues only touched broader policies at the level of social attitudes and analysis rather than policy change itself.

Conclusions and reflections

In the 1980s my interests moved away from the general political issues, and focused increasingly on mothers and children. My study with Caroline New (1985) was published just as this period of my professional life was coming to an end. My own personal experiences of academic life were increasingly leading to my dissatisfaction with it and the extent of equal opportunities in traditional academic institutions. As feminist researchers we all retained our focus on politics, policy change and development and, gradually, became more sophisticated. Our curricular developments drew from the original demands and remained within that sphere. At the same time we were touched by wider theoretical developments towards post-structuralism and methodological developments about how to study these issues. For my part, having developed an interest in the analysis of mothers' relation to children through state regulation, I moved from a historical study through work on understanding childcare to more critical policy analysis. This eventually led to my developing collective feminist studies with colleagues over various aspects of family and education. In this respect we tried to bring together critical policy analysis with studies of mothers' lived experiences of bringing up and rearing their children in a variety of different locales and contexts. In other words, the themes referred to earlier were pursued with varying balances in our collective feminist research and scholarship on family life. We used our personal experiences to study policy and develop social analyses of personal experiences, such as those of motherhood and childcare and education, to understand political and personal family shifts and motherhood.

Hilary Land has been a tireless campaigner and analyst of the ways in which the state has regulated women's family lives especially through financial policies such as income maintenance, social security and other economic policies with respect to work and employment. Her concerns have also ranged over policies to do with care, children and other family members. The balance of issues has been uneven dependent upon the political interests and values of governments in power. However, what has been notable is that, despite feminist campaigning and strategies for change, and although governments have adopted some changes of a liberal feminist kind, women's subordinate position in family and work remains relatively unchanged in relation to men. What is more remarkable is how there has been a shift in social attitudes and approaches rather than in women's economic and social positions.

What I have aimed to demonstrate in this chapter is the key role played by feminist theorising and methodologies on the forming and framing of sociological perspectives on families and family life. I have attempted to do this analysis through an auto/biographical history of feminist thought and contributions within sociology, taking as a continuing central tenet of this feminist research endeavour; the notions of personal experience as being crucial and formative to the kinds of research and political and social engagements. Interestingly the family and intellectual lives of some key feminists have also been formative to the questioning and creation of a particular feminist politics and analysis albeit rooted in personal experience.

CHAPTER FIVE

'Femocracy' and feminist management in the academy

Contexts and challenges

Introduction

This chapter reviews changes in my professional and personal life during the second half of the 1980s and explores my reflections upon these contradictory changes in context, relating them to others' reflections. It was during the mid-1980s that I began to reflect upon aspects of my particular professional involvement, in a couple of invited essays. However, I did not explore much of my family or personal life. I certainly was not then fully aware of how this was growing into a genre of academic writing arising out of feminism and how this genre began to influence and be influenced by other social movements. Looking back and considering the wealth and diversity of scholarship and theories including new methodologies that have emerged from this, it is fascinating to realise just how influential these generations and movements were in spawning transformative concepts and ideas. Yet these have to be set against the changing political context, in which conservative ideas were becoming deeply embedded. By the mid-1980s, Margaret Thatcher had won two general elections and was entrenching deeply conservative and neo-liberal ideas, particularly shifts away from a welfare state towards a market economy and privatisation of public and social services. Similarly Reagan in the USA had entrenched such conservative ideas known as Reaganomics, although in European countries such as Sweden, and in Australia, Canada and New Zealand the forces of conservatism had not yet fully been felt.

Whilst preparing this chapter, I attended two celebratory events that illustrate different but complementary aspects of these transformations in professional life for generations of women and the emergent richness and diversity of academic feminist scholarship around transforming family lives. These linked with new generations of women who, given the expansion of educational opportunities in the post-war era, had access to forms of post-school and higher education. They also bear upon the two threads in my professional life and attempts to keep alive the links between them both personally and professionally, uneasy though these may appear to be at various points. These are academic critical feminist works on family and education and the more political and professionally involved feminist engagements within and outside the academy.

Families and Social Capital group launch

The first event was the launch of a new centre for research on families and social capital, funded by the Economic and Social Research Council (ESRC), at South Bank University. This research group developed out of the emergent and intri- cate work on changing families and family lives, and the links with new concepts that might be found productive in the analysis of these diverse strands and themes. The group planned a series of nine inter-linked research projects about aspects of family lives across three strands, namely ethnicity, education and employment and intimacy, and threaded through with themes which explore the emergent concepts of social capital, namely identities and values, trust and reciprocity, and caring about and for. The notion of social capital emerged in the 1990s from a range of fields and concepts in public and academic life. First it drew on versions of Marxian concepts from economic capital to cultural, as understood by Bourdieu, to social as a quasi-political notion interpreted by Puttnam (2000) in his now classic *Bowling Alone*. It also drew on the rise and acceptance of the notion of communitarianism by New Labour in the political arena in Britain, especially as developed by the American sociologist Etzioni (1993) and around the notion of the parenting deficit.

Examples of the substantive projects were presented in a matrix to illustrate the threads between strands and themes. Three studies of identities were planned: families and young people's diasporic identities; locality, school and social capital; youth transitions and social change, linked to sexual identities. There were three studies of trust and reciprocity; household and family rituals; family, social capital and market labour; strengths and needs for support in parenting And there were three on care; family care and provision in a trans-national world; provision and deployment of care through family, mutual aid and local state; children's understandings and experiences of sibling practices. The methodologies were to be grounded in both qualitative and quantitative approaches building upon new epistemologies about understandings of these complex social and economic processes. This research grouping, spear-headed by Rosalind Edwards, and co-directed by Janet Holland, built upon their inno- vative and feminist work, in using substantive and methodological approaches to aspects of family, such as children and young people's lives, through a variety of lenses. It also brought to bear the radical political economy perspective of Irene Bruegel, the critical policy perspective of Claire Callender together with the post-structural and social constructionist approach of Jeffrey Weeks to alternative families, including gay and lesbian couples, and the substantive concerns of John Solomos and Harry Goulbourne about diasporic ethnic minority families.

This magnificent oak tree grew out of a small acorn of social science research at South Bank that I acquired and augmented when I joined what was then the Polytechnic of the South Bank in late 1985. I was appointed to South Bank as head of the social sciences department, as the third of three women appointees as heads of department. This was an era of widening opportunities for women in higher education, through the policies of the then Inner London education authority (ILEA). The other two women appointees were Jenny Levin – made head of Law and Government a year earlier – and the late Jill Forbes, who was appointed as head of the Modern Languages unit in 1984. As Jenny Levin wrote in Jill's obituary (*The Guardian* July 20th 2001), we were quickly seen as the Valchyries and eventually became proud of that attribution since it seemed to question the very basis of the forms of authority that we had to engage with. We were not formally introduced, nor given help or support with our 'managerial' posts for some considerable time but left to 'sink or swim' as best we were able. Eventually we were subject to various forms of managerial training and management consultants, as the decade wore on, and Thatcherite 'managerialism' became more urgent as a formal part of the organisation. This was reinforced by the then director, a liberal feminist, now Baroness Pauline Perry, who had a particularly strong notion of what public management in education should entail, having spent most of her career in the inspectorate of the government's Department of Education (and then Science). During her time at South Bank she wrote about her style as a leader and manager (in Ozga, ed., 1993).

When I was appointed, I was the mother of two young children and I was offered informal help with finding suitable schools for them within ILEA. Unfortunately, however, my husband planned to remain an academic at Bristol University and we chose to live within easy reach of Paddington station in the only affordable area of the outer London borough of Brent. Thus we were not entitled to send our children to ILEA schools, and chose instead a voluntary-aided school – north-west London Jewish day school – in Brent within walking distance of our house. This appeared to be a solution to accommodate our various needs and 'family' values, although it transpired to be a very traditional school in terms of pedagogy and practices, both religious and secular. It also set us on a particular path educationally, as part of an emerging trend for certain fractions of middle class families (Savage and Witz, 1992; Brown, 1994). This soon became a topic of research interest for me, following, as I continued to do, my children's and my life course events. I return to this later.

My appointment to South Bank set me pondering how to deal with this kind of post and role, new to me. It was to what was by traditional university standards a very large department, almost akin to a faculty, since there were about 50 academics made up variously of teachers and contract researchers and split between various social science subjects. I self-consciously wished to be a 'feminist manager', an oxymoron some might think and others have articulated (Ozga, June 2001 to our EdD students). I wanted, at that point, to imbue my style with feminist notions of collaboration and collectivity, but also drawing on caring practices associated with forms of 'maternalism', avoiding traditional patriarchal forms and cultures of power. I talked to colleagues and friends both within South Bank and at other higher education institutions, across what was then the binary divide (Burgess and Pratt, 1974), and eventually organised a number of meetings of women heads of department in the social sciences, specifically related to sociology and social policy. There were tensions associated with the different practices in universities and the then polytechnics, not only the styles of management but also the forms of organisation related to subject groupings for teaching and linked with research. At the same time, other colleagues were organising and setting up activities, groups and organisations to support and help women with these new managerial roles, including in some places providing forms of 'training'. For instance, Eileen Green and Diana Woodward at what was then Sheffield City Polytechnic organised some short courses through the auspices of their centre for women's studies and eventually reflections on these activities became part of a commissioned series of essays (David and Woodward, eds, 1998). As far as I was concerned, in England, these various activities coalesced into one grouping which was named as *Through the Glass Ceiling,* a network for senior women in higher education and formally constituted in 1990.

Through the Glass Ceiling

The second event was the twelfth anniversary of this organisation, which reviewed the progress, achievements and obstacles surrounding women's moves into forms of higher education (and academic) management over the last decade. It was acknowledged just what sea changes had taken place since those early days, both in more professional activities and involvement and scholarly understandings. How in particular we understand and interpret women in management is now far more sophisticated than our earlier attempts. It can also increasingly be linked to our understandings of wider and global changes in forms of higher education, lifelong learning and what is often now called 'the knowledge economy' (Blackmore, 2002; Peters, 2001) especially conceptualised in Europe, North America, Australia and New Zealand. The changes in access to and participation within higher education have influenced and been influenced by us as part of the post-war generations. As the executive committee put it, in their report for discussion:

Much has changed in the external and internal environments of higher education in the last ten years in relation to: funding; Government priorities; the legislative framework; the changing nature of the student body; the increasing demands placed upon managers and the managed; the increasing professionalism of administration and so on. Our own lives have also become increasingly pressured, and achieving a satisfactory balance between 'work' and 'home' is a recurrent topic for discussion within the Network.

In the light of these changes it seems timely to review the role and title of *Through the Glass Ceiling*. We should consider whether the original aims remain appropriate; whether the target membership group is still the right one; whether the organisation's title continues to reflect the needs of the membership and the changing environment in which we operate. (The Executive Committee, 10th January 2002)

The membership of *Through the Glass Ceiling* nevertheless, continued to represent, for the most part, those women with aspirations to become part of a particular sector and form of higher education in the UK. The initial origins reflected the positioning of the majority of such women within the former public sector, and what had become, over the last ten years, the new (post-1992) universities and colleges of higher education. The old universities had, and continue to have, a more 'collegial' system, in which managerialism, as forms of line management, associated with quality control and assurance mechanisms, had a smaller part to play. The focus was more on research, teaching and administration, rather than notions of management drawn from traditional patriarchal, entrepreneurial and business practices.

In a most contradictory way, the majority of women who secured managerial positions whether academic management or heads of sections, units and institutions, had done so in the new universities and colleges. By contrast, in the old universities, a form of modified patriarchy, as benign paternalism, still prevailed and predominated. At the time of writing, there are only two female vice-chancellors in the old universities who are women, whereas the new universities boast double that, and many more in senior positions, including as heads of colleges of higher education. However, the value of such positionings still differs across the sectors, whereby such seniority is not viewed with the same deference and respect. More importantly these posts and positions reflect other changes in social and familial life, associated with broader educational changes, including participation in higher education amongst students constituting over forty percent of the age cohort, by contrast with thirty years ago, when it was less than ten percent. Mature (and predominantly female) students also added to the new mixed participation in higher education. The composition of staff, both academic and managerial or administrative, does not reflect these wider changes, and the changing constituencies of women in particular. But these kinds of developments have been reflected in some of our considerations, and the ways we tried to write and theorise the embryonic changes, fifteen years ago.

Feminist reflections: early scholarly beginnings

The genre of reflecting upon ones experiences, background and life became a fairly common and increasingly usual approach within the social sciences in the 1980s. However, there were many strands and perspectives on how and why one did it and feminist perspectives tended to foreground personal experiences, rather than the more professional, linking them crucially with aspects of family life. This inevitably built upon the notion of 'the personal is political'. Whilst I was teaching and reflecting on these various perspectives at the University of Wisconsin in Madison, USA in 1999, one of my male colleagues also mentioned that he had begun a similar process in the 1980s, confirming the prevalence of this approach. He gave me a copy of an early piece of his writing which played with the ideas of social science, autobiography and history, entitled *What's in a Research Project: Some Thoughts on the Intersection of History, Social Structure, and Biography* (Popkewitz, 1988). This was formulated and first presented in 1985 but published three years later. Together with much other similar writing this has now become a respectable approach to the genre in education and the social sciences, and, in a different vein, in feminist scholarly practices. However, this is also interwoven with different theoretical perspectives and methodologies. Narrative and ethnographic enquiries predominate, together with critiques of traditional and more quantitative rather than qualitative perspectives.

In the mid-1980s, two colleagues approached me to contribute to two complementary volumes: one about the growing sub-discipline of sociology of education, the other a specifically feminist sociological approach to teachers and education. When invited to write an experiential essay by a former colleague from Bristol University, Sandra Acker, for her edited volume on women teachers, I leapt at the opportunity despite the fact that my professional experiences were not as a school teacher and were as a teacher in higher education. I entitled the essay *Prima Donna Inter Pares – Women in Academic Management*, using a phrase that was meant as a piece of self-parody and yet borrowed from an article on Margaret Thatcher that I had seen in a newspaper. The other essay which I entitled *On becoming a feminist in the Sociology of Education* had been commissioned by a male colleague for a volume reflecting the growth in scholarship within sociology of education, and it was only I who self-consciously considered a feminist perspective for the volume. The two autobiographical pieces came out about the same time (David 1987; 1989). Both were about my professional and academic developments and involvement in the women's movement and academic feminism rather than about my personal, family life and background. They were written from an increasingly personal and subjective perspective, an approach that had been spurned in my formative years of learning sociology.

Apart from these two commissioned pieces, both published in the late 1980s, I had rarely made explicit my intellectual biography but rather had developed feminist qualitative methods (1984a, b and c; 1985; 1986 a, b and c). Having been schooled in positivist social science and quantitative research methods, developing a critical approach through qualitative methods and a feminist perspective seemed in itself daring. Mention of family whether of sexual or parental relationships seemed far too dangerous to contemplate, although others had. It was a measure of how family secrets remained a deeply embedded and seldom reflected upon notion for our lives, although there was a growing body of knowledge, largely by feminist scholars about these 'shameful topics', for example a study on child sexual abuse entitled *Father–Daughter Incest: patriarchy's shameful secret* (Dominelli, 1987).

I did not receive any direct response to the piece in Walford's edited book but *Prima Donna Inter Pares* provoked a major controversy about feminist practices within the academy. To some extent, the debate amongst colleagues over the second autobiographical piece led me to fight shy of further such writing in the academy. Ethical dilemmas were raised as was the growing issue of 'informed consent', particularly problematic in the context of pursuing auto/biography, albeit at the intellectual and academic level. Initially these were raised in a departmental discussion about the ethics and efficacy of writing about one's workplace without obtaining the consent of others involved but eventually they were also resolved by colleagues writing passionately about qualitative research and biographies in a special issue of *Sociology* (Harrison and Lyon, 1993). This all led me to eschew pursuing the developing literature on 'insider accounts', narratives, biographies and life histories and back to more empirical, if qualitative, research on education, gender and family relationships for almost a decade (1990; 1993; 1994; 1996; 1997). But I threaded through here several interlocking interests, namely critical feminist perspectives on policy and empirical studies separately and together with colleagues around our varying practices as mothers in education, developing a form of reflexivity (1996 and 1997).

I did develop a more personal style when I was invited to write a regular monthly column for *The Times Higher Education Supplement* in 1989. I pursued this form of serious journalism, writing as if from my personal diary as a professional sociologist, higher education manager, and 'Jewish mother' combining my attempts at what has subsequently been called a family-work life balance for three and a half years. Yet these, what might now be seen as brief 'insider accounts', were also a digression from the more serious scholarly work on family and education, and my continuing pursuit of issues to do with my, and my children's, life course, contextualised by public and family, education and social policy issues.

Carolyn Steedman's now classic pieces of auto/biography, referred to earlier, pursued far more clearly and explicitly her familial and thus class-based feelings and allegiances and this was published about the same time, becoming a relatively instant classic (1986). She made a good deal of how she felt as she was growing up in the 1950s, focussing largely on the then unconscious, drawing on developing feminist versions of Freudian psychoanalysis. However, she explicitly contrasted her feelings with those of the middle class women whose autobiographies and accounts she had recently read, ones such as Ann Oakley's (see Chapters Three and Four) and a book on fathers by feminist daughters edited by Ursula Owen (1986). She made it plain that her mother's troubled thoughts as a working class woman affected her own wishes and desires. She wrote:

> One of the hardest lessons of my young adulthood was discovering that it was possible to invite people into a household, to have them stay, and that the presence of outsiders did not necessarily mean invasion and threat. But such an anxiety did attach to the practice, and for such a long time, that I have to re-read my childhood in the light of that anxiety, see the refusal of entry to outsiders not as the normality it was experienced as at the time, but rather as a series of covert messages about the impropriety and illegality of our existence . . . my mother had no friends . . . If the doorbell rang when we were eating, we were not allowed to answer it. Years later I read about this reluctance to reveal the poverty of food on the table in several working class autobiographies and thought: yes, that must have been it. I added the monotony of our diet after 1954 . . . to this ascribed sociological motivation on my mother's part and was satisfied. (Steedman 1986: 66–7)

This kind of feminist pursuit was gaining intellectual ground and legitimacy in the USA. Nancy Miller (1990) also reflected most entertainingly on writing personally and autobiographically from her involvement in academic feminism in the USA during the 1980s. Her interest was in:

> . . . two distinct phenomena that have emerged together on the critical horizon over the decade of the eighties – albeit on separate tracks. The first (although it is not practised uniquely by feminists or women) can be seen to develop out of feminist theory's original emphasis on the analysis of the personal: I am referring to the current proliferation in literary studies of autobiographical or personal criticism . . . I read this work as renewed attention to the unidentified voices of a writing self outside or to the side of labels, or at least at a critical distance from them, and at the same time as part of a wider effort to remap the theoretical. The spectacle of a significant number of critics getting personal in their writing . . . is at least the sign of a turning point in the history of critical practices. The other development is a visible trend . . . of attacks on academic feminism – a kind of critical misogyny practised by women as well as men . . . (1990: ix–x)

Miller then went on to argue about the importance of the personal in academic feminism and feminist teaching, saying that it 'tended to produce a great deal of personal testimony' (1990, p. 15). She continued:

> If one of the original premises of seventies feminism (emerging out of sixties slogans) was that 'the personal is political' eighties feminism has made it possible to see that the personal is also the theoretical: the personal is part of theory's material. Put another way, what may distinguish contemporary feminism from other post-modern thought is the expansion in the definition of cultural material. (1990: 21)

Thus as feminism moved from a political project in the sixties and seventies into a more intellectual and academic activity in the eighties, personal and auto-biographical material formed one basis of these theoretical developments (as noted in Chapter Four). However, there were several countervailing tendencies, including revised forms of Marxian theories. Numerous women started to experiment with writing in an autobiographical vein, particularly American feminists, such as Friedan (1987), presenting aspects of their personal experi-ences, although none of them wrote a sustained account in the way that Beauvoir had. What they did was to thread a personal element throughout their writings. Much of it touches on family life experiences and the ways that it influenced their writings, values and politics. As Carolyn Heilbrun argued in *Writing a Woman's Life* (published 1988 in the USA and 1989 in UK) the notion of femi-nism was beginning to change. A more sophisticated notion of understanding not only in the social sciences but also literary theory developed into what she called a feminist undertaking:

> This is a feminist undertaking. I define feminist, using Nancy Miller's words, as the wish 'to articulate a self-consciousness about women's identity both as inherited cultural fact and as the process of social construction' and to 'protest against the available fiction of female becoming'. (1989: 18)

She also argued that writing autobiographies, biographies and memoirs was not new but the extent to which they were published in this period is a reflection of the growth of women's writing and reflections:

> There are four ways to write a woman's life: the woman herself may tell it, in what she chooses to call an autobiography; she may tell it in what she chooses to call fiction; a biographer, woman or man, may write the woman's life in what is called a biography; or the woman may write her own life in advance of living it, uncon-sciously, and without recognising or naming the process . . .
>
> In 1984 I rather arbitrarily identified 1970 as the beginning of a new period in women's biography because Zelda by Nancy Milford had been published that year . . . Only in 1970 were we ready to read not that Zelda had destroyed Fitzgerald, but Fitzgerald her; he had usurped her narrative . . .
>
> With equal arbitrariness I would name 1973 as the turning point for modern women's autobiography. (1989: 11–12)

A new genre of women's writing had begun to emerge in the 1960s and 1970s, although some of this kind of writing had set earlier precedents with the birth of the women's movement and feminism in the nineteenth and earlier centuries. One of the earliest campaigners, for instance, was Mary Wollstonecraft with her *Vindication of the Rights of Women*, first published in 1792. Most importantly perhaps is the role that education, and especially higher education, has played in harnessing women's energies and activities to challenge traditional families and forms of economic dependency. Central to these was the use of several complementary and yet contrasting themes and threads. Simone de Beauvoir's reflections or auto/biography was taken up by several feminist sociologists in Britain in the late 1980s. By contrast other French and Marxist theories were also drawn on to develop feminist perspectives and analyses, so that there was a plethora of approaches.

Reflections on Simone de Beauvoir

As noted in Chapter Two, Simone de Beauvoir was one of the strongest influences on the growth and development of second wave feminism and its uses within academic feminism although she herself did not adopt the term until the 1970s (Moi, 1999). Innumerable works and papers have been written about her both from a sympathetic and also a hostile audience but until the 1980s most of this work was in French as Toril Moi remarked:

> In the 1980s, Beauvoir studies have shifted decisively away from France as well as from so-called mainstream preoccupations with political and philosophical themes. Before 1980, Beauvoir critics were predominantly French: only five out of an estimated twenty-one full-length studies were published in English. The first English language study, Elaine Marks's *Simone de Beauvoir: Encounters with Death*, did not appear until 1973. From 1980 to 1988, however, of thirteen books devoted to Beauvoir, ten appeared in English . . . There are some obvious reasons for this well-nigh total desertion of Beauvoir by the French: in the 1970s and 1980s French intellectual fashions (structuralism, post-structuralism, Lacanian psychoanalysis, post-modernism) have left no space at all for an unreconstructed existentialist humanist of Beauvoir's type . . .
>
> In Beauvoir studies, then, the 1980s are the decade of Anglo-American feminism. But Beauvoir proves controversial for British and American feminists as well . . . Whatever the importance of *The Second Sex*, it ought not to be forgotten that until she was well over sixty, Beauvoir did not think of herself as a feminist at all. (Moi, 1990: 25–6)

This new genre, it has been argued, developed particularly from French existentialism and especially Simone de Beauvoir's work, both her scholarly account published as *The Second Sex,* and her memoirs or autobiographies. This relied on later and more complex feminist and sociological theorising about how to construct a story or narrative about a life, a biography, memoir of a family member such as a parent, or a story about a family. It also linked with the questions of authenticity or fictive accounts and constructions of biographies and memoirs, not necessarily based upon the memories of those involved. Looking back therefore on a history or biography of the influences of feminist thought on sociological theories and methodologies, we also need to consider the changing identities of those who had a critical influence on this kind of thinking as Toril Moi put it:

> When I say I am interested in Simone de Beauvoir as an intellectual woman, it may sound as if I am mostly concerned with biography. Yet my work is based upon the assumption that there can be no *methodological* distinction between 'life' and 'text'. I have always been struck by the fact that Freud, in *The Interpretation of Dreams*, seems unable to distinguish between the psyche and the text: at the same time he gives us a map of the human mind. To read the dream is at once to read the text and the person . . . to all practical purposes, the Freudian subject is a text. In the case of Simone de Beauvoir, whose autobiographies and letters alone run to well over a million words, Freud's discovery is particularly relevant. The intertextual network of fictional, philosophical, autobiographical and epistolary texts that she left us is our Simone de Beauvoir. In addition to this, we have all the texts about her . . . (Moi, 1994: 4)

Beauvoir[1] attracted a tremendous following amongst women and has been the subject of numerous studies, interpretations, accounts, films and biographies. Three biographical works on Simone de Beauvoir were published in the 1980s in Britain and written by feminists. Two are particularly pertinent, since they were produced by feminist sociologists, to popularise her work amongst sociologists and feminists and as a form of reflection on her life as Ann Curthoys did (see Chapter Two). It is significant that the two were produced within a year of each other – the one by Mary Evans in 1985, and the other by Judith Okely in 1986 – and both authors subsequently wrote their personal reflections on their educational lives (Okely, 1991; Evans, 1991).[2] It was as both authors attest a time when feminist scholarship within the academy was burgeoning, and in particular developing into special courses. Mary Evans was jointly responsible for one of the first postgraduate Masters (*sic*) courses in women's studies and she also developed important theoretical perspectives on auto/biography (in Stanley, 1997) and personal lives (in *Sociology* special issue 1993). Moreover, as the third biographer, Lisa Appignanesi, noted:

> For the women of my generation, Simone de Beauvoir took on something of the aspect of *an idealized mother*. (My emphasis) Refusing children of her own, she gave birth instead to a movement, the agenda of which is set out in *The Second Sex*. But daughters, as they come of age, must needs rebel and good mothers be transformed into bad . . . (1988: 2)

Judith Okely's study was what she called a 're-reading' since she had originally read the work in the 1960s and wanted, in 'true' feminist fashion, to reconsider it in the light of feminist theories in the 1980s. Indeed, Okely expressed the issue most cogently writing:

> The author's gender and position as a woman were crucial to her women readers who looked for similarities . . . Today after the creative explosion of feminist writing, a woman reading a woman's text may feel freer to explore the implications of shared gender. Nonetheless, the meeting points depend on the wider context of the individuals and of that re-reading. The reading does not occur in a vacuum but is shaped by history, and the class, age, race and culture of the reader. The text will not read the same for a Black or working class woman as it reads for one who is white or middle class . . . much of her description reflects a very specific experience . . . I have felt free to make use of autobiography partly because of a similar concern within some recent feminist and women's writing. Fear of subjectivity is more a masculine attribute which is concealed behind inappropriate claims to scientific objectivity . . . (1986: vii–viii)

Okely also saw Beauvoir as *'our mother, our sister and something of ourselves'* (1986, p. 1) (my emphasis). Evans was more cautious and equivocal in her assessment of Beauvoir whom she saw as contradictory. She wrote, however, of her inspiration to feminism rather than her direction and influence over it. She also saw her as relatively unique in her ability to be able to ride over the traditional female condition with which she contended, commenting:

> . . . de Beauvoir did not experience any of the constraints traditionally experienced by the majority of women writers. She did not write in the odd cracks of life free from domestic duties or the care of children nor did she have to strive – like many of both sexes – for education and access to the academic and literary world . . . de Beauvoir, therefore, did not share two of the characteristics of the majority of women (and indeed people) of the world – she has been neither a parent, nor poor. On the other hand, unlike many who are neither poor nor parents, de Beauvoir has consistently challenged the taken-for-granted attitudes of western bourgeois society and . . . her association with feminism took some years to emerge; what long predates this is a commitment to, and identification with, left-wing and radical politics. (1985: ix)

All three biographers noted that Beauvoir was born into a patriarchal and bourgeois society. These early family and personal experiences led her to develop the critique for which she has become so renowned. On the other hand, she was the beneficiary of many of the privileges of bourgeois society that others have not been so fortunate to savour. And she was able, albeit not as easily as it appeared, to renounce those privileges and the practices of motherhood and family life in favour of living outside of its conventions. Her active involvement in feminist politics only started in the early 1970s, long after many others in France, Britain and America had already become politically engaged. Swindells (1995) looked at the developments in feminist autobiographical writing, particularly approaching it in a generational and intergenerational way in her introduction to her edited volume about feminist biographies a decade later. Commenting upon the centrality of Simone de Beauvoir to developing the 'tradition' she wrote:

> Simone de Beauvoir is one example of a woman who has only recently received the critical acclaim handed out to sundry men, in the name of the Western European literary tradition. It is possible to see her *Memoirs of a Dutiful Daughter* and her other autobiographical volumes as the works of a writer and thinker who constitutes, belatedly recognised, a key individual of that tradition, though somewhat more radical than most . . . (1995: 205)

A school of thought has also developed and remained influential in a particularly French reading of radical lesbian feminism and subsequently feminist politics through Christine Delphy, a French feminist. Writing together with Diana Leonard, their study *Familiar Exploitation* (1986) developed a particular materialist-feminist approach to family life, demonstrating forms of sexual exploitation through women's family labour and drawing on examples from agrarian and especially French agricultural families. They also applied these ideas to household sexual relations with more general application. Delphy's work in the 1980s remained more within the French structural and Marxist traditions than the experiential perspectives developing at the same time. Delphy has, however, also extended feminism into a political project with the continued publication of the magazine *Nouvelles Questions Feministes*. A memorial conference was organised by Delphy and held in honour of Beauvoir and the fiftieth anniversary of the publication of *The Second Sex* in Paris in January 1999. This signalled the enduring influence that Beauvoir has had on feminist sociology.

It is also important to note the varied and various influences of French sociological thinking that began to percolate through to British works in the 1980s, not only from feminists but also from Marxian schools of thought drawing on Althusser, who taught both Bourdieu and Foucault. Both Bourdieu and Foucault were taken up with varying degrees of influence during the 1980s through critiques of structuralism and developing into what became known as post-structuralism, through the work especially of Foucault, but this only gained ground amongst feminists in the 1990s (Weedon, 1987). Bourdieu was far more influential within sociology and sociology of education, than amongst feminists until the late 1990s, and indeed has arguably been seen as a very traditional patriarchal thinker through his more recent works (e.g. *La domination masculine*, 1998). However, a key influence on feminist developments in Britain at the time were French feminist psychoanalysts such as Cixous, Irigaray, Plaza, and Kristeva which Moi synthesized in an edited collection (*French Feminist Thought* 1987). Moi also developed a critique of the influence of Bourdieu (Moi, 1999) two years prior to his death in January 2002 (Obituary *The Guardian* January 28th 2002). Here it is also important to point to how Moi developed a post-structural feminist analysis and how she has done so in relation to her studies of

Beauvoir. Moi's approach to putting Beauvoir at the heart of the developments in feminism and particular styles of feminist writing is crucial to our understandings of the development of feminist methodologies and how Beauvoir has been central to this kind of writing. Moi argued that:

> For a long time I hesitated to call this book *Simone de Beauvoir: the making of an intellectual woman.* 'It sounds like a critical biography', my friends said. As it had never occurred to me to write the story of Beauvoir's life, their objections seemed conclusive [but] . . . although I was not writing a biography, what I was writing about was precisely the *making* of Simone de Beauvoir as an intellectual woman . . . first . . . by studying her education, that is to say, the institutional structures that produced her as a philosopher and an intellectual in the first third of this century . . . [second] that I set out to study the works that 'made' her . . . finally . . . by using the term *making* I want to emphasis the idea of production or construction . . . as an extraordinarily complex effect of a whole network of different discourses or determinants. (Moi, 1994: 6)

Similarly Judith Butler borrowed from many French intellectuals, feminists and psychoanalysts to construct her feminist philosophical perspective in *Gender Trouble.* Judith Butler also took as her theoretical starting point Beauvoir, writing:

> I read Beauvoir who explained that to be a woman within the terms of a masculinist culture is to be a source of mystery and unknowability for men, and this seemed confirmed somehow when I read Sartre for whom all desire, problematically presumed as heterosexual and masculine, was defined as *trouble* . . .
>
> Precisely because 'female' no longer appears to be a stable notion, its meaning is as troubled and unfixed as 'woman,' and because both terms gain their troubled significations only in relational terms, this inquiry takes as its focus gender and the relational analysis it suggests. (1990: vii, ix)

Standpoint theories for studying women

Marxist and Marxian theories continued to remain influential in developing feminist theories during the 1980s, developing from a variety of different national schools of thought. Equally important, however, were the ways in which feminism was combined with Marxism in rather more traditional ways in both Britain and North America. As noted in the previous chapter, Dorothy Smith's (1987) reworking of Marxism and feminism together became increasingly influential during the second half of the 1980s, with the publication of her *Everyday World as Problematic.* The notion of standpoint theory drew on more traditional methodologies within the social sciences developed from both Weberian and Marxist schools of thought about values and objectivity but became especially useful in relation to joining with subjective experiential accounts which she entitled institutional ethnography (1987). This provided the tools for studying women in particular social contexts, especially families. She subsequently applied this perspective to the study of mothers in relation especially to their children's education and saw this as what she subsequently called 'mothering work' termed in relation to traditional forms of Marxian wage labour. Much of this more recent work, especially of studies of mothers and children's education, has been developed with Alison Griffith (1991 and 1993). As already mentioned I had begun to develop some cross-national collaborations and over the next decade we began a series of inter-related studies on families and education, all of which have related to our more personal experiences.

During this period I also began to extend my work to studies of mothers and motherhood in relation to education, given my children's life course events and especially involvement in primary education, and thoughts about moves to secondary schools, during the late 1980s. Several research students joined me at South Bank and were also engaged in work on mothers and education as a formal and informal institution. Jane Ribbens transferred from her previous higher educational institution to continue work on mothers rearing young children, whilst Mary Hughes developed her historical analysis of adult education for women, and mothers especially. Rosalind Edwards responded to an advertisement for a researcher to study mothers and education, by completely transforming the nature of the study into one of mature mother students in education and their childcare practices. We began, together and separately, to develop our studies of various aspects of women as mothers in relation especially to various aspects of education. By the early 1990s all three women had completed their doctoral studies and theses and we decided to put together a joint publication drawing upon these themes and studies, entitled *Mothers and Education: Inside Out? Exploring family-education policy and experience*.

We had also explored a variety of different approaches to these themes and in relation to this kind of more academic analysis. In particular, we have been influenced by the international debates about how to study and research these various issues. Some of the key contributions have been about how we understand and interpret women's perspectives. Some of the key writers interlaced their methodological interests with their substantive concerns about women and their family lives. We also drew on the work of Dorothy Smith's other colleagues including Margrit Eichler's early feminist research methods and her work on family policies in Canada. Similarly Carol Gilligan's study (1984), *In a Different Voice*, on women's psychological and moral developments became very influential in our thinking during this period as did Belenky and others (1986) on *Women's Ways of Knowing*. Carol Gilligan developed research into women's different perspectives, followed by her work on young women and their perspectives with Lyn Mikel Brown (1992) *Meeting at the Crossroads*. In both of these studies Gilligan explored how women's moral development related to their caring activities and identities. In her second book co-authored with Lyn Mikel

Brown their fascination was with how young women learnt from their mothers
and others. This important work on women's moral and psychological developments became very influential in studies of women and how to study women.
Belenky with others (1986 and 1999) also considered women's differential perspectives from a methodological standpoint. Nell Noddings (1984) also was concerned with women, and especially mothers' moral standpoints in relation to
education and caring. This work has led into major developments in the study of
motherhood in North America, most recently Sharon Abbey and others (1998)
have looked widely at aspects of motherhood as forms of changing identities and
patterns of life. But this is to run ahead of the story of the late 1980s to illustrate
just how fruitful and productive such theories have been in influencing empirical
qualitative methodological studies. I will return to this in Chapter Six.

The debates about the place of ethnicity, race, class and culture also became a
strong theme in our developing studies, especially given our social location as a
higher education institution within inner city London. South Bank was a particular provider of courses giving access to higher education for socially and
economically disadvantaged students. Indeed, for me going to South Bank constituted a number of major life changes, despite the fact that I had considered
these as real possibilities. In particular, I had not been attuned to how to theorise
such changes in my life and those of other women of my generation. The
theoretical excitement and challenges of this period also extended to other feminists especially developing challenging interpretations of them. Although we
were in deeply conservative times in Britain, as feminists we were involved in
international debates, where feminist theories and analyses were flourishing
and growing, despite what subsequently became known as the 'chilly climate'
(title of an Australian conference, 1997).

Femocracy as a concept for capturing the
changes of the 1980s

Feminists, other social scientists and public commentators were quick to note
economic and social transformation and the resultant changes in women's lives
both inside and outside the family, as wives, mothers, and 'workers', whether as
functionaries, professionals or, even especially recently, politicians. How these
various changes have been theorised at various stages and in relation to feminist
theorising more broadly is of considerable interest. In the 1980s theoretical
diversity began to flower, and in respect of women's diverse forms of employment, and the part played by feminist political activists, were more hidebound in
Britain than in other countries, given the Conservative administrations. Thus
particular changes were noted especially for countries other than Britain. In
particular, Australia experienced great changes in women's lives in the 1980s and
a Labour government responded there to the 'demands' of feminists and other

social movements. Indeed, as Yeatman (1990) noted a new term – 'femocrats' – was coined to describe the involvement of women in public life and public bureaucracies pursuing a feminist agenda. She also noted the influence of particular Labour governments in Australia in the 1980s, willing to take up the issues, albeit ambivalently. Thus she argued that:

> The term femocrat appears to have been an Australian neologism invented to refer to a *feminist bureaucrat* (my emphasis). The neologism is possibly an Australasian one since it is a term used also in New Zealand, though there is some evidence that it is coming into North American usage (see Weir, 1987:98) and Scandinavian feminists have developed the term 'state feminism' . . . The term originated to refer to official or state feminists, namely women who are employed within state bureaucratic positions to work on advancing the position of women in the wider society through the development of equal opportunity and anti-discrimination strategies of change . . . Femocrats are viewed as owing their positions to movement pressure but as giving their ultimate loyalties to the employing government body. (1990: 64–5)

Femocracy as a term has not entered public discourse in Britain. However, the term could be applied in Britain to the growing activities of women in certain public bureaucracies, such as the Inner London education authority, of which the Polytechnic of the South Bank was then a part. In Australia the term was used – femocrats were indeed feminists in public life, aiming to implement equal opportunities for work and pay, especially in education and other forms of public employment. As Yeatman put it:

> In the various discussions of Australian femocracy it is common to find some acknowledgement that the privileged access of femocrats to well-paid and high-profile employment positions creates a significant difference between them and the majority of Australian women . . . This kind of questioning can apply not just to femocrats but to all women who have been fortunate enough to establish access to well-paid, full-time professional and managerial positions. Does this . . . enable them to escape out of their gender-class-determined position of economic dependency on men, either as individuals or in their corporate expression as the patriarchal state? . . . femocrats . . . are paid advocates of the interests of women as a gender class. This distinguishes them from other women professionals and managers . . . and represents the existence of a political feature of the femocrat labour market . . . which depends on the persisting legitimacy of the ideology of feminism. It is the political force of feminism which leads governments to create these advocacy positions and which demands of their female occupants a commitment to feminist ideology. In this sense femocratic positions demand a convergence between the material interest of women professionals or managers and the ideal interest of feminism. (1990: 4)

We in Britain tended to see ourselves as concerned with attempts to combine our feminist interests with more socialist concerns, largely seeing ourselves as socialist-feminists, and with respect to issues about the family to questions about women and work. We were concerned more about women's relation to the public sphere and how that was regulated through both policies and practices. With the benefit of hindsight and much collective reflection on the growth of academic feminism and sociology, it is now possible to summarise the academic developments around women's family lives into somewhat disparate themes about gender and generation and explanations for women's oppression within the family. These all draw on theories and international developments from the USA, Australia, Canada and parts of Europe, especially as already noted French feminism. They are also interwoven with each other, but can be viewed as relatively separate in terms of strategies and analyses.

There have been many commentators, including feminists, who noted the unevenness (especially in terms of class and race) of the supposed changes in family, as seen in marriage, and/or parenthood and in relation to forms of employment. There have been many more political commentaries on the morality or not of some of the key changes, such as the growth in the percentage of children now born out-of-wedlock, and increasingly frequently to single or lone mothers. Thus much of the debate is suffused with questions of morality, whether religious or not, and the effects on children and future generations of such changes in the legal status of marriage, divorce, parenthood and forms of childhood. This has even infected the public policy process such that social and other policies have been applied, by conservatives, to try to stem the tide of change and by social democrats only to slow the process. Some applauded whilst others were appalled by changes in women's lives and those of their children and especially in women's various forms of involvement in employment. These rich and diverse approaches to family life, and in particular the contribution that feminist methodologies and theories made to our understandings, perspectives and approaches both to social life in general and family life as an experience, were beginning to take hold in the late 1980s. Standpoint theory or experience, as it is known, was complex and complicated, consisting of both being mothered and/or parented and of learning about ourselves through lives in families and how we live our lives, as women. Thus increasingly it was possible for some to think the term femocracy appropriate to the diversity of women's lives in various forms of work. By the late 1980s, many of us were beginning to reflect upon our personal experiences in family, in family changes for us as mothers, wives, divorced or separated, cohabiting and clearly involved in employment. In particular, our lives as academics and in the academy were, for some, getting stronger and more secure, whereas for others they remained tenuous as contract researchers and teachers. And the presence of feminists and feminism in the academy was increasingly being seen as a given, despite the fact that we continued to contest those ways of understanding and knowing about our lives, which remained relatively invisible.

Reflections by two generations of 'femocrat academics' on family and educational changes

By the late 1980s there were at least two if not three post-war generations of women who were feminist and involved either directly or indirectly in the academy. Feminist and what might be called pro-feminist (Lingard and Douglas, 1999) writing about family and auto/biography was increasingly common and increasingly used as an essential part of the academic fare of feminist courses in the academy. It was significant that education assumed a central role in these women's lives and their accounts. This may also be because of the generation of women who remained within the academy and pressed for the inclusion of such feminist approaches and at the same time achieved seniority albeit at some personal cost and with considerable efforts and challenges to the traditional academy. For instance, over time our efforts to create a support group for women in senior academic positions in the social sciences bore fruit. It led to the creation in 1990 of the *Through the Glass Ceiling* network not only of women in the social sciences but from higher education, curiously perhaps largely from the public sector of what became the post-1992 new universities rather than the traditional universities such as Bristol (see previous chapter). Given the growing popularity of biographical accounts (see Chapter Seven) two of us feminist academics (David and Woodward, 1998) decided to ask some of the women in the group to provide autobiographical accounts of life in the academy. We also invited a few other senior sociologist/social scientist feminists to provide personal reflections on their academic lives. We chose a variety of women from across a range of countries. We were eager to obtain reflections from women who might be considered 'femocrats' because they were self-consciously concerned with women's lives in the academy, although not all of them would chose the term feminist. We asked the women deliberately to think about family and education in their lives. Two generations of women characterised by their ages, education and subsequent family formations were invited to contribute – those who were embarking upon adult careers and those born in the aftermath of the Second World War. Although the generation of women then in the 'twilight' of their careers, in particular Dulcie Groves, Hilary Rose, Margaret Stacey and Dorothy Wedderburn, were the more upper middle class and well-educated, their struggles to meet the challenges of patriarchal universities and/or higher education institutions were the more poignant. Some of the younger generation of women (who were born at the end of the Second World War and into the early 1950s) were able to combine children and/or family and careers in more complex ways than the older generation.

What emerged from their accounts was the importance of family and traditional family in their early and young lives, and its enduring importance, throughout their education. What happened, quite by chance or serendipity, was that our two generations of women and those in the midst of their careers divided in terms of both social class, family backgrounds and education. They cannot be easily differentiated, however, in terms of their own families of creation, except for the timing in relation to education and employment. First of all, all the 'twilighters', as those American and Scandinavian women have since referred to themselves such as Jane Roland Martin (1999) and Inge Salzman Enquist (1998), were from upper middle class family backgrounds and attended relatively elite schools. They themselves chose family over education in the first instance, with the exception of one, who followed more faithfully in Beauvoir's footsteps and renounced marriage. For the rest relatively large families, in the context of a traditional or rather legal marriage, were the norm. And their children were all born before careers were fully embarked upon. For the 'younger' generation, mixing marriage, motherhood and careers was far more the norm, from this mixed social class group. However, one element of constancy amongst these two generations of academic women was 'family break-up' rather than marital stability, illustrating an element of social change amongst these women.

What emerged equally significantly from our personal reflections were the two themes of the extent of family change emanating from relatively traditional family backgrounds, whether upper middle class or more middle and working class backgrounds of the second generation and the role of education, especially academic education, in providing the challenges and sustenance for these family changes. At an anecdotal level there was a quickening of the pace of particular forms of family change, especially around marriage, divorce and cohabitation during the late 1980s. Thus Simone de Beauvoir's unique but influential pattern became less unusual amongst these generations. Our personal experiences in families, of being mothered, fathered and parented, of learning about our sexualities, our feelings and being, our emotions can all be said to be important, if not crucial, to how we defined ourselves in relation to others and as adults. The extent to which we define ourselves as social beings is also relative, dependent upon our family and early experiences. Our biographies and our experiences began to capture imaginations as an approach to our understandings of family and social life. A new genre of research and writing developed which drew on personal experiences and biographies or autobiographies as ways to capture the essence of family life and its relation to social life, social and economic transformations and social structures.

A New Era? Critical policy analysis and changing family lives

The academic feminist theme of the late 1980s in Britain remained that of critical feminist analysis as Thatcherism continued to hold sway with three successive electoral victories. The third term of Thatcherism brought with it increasingly conservative measures around family and consumerism, with clear measures to increase rather than reduce inequalities between families. Whilst it was clear that social and economic policies were allowing for women's involvement in paid employment, including for educated women, opportunities for continued involvement in levels and stages of education, including higher education, this did not affect the majority of women. Thus there were a plethora of perspectives, themes and approaches to feminist analysis and study, which could no longer be bracketed together into any simple formula about feminist theories. In an intriguing and contradictory way, conservatism generally and Thatcherism in particular ushered in a whole host of new measures and approaches to the increasing diversity of women's lives inside and outside families, employment and public and private situations. Thus it was becoming increasingly possible to theorise women's involvement in public forms of employment, in public life and in the academy as forms of femocracy.

It was also the case that feminist academics and sociologists in particular began to sharpen their tools of analysis to consider the effects and impacts of measures to transform state regulation of families and the economy. In developing this into a more academic analysis within the academy this theme largely focused on issues to do with the family in relation to state policies and their developments around women as wives and carers of men. This kind of detailed policy analysis and critical scrutiny remained a dominant theme within the sociology of the family and family life, using a rather more traditional form of Marxian analysis and here particular methodological approaches for the most part have remained within the social scientific tradition. Fiona Williams' critical social policy analysis was published in 1989, which had been the subject of her thesis by publication, for which I was one of the external examiners. (Madeleine Arnot's thesis, revised and published as *Reproducing Gender* (2002) was examined the same year.) Collecting evidence of a statistical nature, for example about the proportions of married women involved in paid employment, or lone mothers dependent upon state benefits, remained a dominant method within this theme. The theme has tended to involve less reflection of a personal kind and more traditional analysis over a more varied set of themes and issues, from sexuality and marriage, through to parenthood and employment, and family and education.

A theme that I continued to pursue, together with colleagues, was the influences of conservative policies on aspects of family lives in relation to education. I decided to concentrate on issues that linked with my family's life course events and my own personal trajectory as a mother and professional woman, albeit still also a worker. Thatcher's third term was characterised by moves to increase consumer choice with what were ostensibly still public services. In particular, these moves to introduce economic and business measures into the educational arena, from early childhood through to higher education, was a strong theme. For instance the development of policies was increasingly referred to as educational reforms and attempts to deal with wholesale changes seen as measures to bring about a new era, through a unique piece of legislation known as the Education Reform Act (ERA), 1988. Different from the US version about the Equal Rights Amendment but using the same acronym, ERA, less than a decade earlier, which had provoked a huge debate about the proper roles of men and women in relation to war, combat and conflict, this piece of legislation was nevertheless quite dramatic. It threatened to transform family lives in relation to education, over-turning sacred shibboleths about equality of opportunity in relation to family background and social class. Although couched in the now gender-neutral language of families and parents, it threatened to transform family lives through market forces, privatisation of public services and new forms of institutional autonomy.

In a myriad of ways this legislation represented critical shifts and changes in the landscape of women's lives through education and educational institutions at all levels, many of them contradictory. A whole generation of feminist and critical researchers began to develop studies of policy developments, in which new forms of critical analysis were increasingly brought to bear over the next decade, mushrooming eventually into what is now commonly known as post-structural feminism. Again, I run ahead of the story. Back in the late 1980s we developed critical studies of ERA 1988, and especially the new meanings and understandings of consumerism and parental choice in education, from a variety of perspectives and methodological approaches. I developed a text about such transformations (David, 1993) and also began to embark upon new forms of empirical work about women's role in such choice processes. We began to focus on the twin aspects of mothers versus fathers' involvement as aspects of parental involvement and family changes towards single and lone parenthood (David, West and Ribbens, 1994). In these increasingly harsh times, it was interesting that feminist studies were relatively overlooked by comparison with the more traditional studies of a social class analysis of the effects of such policy develop-ments. Thus even now a sophisticated review by a key educational sociologist of the myriad developments of the period can render invisible these social changes (Tomlinson, 2001).

With regard to the USA this kind of critical policy analysis remained more focused on single issue politics of family than in Britain, most recently however by providing detailed critiques of what have become known as 'family values'. For instance Judith Stacey (1996) who had been one of the early feminist writers and academics in the USA and who wrote on girls and young women, has lent her recent analysis to the study of family values (*In the Name of the Family*). In this respect she provided a strong rebuttal of the backlash against feminism and the moral panic about the demise of the traditional family. However, together with colleagues Madeleine Arnot and Gaby Weiner, (1999) I too developed an overarching analysis of social transformation and educational change in the post-war period, which attempted to account for how and in what ways women and the women's movement had influenced the changes. We too discussed the changing role of family values in respect of the period of Thatcherism, arguing that the shift from Victorian values to 'modern' views of family life was one of the most significant reasons for the social and sexual transformations brought about during this period.

Moreover, for Britain at least there have been shifts in the central concepts used about how to study and analyse family matters, shifts which began to occur in the late 1980s, in response to a conservative agenda. In the initial phases of this analysis, using concepts drawn from the women's movement and political activism meant a direct focus on women as the centre of attention across the generations – women as wives, as workers, as carers and as daughters, sisters and mothers. Part of the approach was to consider and make explicit sexual divisions in approaches to the study of family life. As these issues were introduced into the academy, however, the concepts became hotly debated and contested within disciplines and subjects. In sociology and social policy and indeed across the social sciences, the question of the concept of gender rather than sex, sexuality, sexual divisions or relations, was raised as a more inclusive concept of analysis during the 1980s. By the end of the period gender had become the more usual concept rather than the category woman. Indeed a focus on women qua women was frequently disdained during this period in reaction to the increasingly reactionary political mood.

At the same time, and alongside the expansion of higher education, women's studies was also becoming a subject for the undergraduate and also postgraduate curriculum. As the marketisation of higher education began to grow, in response to conservative policy shifts and changes, women's studies began to appeal as a subject and discipline in its own right. Hitherto, it had developed outside of the formal academic walls, in extra-mural departments and courses, and as part of the Workers Education Association (WEA), but in the second half of the 1980s, some creative institutions began to allow for the offer first of postgraduate, later undergraduate, courses in women's studies. As mentioned above, the first such postgraduate MA was offered at Kent University in 1980s, followed by a pro-liferation of such degrees. The establishment of the Women's Studies Network (UK) Association signalled this major development and the initiation of feminism as a subject rather than approach to studies. Topics which do require explanations drawing on issues to do with family, such as domestic violence or violence against women, occasionally referred to by non-feminists as 'spousal' violence, sexual abuse and/or child sexual abuse have become more the purview of women's studies. Moreover, many issues have also been included in the curriculum of women's studies courses rather than sociology of the family *per se* and many such feminists do not include themselves in this particular intellectual arena. For instance the debates over radical feminism which address questions of sexualities and particularly lesbianism have not been seen as to do with the sociology of the family. Yet again, feminist studies of work and employment, health, including mental illness and some aspects of studies of sexual relations, have also been limited and not seen as part of the sociology of family life. Similarly the development of feminist analysis and debates on gender and education whereby central studies are about girls and/or boys and schooling have not traditionally been viewed as within the purview of then sociology of family life. This is despite the fact that there is a relation between the family and education as Smith and I amongst others have noted. This may also have to do with the concepts that have been used and developed as feminist academics have framed and developed such courses. This all also illustrates the diversity and richness of approaches during the period traditionally seen as dominated by conservatism.

Reflections on the late 1980s

The period of the second half of the 1980s was characterised by contradictory economic and social changes and contexts, especially for women's lives inside and outside families and as understood through academic analysis. My own professional life may be said to have blossomed as I moved from a lectureship at the elite and prestigious University of Bristol to become head of department at the cosmopolitan but inner city Polytechnic of the South Bank in London. I became a professional working mother, responsible for two 'families', those of my 'biological' family and also for the department of social sciences. Both seemed to me to constitute large and unwieldy groups: my family of origin and my 'in-law' family had been distant until my return to London and I was now confronted with regular engagement again. At the same time, I had to contend with a department of fascinating and able academics who were resistant to change and whose behaviour was described to me in these terms by a management consultant who was employed to help foster change in the organisation. The ebbs and flows, however, of intimate and personal change around my family coincided with the ebbs and flows of change amongst the academic department of which I had charge. At the same time, the wider social and political context was subject to constant change with the more insecure and yet routine involvement of women in public and political life. Our studies and analyses increasingly reflected this diversity and development: women's studies and feminism in Britain came to the fore at the same time that Thatcher's fortunes were waxing and waning. Interestingly, the *Through the Glass Ceiling* network was formally constituted at the beginning of 1990, the year that Thatcher was forced to resign. Although her resignation on November 22nd signalled her personal nemesis or rather demise, it did not signal either the demise of conservatism or of women's role in public and political life or employment. In fact, both conservatism and women's public involvement continued unabated throughout the next decade. This is the subject of the next section of this book, signalling the transformations in family lives, women's working lives and the various forms of analysis drawing on theories and developments more globally in the light of global economic and educational changes. Moves towards a knowledge economy, in which women's lives feature more prominently, and feminist theories and analysis have a recognised if not secure place is the emblem of the *fin de siècle*.

The methodologies and the notions of looking at women's changing lives through auto/biography are particularly evocative and moving accounts of the feelings and understandings about such changes and took off during the 1980s. Indeed these are the quintessentially feminist approaches to more academic understandings of both the feelings associated with changing and challenging traditional notions and ideas and attempting to break out of oppressive patriarchal structures and processes. In many such efforts even the traditional concepts of family and family life are avoided, although the routines of everyday life as discussed through auto/biography must perforce entail accounts of childhood in families and the regular processes of growing up and developing understandings from the family and home context. It is thus perhaps no surprise that this melange of methods and methodologies should characterise and illustrate continuities and changes in family lives that began to take off dramatically in the 1980s. Indeed, the writings of Beauvoir, the relation to changing personal lives and the role of education had rarely been connected in texts on the family. Julia Swindells in her edited collection from a feminist conference in Cambridge in 1994 made the point:

> This commentary on the uses of autobiography is . . . to indicate . . . ways in which an understanding of the social, educational and political uses of autobiography can help critique subject specialisms and authoritative accounts, where these rely on particular kinds of social and individual exclusion. The overarching aim is to identify and change educational and cultural processes, where these operate against oppressed and powerless groups. The crucial and intriguing dependence of most kinds of educational and professional process on the account of a personal life, or aspect of it, signifies a need for a detailed study of that dependence, with a view to enabling us to understand and activate autobiography around the political and educational intervention of our choice. (Swindells, 1995: 10–11)

Thus the 1980s signalled profound familial and social changes which seeped into all aspects of personal, social and political lives and feminist analysis in the 1990s. Femocracy was but one way of characterising aspects of the incorporation of feminist ideas into public life, and challenged by the conservative and neo-liberal agendas which were gathering force and entrenching traditional 'family values' in the public arena. It is to these contradictory contexts and challenges that we now turn.

Notes

1. Simone de Beauvoir was born in 1908 in France into a bourgeois Parisian family and became an intellectual in the 1930s when she met at university and developed a partnership with the philosopher, Jean-Paul Sartre. They pioneered existentialism, new ways of living without conventional rules of sexual fidelity, marriage or children. Beauvoir was one of the first generations to be able to enjoy a sexual relationship uncoupled from the constraints of marriage, and with the possibilities of modern techniques of birth control, rather than the more traditional methods, associated with traditional religions. Her birth in the first decade of the twentieth century was thus highly significant for the slow glimmerings of the economic and social changes to come. But her ideas were by no means typical of women of her generation; mothers and grandmothers of my generation. My mother was born a year later than Simone de Beauvoir although she too benefited from having been born into a (petty) bourgeois family and attended university (albeit not the Sorbonne) she did not make the same choices or face the same dilemmas as Beauvoir. Although she saw herself as a liberal 'feminist' my mother did not choose to renounce either marriage or family and indeed remained economically dependent upon my father from marriage until widowhood (and through widowhood mainly dependent upon his pension). My mother's (du Bois-Reymond 1998) 'normal biography' was altogether more typical of her generation than that of Beauvoir, although we have no recourse to autobiographical accounts by Beauvoir's own biological 'dutiful daughters', although she did have an adopted 'dutiful daughter' (Moi, 1994).

2. The two women sociologists also wrote personal reflections on their own childhoods and education (Judith Okely, 1987 and Mary Evans, 1991) about education rather than family in their lives and creation of their feminist identities. In *A good school: life at a girls' grammar school* Evans (1991) focused on her educational formation in a particular type of state secondary grammar school. Okely (1987) also wrote about her educational background and life in an upper middle class boarding school in the 1950s. The third biographer is Appignanesi (1999) wrote a family memoir of her life interlaced with her mother's life (*Losing the Dead*).

CHAPTER SIX

Changing social conditions and feminist theories

From post-socialism to post-structuralism

Introduction

In this chapter and the next, I reflect on the subtle shifts from economic towards neo-liberalism internationally from late 1989 and the equally subtle shifts in our personal lives and responses to the various changing and diverse family lives that developed in the academy. I look here at the period from 1990 to about 1996 during which time we developed critical and feminist research specifically on mothers, children and young people, their changing identities and understandings in relation to the changing policy contexts and the new sociologies of childhood and the family. Personally, my life also began to change as I became more of a public intellectual, writing regularly for *The Times Higher Educational Supplement* (THES) and becoming director of the Social Sciences Research Centre at South Bank University. I also went through a divorce, and two years later my mother died.

This is the third phase of feminist thought, theories and activity, as the notions became entrenched in academic life but also reflected our own ever-changing personal experiences and circumstances. There are, therefore, two threads to this reflective analysis: the first is how we as academics collectively tried to develop new feminist perspectives and methodological approaches, albeit with different balances given the mushrooming of social and feminist research and ethnographies, especially around notions of reflexivity, reflecting the changing social times. These changing times also had their influences on our personal and family circumstances. The second thread is about the changing social conditions, and what Fraser (1997) has called 'the post-socialist condition' whilst it was also becoming clear that forms of what are now known as 'neo-liberalism' were here to stay.

The beginning of the 1990s can be characterised by these two inter-linked threads: namely massive ideological and contextual shifts and a variety of methodological perspectives on these shifts, making for what has been named as critical social theories and feminist ethnographies. By the beginning of the twenty-first century these approaches to social and feminist analyses and research arguably are deeply embedded in the psyches and perspectives of social researchers. Whilst there is still controversy and conflicts about how to approach such studies, there is a measure of agreement about the importance of personal understandings, subjectivities and identities in understandings about these social transformations and their impacts upon emergent diverse families and social, racial and sexual relations. Personal experiences and reflections upon this had become germane to these theories.

Fraser (1997) pulled together these two threads in her analysis of the links between social transformations and maintaining a critical stance, defining the 'post-socialist condition' as 'an absence of any credible overarching emancipatory project despite the proliferation of fronts of struggle; a general decoupling of the cultural politics of recognition from the social politics of redistribution; and the decentering of claims for equality in the face of aggressive marketization and sharply rising material inequality' (1997, p. 3). She had developed the notion of the post-socialist condition in terms of a post-structural analysis and I use her feminist theories in association with post-structuralism around women's lives as a marker of these developments in the 1990s. My critical reflections map onto hers since she was concerned about the wider changing social and political context and how it affected the development of a socialist politics. She elaborated three features of a critical policy perspective; namely the lack of progressive vision of an alternative, shifts in claims from a focus on social equality, or from a 'socialist political imaginary' in which the central problem of justice was redistribution to one in which it was 'recognition' of social groups, rather than social class, and the 'third defining feature . . . is a resurgent economic liberalism':

> As the center of political gravity seems to shift from redistribution to recognition, and egalitarian commitments appear to recede, a globalizing wall-to-wall capitalism is increasingly marketizing social relations, eroding social protections and worsening the life-chances of billions.' (1997: 3)

Fraser was more concerned to analyse critical political theories and policies rather than their application to studies of women's lives in and out of families. Yet she centred her study within a critique of 'economic liberalism' or what has now been referred to as neo-liberalism. Others have developed a more targeted analysis. As Valerie Walkerdine (2002) argued, the issue centred upon how we understand and study subjectivity in relation to how we also study 'neo-liberalism', and yet it is 'personal choices' that are paramount in these understandings and parallel policy reforms and initiatives. Ruth Lister (2002) argued in a similar vein in a lecture to a meeting of the gender research forum organised by the Women and Equality Unit (WEU) of the New Labour government's cabinet office. She made the point that feminist research was now crucially and centrally focused on understanding the perspectives of poor women as mothers and carers, subject to the constraints and constrictions of policy developments through what might be called neo-liberalism. She highlighted a number of fundamental propositions in arguing for feminist research continuing to attend to the subjective experiences of women in the context of policy reforms that may militate against women's autonomy and independence in relation to children and caring.

Modernities and neo-liberalism: understanding social and political changes

In Britain the subtle shift to neo-liberalism as a moment was signalled by Mrs Thatcher's resignation as Prime Minister and her replacement by John Major, an equally committed neo-conservative. Whilst Mrs Thatcher's resignation was forced, as she herself stated in her autobiography about the events on a momentous November 22nd 1990, it did not signal any radical shift in political ideology but rather the demise of a once powerful and iconic personality (Arnot *et al*, 1999). In most respects it indicated continuity with economic liberalism as Major elaborated a more explicit approach to consumerism through the citizen's charter, and individual charters for public services, such as the parent's charter for education. This ensured continuation of a particular conservative social agenda with its implications for poor women and children.

The enduring conservatism of the US government was signalled through Reagan's replacement in office by George Bush in 1989, and continuing through until the end of 1992, only to be replaced by Clinton, as a Democrat, with a relatively fresh perspective on a social agenda in 1993. During that time a number of writers were still aiming to understand and theorise 'liberalism' or neo-liberalism as an extension of the policies developed under previous conservative administrations in terms of sexual relations (Zillah Eisenstein, 1996).

In other advanced industrial or capitalist societies, such as Australia, Canada and New Zealand as well as many countries of Europe, namely Denmark, France, Germany, Italy and Sweden, political ideologies remained more leftist or socialist during the 1990s. However, most countries of Eastern Europe, such as Czechoslovakia, Hungary, Poland and Yugoslavia reneged upon their communism in the late 1980s and early 1990s, culminating in the overthrow/demise of Gorbachev and the Soviet Union in 1991. Thus the beginnings of the 1990s were characterised by a number of major international political shifts, not all of which went in the same ostensible direction. With hindsight, it can be argued that they all tended in the direction of what is now named, by many social scientists, as 'neo-liberalism', that is a politics based around the themes of market forces,

consumerism and choices within public services. Although these transformations took place globally it is difficult to refer to them as one single process, since
they took many different economic and social forms, thus they are not, as Held
(2001) has argued, a singular or single phenomenon.

These shifts also bear with them changes in public-private balances, especially in
relation to families and social and welfare services, and the institutions known
broadly as the welfare state. In particular, moves away from social welfare as a
means of providing protection from adversity for individuals and families, such
as family poverty and violence, have been significant transformations in political
life in this period (Beck, 1992; Giddens 1998; 2000). Some theorised these
changes in what in the USA first was called 'welfare dependency', meaning
significantly here the dependence of particular categories of people, mainly
single mothers with dependent children on the state, to dependence upon work
or employment. The rate and pace of change has varied and been targeted on
particular categories, but most usually women as mothers, have been 'named'
and 'shamed' and expected to bear the brunt of these changes (David, 1998).

Memories, reminiscences and revised reflexive understandings

At the end of the 1980s, I was invited to contribute a regular column to the
THES, by the then editor Peter Scott, whose writings I admired greatly. I was
flattered to be invited to do this, and did not hesitate to accept, although several
people subsequently commented that they were surprised that I would want to
take on this kind of writing. However, it gave me the opportunity to write more
reflectively about the entwined issues of family, academic life as divided between
administration, teaching and management. It was also a discipline about writing
in this reflexive mode that I came thoroughly to enjoy, and honed my skills at
writing in a direct and serious journalistic fashion. In any event I had regularly
counselled my students of social policy that I thought that 'serious journalism'
was a style that they should aim to achieve, being able to critique, evaluate and
criticise policy developments. I continued to write this column for three and a
half years, to the beginning of 1993, although I had initially anticipated that I
would only do so for six months. During this time I aimed to combine consideration of research questions and issues with the finer and more regular routine
issues of family and academic life. I was concerned to elucidate and describe the
various forces and influences on gender relations in public policies and private
families.

During the late 1980s South Bank, like many other polytechnics at the time, had
also instituted a system of professors to accord with academic seniority within
the traditional universities. I was chosen as one of the first eight professors in

the inaugural round in 1988, and the first and only woman. My scholarship on families, gender and educational policies was the reason for this appointment. Thus my inaugural professorial lecture, entitled *What is Education for?* given on November 7th 1990 illustrated how the enduring themes of unequal educational opportunities were closely linked with wider public policies (a revised version was subsequently published in Floud, 1997). I threaded through an historical analysis, with a case study of the history of South Bank, and its origins as Borough Road training college, through the Fabian influence on its development into a polytechnic institute in the late nineteenth century, to its emergence as an inner London polytechnic providing educational opportunities for working class families. In particular, I pointed to differences in provision for men and women, across and within different subjects and with different purposes for their adult lives.

This kind of approach to critical policy analysis across a range of public policies of social welfare, from a feminist perspective, remained my emphasis although I was beginning to return to a more empirical approach to studies of contemporary policy reforms of social welfare. During the early part of the 1990s, I embarked upon a series of research studies, both with colleagues within South Bank and in other higher education institutions in Britain, and also developed several international initiatives around studies of families and family policies. These culminated in the setting up early in 1992 of the Social Sciences Research Centre (SSRC) at South Bank of which I became director. I changed roles from my position of head of the Social Sciences Department, given the managerial shifts and changes in the polytechnic becoming a university in response to Thatcherite policy changes. Curiously I became responsible for developing social science research in a period when there was great scepticism about this activity for the new universities. At the same time I was invited to become a member of one of the then Universities Funding Council panels for the Research Assessment Exercise (RAE) for sociology, a part of the growing managerial process of quality assurance in British higher education.

The aims of the SSRC were around the themes of critical policy analysis of developments in neo-liberalism, developments of charters and consumerism, and the empirical studies of people's lives, women's lives especially in relation to these policies. We brought together in the SSRC a number of critical perspectives on a wide-range of policy issues, from education and family, to health, housing, social care and welfare. What united us was a desire to develop a critical social analysis of public policies being developed in the name of economic liberalism. The centre was based within the Social Sciences Department, and whilst its core was half a dozen dedicated researchers, specifically Rosalind Edwards and Phillip Gatter, together with Linda Mulcahy and Jonathan Tritter, there were several colleagues who were also involved, namely Judith Allsop,

Norman Ginsburg and Jeffrey Weeks. Our approach was to twin methodological perspectives with substantive areas. We developed our theme around research on families, using feminist and social constructionist perspectives. We drew on earlier work associated with a variety of colleagues, specifically around childcare (with Pam Calder), education and families in an international context and also with a particular expertise on work on AIDS, which drew on earlier innovative studies by Peter Davies and colleagues on socio-sexual investigations of gay men with AIDS – the SIGMA project and work on families of people with AIDS by Rayah Feldman.

We continued to build upon the scholarly and empirical work we started in the aftermath of Thatcherism, bringing together work on diverse families. The work of research students such as Jane Ribbens and Rosalind Edwards contributed to the feminist perspectives on changing families in terms of how such families developed perspectives on the neo-liberal notion of parental choice of school and around social welfare issues in relation to childcare for lone parents. I developed my research around my own biography and those of my children, especially in relation to their education. Choosing schools for them had continued to be a major issue, in terms of attending secondary school, since they both transferred in the aftermath of the ERA, 1988 when 'parental choice of schools' became a major new slogan. The moves away from state education providing for equality of educational opportunity towards parental choice and marketisation were dramatic, particularly in London at the height of Thatcherism. This was when education became a political football and the evidence about children's educational successes were linked to quality of schools in terms of what we later called the 3 Ps – performance, proximity and pleasant feel (David, West and Ribbens, 1994).

Researching and choosing schools became a personal and family dilemma and my maternal guilt was huge. My daughter Charlotte was initially unhappy at her primary school in London when we moved in 1986 and although she settled and became happy she was invited to take an entrance examination and on successful completion went to a girls' single sex school in the winter of 1988/9. My son Toby transferred to a boys' independent school in the summer of 1989. Later university choice became an issue and topic for further research. From my divorce in 1994, a myriad of other changes set in train, although we had settled for a stable approach to our children's education such that I remained in the family home, whilst both completed their education at school. My son Toby finished his A levels in 1996 and after a gap year working, travelling in Australia and studying in Israel for 6 months, entered university in 1997 to study politics and modern history. My daughter completed her A levels two years later and took a similar gap year working, travelling in the USA and studying in Israel for 6 months, entering university in 1999 to study modern foreign languages. I did not, however, consciously consider studying more personal issues for them, around questions of children in divorcing families although I was well aware of the wealth of research emerging on these topics at this juncture both important studies by Smart and Neale (1999) and from the USA.

Our research increasingly took on an international flavour, with visits too and from the USA, Spain in the summer of 1991 and Israel for the women's studies tour in November 1991. This illustrated the widening sphere of feminist studies internationally and yet its more problematic political context. However, as we later demonstrated (Arnot David and Weiner, 1999) there were serious contradictory effects in the widening of spheres of individual choices and the opening up towards more chances for women and yet the lack of opportunities for women in the public spheres. The evidence of women's participation in higher education and the shifts over 25 years proved dramatic.

My memory of some of the global political shifts in the early 1990s is strong. I was attending a European feminist research conference in Aalborg, Denmark, when news came through of Gorbachev's house-arrest in the summer of 1991. I was giving paper on mothers and education: issues in family-education policy with a particular focus on childcare. I shared a platform with a number of women from the Eastern bloc, who had very different perspectives on women's rights and responsibilities, for example, many appeared conservative on issues of abortion, to our Western ways of thinking. About a third of the delegates to this conference were from Soviet-bloc countries and our attention was diverted from the original themes of the conference, largely about women in relation to sexuality, family and public policies by the need to support their rapidly changing circumstances. Some of them feared that they would not be able to return home, and indeed they were not, confirming the brusqueness of these changing regimes. However, the conference remained committed to rather traditional forms of feminist research, and Christine Delphy was one of the keynote speakers, arguing for a material-feminist perspective.

Emergent feminist theories compete with post-structuralism and high modernity risk societies

The beginning of the 1990s was a time of great intellectual and political turmoil and contested social theories abounded to provide explanations for the multitudinous social transformations including family changes. Traditional feminist, especially socialist or Marxist, theories clashed with more philosophical and post-modern or post-structuralist theories. Fraser's concerns did not encompass all. Thus she argued in her *Justice Interruptus: critical reflections on the 'post-socialist' condition*:

> Scarcely a definitive negative verdict on the relevance and viability of socialist ideals, it is, rather, a skeptical mood or structure of feeling that marks the post-

1989 state of the Left . . . this mood expresses authentic doubts bound to genuine opacities concerning the historical possibilities for progressive social change. Yet it is laced with ideological elements, which are difficult to disentangle and name . . . (1997: 1)

Hilary Rose's clear critique of these complex theories and their adoption within studies of social welfare and feminism helped in particular with these emergent critiques (Rose, 1994). She argued for an approach to thinking from caring, using feminist perspectives, and from a critique of post-modernism entwined with critical realism (and no references to Giddens!). She wrote:

> . . . for those of us living in Britain, an old industrial society with a problematic economy and a growing culture of social indifference, the changing context of the 1980s and 1990s has seen those fierce divisions of radical and socialist feminisms diminish; the body and gender are now central issues of feminism. The significant difference is that now feminist materialism is itself having to compete for intellectual space against a strong poststructuralist current. It has been in and against this changing context that the present book has been all too slowly written . . . (Rose, 1994: xi)

At the time, understandings and perspectives on these multitudinous changes were varied, and feminists, as other social scientists and researchers, developed a variety of social analyses, linked with perspectives on social and political change and context. On the one hand Walby's *Theorising Patriarchy* (1990) pointed to what she called dual systems theory, linking capitalism and patriarchy and breaking down previous distinctions between the three traditional strands of feminism, namely liberal, socialist and radical. Her work has led her towards a position identified as 'critical realism'; a Marxist materialist methodological perspective (Walby, 2001). On the other hand, post-modernist and post-structuralist perspectives critiquing traditional concepts and approaches and relying on radical psychoanalytic approaches were gaining currency.

Perspectives had, for the most part, shifted away from a focus on sex to gender, as the unit or category of social analysis. Christine Delphy (1993), however, wrote a strong critique of these moves, arguing that 'most feminist work on gender has been based upon an unexamined presupposition: that sex precedes gender' (1993, p. 1). She argued that such an approach failed to recognise the naturalistic assumptions in gender analysis and that these were linked to values around notions of hierarchy and division. She argued for a more thorough-going analysis of both sex and gender as socially constructed: 'we shall only really be able to think about gender on the day when we can imagine nongender.' (1993, p. 9)

It is possible to argue that these changes were linked to various forms of discursive analysis, stemming from complex French traditions of analytic and political thought. Indeed, these French theories, drawing largely on social philosophies, including structuralism, post-structuralism and psychoanalysis, were beginning to be taken up in feminist theorising within the academy across the globe. For instance, the American feminist Judith Butler's work in the humanities, and her book *Gender Trouble* published in 1990 became an instant classic arguing for gender as a category of analysis, using both psychoanalysis and other French philosophical traditions, including the work of post-structuralists and Foucault in particular. However, Butler's feminist project was not to understand familial change or how women have tried to change their lives but was rather a philo-sophical project to theorise notions of being a woman. She drew on a range of post-structural and post-modern theoretical developments to theorise the cate-gory of woman, albeit that many aspects of this categorisation relate, as she argued, to notions of family positions. She concluded her essays with the comment:

> . . . the very injunction to be a given gender takes place through discursive routes: *to be a good mother, to be a heterosexually desirable object*, to be a fit worker, in sum, to signify a multiplicity of guarantees in response to a variety of different demands all at once. The coexistence or convergence of such discursive injunctions produces the possibility of a complex reconfiguration and redeployment; it is not a transcen-dental subject who enables action in the midst of such a convergence. There is no self that is prior to the convergence . . .

> I have tried to suggest that the identity categories often presumed to be founda-tional to feminist politics, that is, deemed necessary in order to mobilize feminism as an identity politics, simultaneously work to limit and constrain in advance the very cultural possibilities that feminism is supposed to open up . . . (1990: 145; 147) (my emphasis)

Butler questioned the very category of 'woman', especially in relation to identity. Her questioning grew out of a more insistent questioning of other categories of identity too; in particular the dominance of white middle class accounts, even in feminism. This theoretical project takes us beyond the project of understanding changes in family life and the role that feminism and feminist politics played within that. It is very important theoretically but it is critical of much of the feminist politics that sought to consider changes in family life. Much of the original campaigning of feminists centred on children and childcare. It was also part of a strategy to change living arrangements. It also signals the dominance of a particular generation in the forming and framing of a particular feminist politics and later theoretical developments. However, these politics have shifted and altered as more generations contribute to theoretical debate and policy analysis. Nancy Fraser's analysis used a combination of Marxist and Foucauldian or post-structuralist approaches.

In the early 1990s Giddens (1990; 1991; 1992) had begun a long process of theorisation about the characteristics of what he called modernity and especially late modernity, as the current period. He related these developments to notions of self-identity, and how individuals were increasingly expected to construct their own identities within the contexts of modern societies. He also grappled with changing theories about sexual relationships and love, specifying new perspectives on couple and marital relationships and feelings within late modern societies. Although he explored these theoretical developments by interrogating a variety of social theories about intimacy, including his sympathetic understanding of social constructionism, and post-structuralism, he did not grapple with feminist theories around family, and nor did he consider issues in relation to children (Giddens, 1992). Although he was sympathetic broadly to psychoanalytic perspectives, his emphasis was increasingly upon the ways in which late modern societies constructed individual identities and provided little protection for social risks and hazards of a constantly changing context. Working together with the German sociologist Ulrich Beck he began to explore notions of the risk society, and identities in relation to these changes (Beck, Lash and Giddens, 1996). Whilst many feminist sociologists did also explore the implications of these notions at that time, I remained wedded to a more traditional form of feminist political analysis rather than sociological theories.

Extending work on motherhood in relation to policy and practices

I was not in the forefront of those adopting these new perspectives on understandings, and uses of French political philosophy, although I had used Althusser, a French Marxist over a decade earlier, and Althusser had been Foucault's and Bourdieu's teacher (David, 1980). I was sympathetic to the uses of psychoanalytic thinking within feminist theorising, but was unable to see its utility in interpretations of social and political change, a position that I have subsequently come to revise through the more imaginative uses of these perspectives by a range of social and feminist theorists, such as Walkerdine, Lucey and Melody (2001), Shaw (1995, Williams 1989). In particular, Shaw's uses of psychoanalytic notions for understanding educational processes around anxiety and their impacts upon children, parents and teachers, in terms of gender is particularly illuminating. It is also useful for studies across education and families.

As feminist sociology matured into the 1990s more interest was taken in developing a more reflective and indeed reflexive approach to studies of family life and influences on our lives and our identities. This was part of the complex picture of the growth and development of sociology in tandem with feminism. As the first generation of second wave academic feminists matured we began to reflect upon our personal lives as feminists. There have been several distinct approaches across the various generations involved in academic feminist sociology with auto/biographical accounts, reflections on life histories and narratives about feminism. The importance of diverse, fractured and hybridised identities and subjectivities in framing appropriate methodologies has become predominant. As I have noted before, I was interested in two interlocking perspectives; namely critical policy analysis of developing neo-liberal policies on families and education, including sex and social policies, and more theoretically informed empirical studies of families, especially mothers and children, in a variety of socio-economic circumstances and family backgrounds. Sue Lees (1986; 1993) was a pioneer of studies of young girls and their perspectives on sex and sexuality at school. Studies of children and young people became a part of the emergent sociology of childhood. Studies and theories abounded but how motherhood, mothering and families should be studied in relation to both children and work, and equally how public policies should be critiqued became the subject of much controversy. On the one hand, the academic debates about feminism were originally suffused with questions about maternalism as a form of essentialism rather than such ideas being ideologically and socially constructed. Thus those that developed such concepts were developing what might be called 'maternal feminism' an essentialist theory of women. Sara Ruddick's (1989) study of maternal thinking became very influential in the debates about essentialism versus social constructionism or post-structuralism, as it subsequently became known. Ann Snitow (1992), an American feminist, inaugurated a debate about these issues and matters in *Feminist Review* nearly 10 years ago, on the grounds that the mothers and maternalism had largely been ignored by feminists but pointing also to the essentialist 'nature' of the debates.

However, this strand of development of mothers writing about relations with and to children has developed more as part of feminist work and studies in the academy, becoming known as critical ethnographies. There was also excellent carefully crafted work being developed around young mothers and mothers' practices and ideologies in the UK (Phoenix, 1991; Phoenix, Woollett and Lloyd 1991). This kind of work drew on race and minority ethnic agendas and perspectives, as much as with social class. Mirza's (1992) excellent study of young women and their educational perspectives, added to these debates, as did work by Tsolidis (2001) on hybridised identities of young women in education. This has led into rich and detailed work on different identities of both young people and mothers. Phoenix's scholarly work has been imaginative and she extended her studies of black young women and mothers with Tizard (1996). More recently, she elaborated her studies of young people in relation to theories of childhood and drawing on more sophisticated notions of gender studied masculinities and race/ethnicities with Frosh (2001).

Similar critical feminist ethnographies were developed in the USA and Canada by Dorothy Smith and her team of researchers (Griffith and Smith, Ann

Manicom, Gillian Walker and others) and in Australia (Kenway, 1990) and in New Zealand (Sue Middleton 1998). Many of these critical studies were of mothers and women in relation to health and social care as well as education, and studies of women in various social locations and locales, with caring responsibilities.

Moreover, during the early 1990s, conservative agendas were increasingly developed about different kinds of motherhood, especially young and single mothers, who were 'named' and 'shamed' and linked to welfare transformations. The early 1980s approach of Reagan through his adviser, George Gilder, whose text *Welfare and Poverty* had been subject to critical scrutiny, was reinscribed in the early 1990s, in both the USA and UK. In particular Charles Murray, Gilder's successor as scourge of the welfare poor, began to make impassioned visits to the UK, and develop policies for Britain by analogy with the USA. His work on welfare mothers and poor families, whom he dubbed 'the new rabble' by contrast with the 'new Victorians' (1994), and his predictions that the trends would reach astronomic proportions by the turn of the century was taken up by policy makers and policy critics alike (Lister, 1996). This kind of approach became the basis for further critical analysis. Some of these studies fed into more critical perspectives on policy analysis, being developed *inter alia* by Kiernan Land and Lewis, (1998). This was also part of the emergent critiques of policy specifications around notions of 'the parenting deficit' (Etzioni, 1995) and social capital and communitarianism (Etzioni, 1996), including the more conventional policy analyses by public policy think-tanks such as the Institute for Public Policy Research, established in the early 1990s.

There were also emergent new studies using post-structuralist analysis and reflexive sociological methodologies for studies on new generations of women. This new sociology produced a wealth of scholarship on young people and women; exemplified by Sue Lees (1986; 1993) Tuala Gordon, Rachel Thompson and Janet Holland (1996) on young women; Sue Scott and Stevi Jackson (1999) on risk anxieties and ethics amongst young people; Kenway, Willis, Blackmore and Rennie on young women in school in Australia (1997). By the mid-1990s, feminist theories had become embedded within sociological thinking (Skeggs, 1996) and questions about sexualities paramount. The BSA conference in 1996 was devoted to the topic of sexualities, and four volumes of conference papers were subsequently published, demonstrating the prolixity and proliferation of writings about these themes. The themes interlaced throughout many of the conferences were feminist and pro-feminist analyses. For instance, the BSA conferences in 2000, 2001 and 2002 had themes about family studies and gender and sexuality.

As noted in the previous chapter, together with several colleagues and students, we had embarked upon a series of studies of mothers' lives in relation to education, and particular policy developments such as the Education Reform Act (ERA) 1988 and the extent to which it was creating a new era. A series of studies, both critical policy analysis (David, 1993; David, *et al*, 1993 and a research project on parental choice with Anne West and Jane Ribbens, 1994). Together a new approach to family and education both substantively and theoretically and methodologically slowly emerged from these collegial interactions. We gave consideration to a variety of aspects of mothers and education both in relation to state policies and women's experiences of living through those situations. This marked the beginnings of our attempts to develop a post-structural analysis with forms of discourse analysis.

The initial studies taking these various perspectives and drawn from various studies were published in *Mothers and Education: Inside Out? Exploring family-education policy and experience*. Each of the four authors addressed a different aspect of the issue drawing on their own research studies that were also each published separately. Rosalind Edwards had studied mature mother students, Mary Hughes aspects of the regulation of women in adult education, and Jane Ribbens had studied mothers' child-rearing practices in relation to young children. I presented work on the relation between mothers and schooling drawing on work previously conducted with other colleagues. We wrote:

> The themes of this book have grown out of our joint and several concerns with the issues of mothers and education, since we are all mothers and feminists. We came together . . . given our shared academic interests in family and education debates. We were all working separately on questions around these themes, having come to them from our personal concerns and intellectual interests in broad questions of feminism and social research . . . (1993: 4)

> Our book aims to reveal the gendered nature of, and issues of power in, the relationships between mothers and education . . . We will explore policy understandings and prescriptions to demonstrate how they are constructed on public world ways of knowing and professional and social scientific agendas. We hope to show that they do not necessarily relate to the realities of women's family-based lives. We will also explore how being a mother can mean different ways of knowing and experiencing the world from these public world points of view. On the other hand, we will also argue that unless mothers have access to place and status in the public world, as things stand they may find it difficult to make their voices heard and influence changing agendas. (1993: 26–7)

Together we also pursued a number of policy-oriented and policy-relevant funded studies from a critical policy evaluation standpoint, applying a range of qualitative methods. Some of the studies have been rather more traditional in social scientific method with the aim of influencing policy-makers and the policy making process. Thus the Conservative educational reforms of the late 1980s, and specifically the Education Reform Act 1988 that avowedly aimed to create a new era, were the occasion for the engagement with critical policy analysis. First studies of the ostensibly new policy of parental choice of education were funded. In *Mother's Intuition? Choosing Secondary Schools* West, Ribbens and I presented our findings from this study in London of the ways in which mothers of primary school children went about the process of thinking about and choosing secondary schools for their children. Here we wrote:

> In summary, we have found that the processes and the procedures for parents making a choice of secondary school are indeed complex and complicated. However, we can summarize our key findings by saying, first that *mothers* are almost invariably involved in the those processes and procedures whatever the kind of family and child. And given the complexity of the processes and stories that we have presented, the mothers' involvement is more than based upon their intuition. On the other hand, fathers are *not* invariably involved and, when they are, it is largely to do with the social and cultural characteristics of families, but not necessarily to do with the family structure, that is the fact of being a lone parent family.
>
> We are not aware of any past research that has looked at the processes of either educational decision-making or school choice in terms of the gendered nature of parenthood. Neither has there been any research in Britain at least, as far as we are aware, on the ways in which family structures and new family forms may affect educational choices and decisions. We do know that work, variously by Dorothy Smith and Alison Griffith (1990) in Canada and Annette Lareau (1989) and Joyce Epstein (1989) in the United States, shows how difficult it is for mothers from single-parent family settings to be involved in the regular and routine activities of schools. (1994: 130–131)

Thus we also tried to develop a number of more internationally and theoretically informed studies of parental choice and mothering work (Smith, 1990) in collaboration with these colleagues. Similarly we also developed a more international focus by considering comparative educational and feminist perspectives, drawing on the work of Gail Kelly (1993). We also considered a range of theoretical and methodological developments. Beverley Skeggs' (1996) work was of great significance in demonstrating the complexities in studying subjectivities and women's raced and classed lives.

Our studies also mapped on to the critical work on the impact and effects of market forces and choices. A group of us met together regularly through a seminar series entitled 'market forces' to share work and perspectives and concerns. Thus Whitty's (1992; 1993; 1996) various studies together with Fitz, Halpin, Power, Edwards and Gewirtz on studying changing educational policies and practices, and those of Ball and his colleagues (1993; 1995; 1998) all contributed to our changing perspectives on policy reforms in relation to families. However, a feminist perspective tended to be ignored, although Ball pioneered a more Foucauldian approach (1994). His studies with Bowe and Gewirtz (1995) said little about gender and mothers but focused more how these policies affected working class families. However, more recently we have tried to integrate feminist and post-structural perspectives in a study of families and higher education (Reay, 1998; Ball, Reay and David 1999; 2001).

Consideration was also given to how our various studies of mothers in relation to children's education were similar to and even paralleled those of Dorothy Smith and Alison Griffith. Thus we aimed to develop a comparative study, but found difficulties in translating American predilections into the British context. Eventually we found it impossible to replicate the study and found ourselves providing a more methodological critique of these approaches towards mothers and children. We wrote:

> We are a group of feminist academics, all mothers, researching and writing about women in relation to families, family structures and forms such as lone-mother families, and in relation to bringing up children and their education in schools. We are concerned to explore, from a feminist perspective, whether and how mothers choose to bring their children up and their relation to schools . . . (David *et al*, 1996: 208)

> Researching motherhood as full-time academics and mothers raises painful issues about the gaps in researchers' own mothering (Smith and Griffith, 1990). We have all at different times had to contend with guilt in the research field, but our response to other mothers is much more varied than simply feeling guilt. Feelings of association and antipathy influence researchers' relationships with the researched in subtle yet powerful ways. Tales of juggling different roles and never having enough time lead to empathy and identification, while stories of full-time mothering often result in a complex mixture of envy, condescension and disbelief . . . Our very commitment to feminism means that often our interpretation of the social world is very different to those of some of the mothers we interviewed . . . As feminists we have all struggled to adopt the principles they suggest in our own research practices. However, there is an inherent problematic in making clear a feminist epistemological position and recognising our role in the research process. Too often it is read as bias within the malestream research world. Within academia, feminist researchers are constantly working with, and caught up in, malestream epistemologies which give primacy to male views of the world. Far from challenging the system, all too often we find ourselves inevitably colluding with it.

> The difficult choices that we face as feminist academics are magnified for mothers in the sphere of parental involvement. Neither mothers' involvement in their children's education nor mothering more generally are seen as worthy substantive or theoretical topics by academics working in the mainstream . . .

> In other words, we argue that choices take place in particular socially and economically structured contexts, which means that all individuals are to some extent constrained from being entirely free to choose. This can be as much the case for ourselves as feminist academics as it is for those whose lives we study . . . (David *et al*, 1996, in Morley and Walsh, (eds.): 210–211)

We also tried to develop the notion of reflexivity in relation to our own work as mothers and involved in higher education as academics; this was subsequently through work with Rosalind Edwards and Diane Reay. Diane Reay's thesis, subsequently published as a book (1998) was a reflexive account of mothers' work in relation to children's schooling. We were building up a 'school of thought' or feminist perspective on mothers and their work in relation to children, through specific substantive doctoral studies of mothers in different social locations – lone, single divorced, black, working class (Reay, 1998; Kay Standing, 1999; Tracey Reynolds, 2002, Val Gillies, 2002) and work of other associates (e.g. Pam Alldred, 2000) about diverse families. Thus we attempted to develop a more methodological critique of how we were working and in particular considered our involvement in the issues in relation to the academy. We also drew on our various substantive studies of mothers in a range of contexts with children and their education, in which working class, lone mothers, black and ethnic minority women were given consideration:

> Mothers' experiences of the processes of bringing up and educating their children are not at all in harmony with the public policy discourse of their being free to choose . . . Lack of resources is the key structural constraint on mothers' possibilities but so too are gendered moral rationalities (Edwards and Duncan, 1996) . . . These diverse but rich accounts illustrate just how constrained mothers' lives are in bringing up children . . . Despite the public discourse of individual choice, this is commonly experienced by mothers, as a further tightening of constraints, whether structural or moral, on how they live their lives and rear the next generation – a far cry from freedom of choice. (1997: 409–410)

Diane Reay developed a variety of studies together with Heidi Mirza on Saturday schools (1998; 2001). Mirza and Edwards also worked together with Tracey Reynolds on black mothers' perspectives. Edwards, with Duncan (1997; 1999;) and with Carling, (2002) also pursued studies of lone parents in international contexts and their 'gendered moral rationalities', and Edwards with Ribbens and Gillies (2002) studied step-parenting and also developed specifically an approach to feminist qualitative research. Studies were also commenced on young people and their views of parents, mothers especially drawing on the important work around divorce and women and children's changing identities and perspectives. (Smart and Neale, 1999; Smart, Neale and Wade, 2001))

Changing families and changing lives: research and practice

During the course of this exciting and intellectually productive work around diverse and changing families, I went through a divorce (1994), and then my mother died in 1996. I have often wondered whether the effect of doing research on changing families was to hasten my own changing family life or whether it was the other way round. In any event I found myself studying a diversity of issues around women's changing lives.

Another study, also developed through the SSRC was a study commissioned by the Equal Opportunities Commission (1996) on gender equality in schools. The report of this multi-methods study of both statistical evidence of boys' and girls' educational achievements and case studies of school policies and practices appeared in 1996. It led us to consider the more complex and historical reasons for changing patterns of gender equality both in schools and in the wider society. This led us to a more theoretical and wider consideration of changing families and gender, in which we studied both social policies and global economic trans- formations in the post-war period to account for these changes in gender patterns in family and education (Arnot *et al*, 1999). Meanwhile we also under- took more complex and complicated studies of parental choice, parental involve- ment and expectations of achievement in schooling. This study reviewed the complexities of mothers and fathers relationships in different family and school settings over their children's education. Again, with West, we wrote:

> This paper is specifically concerned with . . . parents' involvement in their children's education. The study was carried out during the period of Conservative government reforms that were designed to raise the standards of educational attainment through the introduction of market forces . . . A similar philosophical approach is continuing with the Labour Government . . . (1998: 461)

> It is clear that the mother generally assumes overriding responsibility for children's out-of-school and other educational activities . . . It might be argued that the inter- viewees, the majority as mothers themselves, were not accurately reflecting the true position . . . it seems unlikely given that it was the mother who agreed to be interviewed in the majority of cases . . . (1998: 461)

> Overall, the results point to more highly educated mothers trying to ensure that their children's chances of success in the education system are increased. The implication is thus that these mothers perceive that there are benefits to having higher levels of educational qualifications – that they themselves already have – and that they have the capacity to contribute to those benefits. Their own cultural capital and often financial resources mean that they are in a position to seek to maximise their children's chances of educational success. (West *et al*, 1998: 482)

These studies led to further theoretical consideration and developments within both the sociology of childhood (Jenks, James and Prout, 1996) and the new sociology of families (Skeggs, 1996; Scott and Jackson, 1999; Scott, Jackson and Beckett-Milburn 1998). In terms of the sociology of childhood, we undertook, through a broad programme of studies of children 5–16 funded by the ESRC, a study of children's understandings of parental involvement in education (with Edwards and Alldred, 1999; 2001). This linked theoretically and substantively with studies by James (1999) and Scott and Jackson (1999) and with Diane Reay with Helen Lucey on children's involvement in choice of schools (Reay and Lucey, 2000). It also contributed to detailed studies with Diane Reay and with Stephen Ball on aspects of parental choice of higher education. Here we attempted to theorise these questions by drawing on Reay's work which had drawn on Bourdieu on familial and institutional habitus (Reay, 1998 a and b).

Writing about generations of young women's personal lives

Many feminist researchers internationally had become interested in researching the lives of young women growing up within the changed times and social and economic transformations. This work fills in the questions that Curthoys (2000) raised about exploring the influences of feminist thinking upon subsequent generations of young women. Thus feminist researchers have also been interested in the question of the impacts of feminist amongst other ideas on how such young women learn to develop their personal lives, across social class, ethnicity, race and culturally, drawing on a range of concepts such as hybridity and subjectivity. At least a part of that has been an interest in how children have responded to the social changes that feminists have been involved in working towards. Many feminist academics, particularly within educational feminism have begun to study these issues taking as their starting point the concern about the influences of feminist ideas on succeeding generations. (Sue Lees, 1996; Jenny Shaw, 1994; Wendy Luttrell, 1997; Lyn Yates, 2000 and with Julie Mcleod; Jane Kenway, 2000; Kari Dehli; Carol Smart and Bren Neale; Fiona Williams)

Valerie Walkerdine has written some of the most important theoretical work to understand young women's subjectivities. Basing her initial interests on her own working class background, she sought to understand the complexities of influences and meanings drawing on a range of theories, including the use of psychoanalysis. Amongst her several important studies, she first explored, with Helen Lucey, (1989) through a re-analysis of studies conducted by Tizard and Hughes (1984) the importance of the ways in which working class mothers constructed and were constructed in their relationships with their young pre-school age children. This study complemented the kinds of studies that I had conducted and led into similar studies of younger generations of women. Her work has been particularly important for revealing the social class and 'race' approaches to young women's search for new and meaningful identities, much in keeping with the new traditions of finding and exploring girls' voices in relation to their being of a new generation. In *Daddy's Girl,* Walkerdine (1997) explored working class girls' relationships with their fathers and how these represent threats to men and in a wider context to education. She wrote:

In . . . television presentations of children the eroticization of little girls is presented as . . . as profoundly classed . . . the blonde-haired girl to be protected is
inevitably middle-class and the little seductress is the working-class girl who
presents the danger of the fecund masses . . . Because I grew up in the post-war
British working class, those stories have touched me profoundly and because I feel
implicated in them, I want to interrogate them . . . they are . . . failing to take
account of how else we might think about the relation of subjectivity to popular
culture . . . (1997: 5)

My aim is to explore . . . an understanding of the subjectivity of 'the working class'.
To do this, I blend theoretical discussion with actual case material, bringing in my
own subjectivity as part of my method ... (1997: 8)

She extended this analysis in her work with Lucey and Melody (2001) and
argued about different girls' voices and identities, using the tools of post-structuralism and the approaches to understanding how young women cope with constant re-inventions of the self and the wider uncertainties in the social and
economic context. Young women's lived experiences were examined against a
backdrop of constantly changing social life, a fluidity of social change and risks
that lead to a reflexive concern with challenging and changing social identities.
Walkerdine located her initial concerns with her own identity as a white working
class woman; yet another quasi-autobiographical search for meanings and
understandings. The studies sought to understand the differences in class-based
experiences of young women, growing up in England at the turn of the century,
drawing upon a study of young women originally studied in the early 1980s and
who became 21 in 1993. It explored changing generations of younger women and
the interrelationships between their family, educational and employment identities within the wider contexts of massive social, economic and global transformations. The authors identified the massively different life trajectories of the
middle class from the working class women and pinpointed the very different
fears and fantasies of these two groups. The middle class girls all became very
highly achieving academically but routinely saw their performances as ordinary
and had great anxiety about balancing their cleverness with their femininity.
They routinely saw themselves as 'not good enough'. However, their femininity
was not about being wives and/or mothers but about sexual attractiveness and
yet also the search for men and employment. Fecundity was associated in their
minds with stupidity. Their anxieties contrasted remarkably with those of the
working class young women, whose anxieties remained rooted in their family
lives, albeit that many of them became single mother families, and searched for
their identities within another context of broader social changes. Thus sexual
relationships took on new meanings for these young women, interlaced with
their educational developments.

Education, and high academic performances both at the end of school and on entry to university, became routine amongst the young women from the middle classes but also contributed to their struggle and search for new identifications and balances in their family and work lives, which were unthinkable only a generation or two previously. A critical point was the extent to which changing social and economic contexts have contributed to educational transformations on the basis of gender. These women's lived experiences in family, personal and public life have already become substantially different from those of their mothers and previous generations. On Walkerdine, Lucey and Melody's reading of their evidence the subtleties of the changes and the increasing emphasis on the search for self-identities nevertheless led to a relatively common set of new patterns, in which sexual anxieties and fantasies had become more pervasive. The patterns are not ones that mirror those of previous generations of women and their mothers. They concluded:

> We have told a story in which class differences between young women figure as largely as they did 20 or 30 year ago, despite the face of class having changed considerably . . . transformations . . . had a huge impact on women's as well as men's employment . . . There is no doubt that the notion of self-invention and self-regulation offers a way to understand the social and psychological changes that have been central to an understanding of the changed times for young women and their families. It is the fragility of the arrangements for all subjects that is highlighted . . . subjectification works not only on complex conscious and rational processes but also on desires, wishes and anxieties and creates defensive organisations through which participants live their inscription into discursive practices that make up current sociality . . . Women's position in the new economy is not comfortable. Young women watch their mothers struggle and do not want to have to combine work and family, but know very well that is the future they face. Indeed more than that, they may also have to cope with men who are feeling intensely the loss of previous modes of masculinity. In these circumstances it would be difficult to say that the female future is rosy. (Walkerdine, Lucey and Melody, 2001: 211, 212 and 216)

These rather dramatic findings and theoretical notions elaborated and extended similar studies by other feminist researchers in other cultures and contexts (Lees, 1996; Luttrell, 1997; Kenway *et al*, 1998; Yates and Mcleod, 2000). Accounts combining gender, race and class as hybridised ways to understand subjectivities have begun to emerge (Brah, 1996; Skeggs, 1996; Kuhn, 1996; Razool, 1997; Bhatti, 2000; Tsolidis, 2000).

Concerns about changing sexuality and sexual identity, particularly the implications of young motherhood, became urgent policy questions amongst many late modern regimes, for instance studies of teenagers and teen pregnancy in Canada (Deirdre Kelly, 2001; Jane Gaskell, 2000) and the USA (Pat Burdell, 1995/6) and in Britain by Sue Lees (1993; 1998) and Measor, Tiffin, and Miller (2000). Another way in which these studies were complemented was by Jane Kenway's work with Bullen and Hey (1999) on young people women especially as mothers/teenagers and learning to become women, through their construction through policies about teenage pregnancy. Lyn Mikel Brown (1998) addressed similar concerns about how to study and write about adolescent girls' voices out of her work with Carol Gilligan (1992). In *Raising their Voices: the politics of girls' anger* she presented her studies of two communities of young American girls – one working class and the other middle class. Her personal and methodological concerns were in debate with Walkerdine (1998, pp 37–39) She wrote:

> As I have listened to the voices and witnessed the interactions of the girls in this study, I have had to confront my own preparation, or lack thereof . . . I sit uncomfortably between two groups of girls who echo not only different periods in my life, but also complex and contradictory class fractions and voices that have existed within my family throughout my life. These girls both represent and contest the ordinariness of my own journey from working poor to working-class to middleclass . . . Because so much in these girls' lives was familiar . . . knowing, understanding, and respecting the differences between my past and their present was a constant challenge . . .

> As silencing or speaking on behalf of the Other has been used in patriarchal culture to mute or shape feminine experience, so have these same strategies been used by academics to mute or shape the experiences of the poor and the working class.

> My struggle has thus been against a temptation to either idealize or pathologize these girls, or to give them, attribute to them, knowledge, desires, or wants that are more about my experiences, my thoughts and feelings, my fictions and fantasies, than about theirs. My hope is to widen the scope of understanding . . . (Brown, 1998: 37–9)

Brown reached sensitive and challenging conclusions about these young women's struggles:

> The girls in this study, balanced on the precipice of full-blown adolescence, reveal the difficult transformations of public language into private consciousness through their struggles to come to terms with the tensions between local and dominant notions of femininity, between their experiences and the unattainable ideal . . .

> Feminist writings about powerful learning experiences underscore the importance of expressing passionate emotions such as anger . . .

> What is important is that we recognize the *potential* power of anger if and when it is heard, understood, and engaged in dialogue. (Brown, 1998: 209–10)

This led her to her conclusion about the potential for change amongst this emerging generation of young women, women schooled within a culture where feminism is a potential value and ideology, and where changes in family lives are now irrevocable, albeit that they may not be extensive. She concluded:

> Appreciating the ways in which girls from very different experiences and backgrounds capitulate to or resist appropriating the intentions of a patriarchal

discourse about femininity is central to understanding not only girls' psychological health and development, but also the complexities of social reproduction. Girls at early adolescence, in the process of negotiating their connection to the wider culture, have the potential to contribute alternative visions and voices, but they have to recognise themselves as complete and whole beings, with a range of feelings and thoughts connected to their experiences. (1999: 224)

Mikel Brown (1998), Walkerdine, Lucey and Melody (2001) and other feminist researchers, such as Kenway, Willis, Blackmore and Rennie (1998) and Jones (2001) pointed us to the complexities of understanding the processes involved in developing new identities and subjectivities. Kenway *et al* tried to study how these subjectivities were connected to and embedded within educational processes by studying how schools in Australia facilitated girls as compared with boys in equal opportunities.

Changing feminist theories and methodological concerns

These studies have pointed us to the rich new ways in which transformations in family life and the ideas that have contributed to some of these social changes can be theorised. They persuaded us to take the starting points in our own and others biographies and personal experiences and consider how these changing ideas are reflected in our changing lives and those of our and subsequent generations. The ideas that influenced the feminists starting to create and develop second-wave feminism have spawned whole new debates about how to study and understand these both deeply personal and private familial developments. Not only have they given birth to major debates about these studies and understandings but also how to develop these ideas and studies within not just the wider public world but that public world of the academy. This has also led into considerations about what it is to be a woman, first through the theoretically sophisticated work of Judith Butler amongst others, to more in depth consideration of the diversity and differences in terms of class, race and culture of our varied and various personal lives. This emphasis on what it is to be a black woman, or a woman with a hybridised culture and identity has brought far greater nuanced and complex theoretical understandings. Although these concentrated on differences in private and public lives, these are usually refracted now through the lens of academic lives rather than the more public and social worlds of politics. Thus at the same time as the growing complexity in social transformations of families and public worlds there has been a sophisticated growth in our varied understandings of these changes. Family lives are no longer just about our youthful concerns around sexuality, love, intimacy and marriage and/or divorce and the moves to motherhood; they are also about the problems of continuing relationships including with mothers, and ageing and all that is entailed. This not only signals a growing maturity amongst feminist sociologists but also a growing maturity of perspective to the kind of work that is currently key in feminist sociology of family lives.

Others, however, have attempted to study how familial and political changes have influenced generations of younger women, and considered the extent to which these changes are now part and parcel of younger women's subjectivities and lived experiences (Kuhn, 1996). Feminists wrote about and researched on children and have now altered their approaches to take account of children's views. Their methodological concerns about narratives, stories, voices and about daughters' writings about their mothers' lives. In more auto/biographical accounts the predominant concern has shifted from that of young women, and their various relationships with sexuality, men and issues to do with 'family planning', that is maternity child birth and children; or contraception and abortion to more general concerns.

Ribbens and Edwards (1998) began an association in which they addressed questions of feminist qualitative methodologies in relation to family, whilst at the same time also developing further research studies of families in various new situations, entitled *Feminist Dilemmas in Qualitative Research: Public Knowledge and Private Lives*. The women who contributed to this debate all gave consideration to how their own lives, and particular aspects of their own lives, mapped on to their research interests and how they would/could study them. Edwards and Ribbens wrote, by way of introduction:

> As women researchers concerned with domestic and intimate 'private' lives, the contributors to this volume have together explored their shared concerns about how to proceed in academic research when the theoretical, conceptual and formal traditions in which we are located are predominantly 'public' and 'malestream'. Questions of how to gain access to, interpret, analyse, and theorize research participants' experiences and accounts have formed a concern of qualitative researchers across disciplines and substantive topics for many years. As feminist researchers, we want to highlight the issues involved in doing this when applied to a sphere that has been characterized as 'female' or 'women's matters' . . .
>
> Thus, in our research, we have examined 'private' and 'personal' social worlds, which we then make 'public' for academic, and perhaps professional, audiences . . . As researchers we embody and directly experience the dilemma of seeking knowledge and understanding on these edges even as we seek to explore other people's private lives and translate them into the format of public knowledge . . . (1998: 1–2)

The essays in Ribbens' and Edwards' edited volume were careful to attend to personal experiences from locations that are 'raced' and 'classed' as well as gendered (1998, p. 8) and considered the notion of post-colonial theories. Nevertheless, all the contributors were involved in aspects of family research, having been involved in the women's workshop on qualitative family/household research (1998, p. 5) The editors added:

For members of the Workshop, the threshold between these social worlds has been especially difficult because we have often chosen to research topics to which we have a particular personal attachment, based upon our individual experience and knowledge. The Workshop thus contains women with a special type of commitment to their research, which then raises dilemmas for the ways in which its academic production affects the knowledge produced . . . (1998: 5)

While the contributors to this volume may not all agree with the totality of our arguments here about the constitution of, and relationship between, public, private and personal knowledges and ways of being, all acknowledge that theoretical and practical dilemmas and challenges are involved when we are concerned with hearing, retaining and representing research participants' 'voices'. At every point they reflect on the issues we experience as feminist researchers concerned with the qualitative exploration of intimate, private and domestic lives. (1998: 20)

Ribbens (1998) also tried to write an autobiographical account to contribute to qualitative methodological concerns. Entitled *Hearing my Feeling Voice? An autobiographical discussion of motherhood* her focus was centrally on her own constructions and feelings about becoming a mother and her research on mothers:

In this autobiographical discussion, I have sought to pay attention to the 'internal' processes of voice, while also recognising their fundamentally cultural construction. But I am not only seeking to find my own voice in my mothering. I am also committed to hearing the voices of others (women and men) rooted in their own experiences and understandings, about their lives with children. I want these voices to be heard within the public domain. (1998: 37)

The experiences recounted in the book ranged from discussions of sister and sibling relationships, to childbirth, childcare, children's voices, to mothers and lone mothers especially. In particular the authors argued that the specific circumstances of their locations as mothers with children had important effects upon the ways in which they research and argued:

. . . for many of us, the presence of children in our lives has significantly affected the ways in which we think about the position of women in our academic work. Even if we are central participants in the privately based social worlds we study (as mothers, sisters, wives or partners, and so on) or our topic has formed part of our biographical history (for example as children or mature women students) or we have strong privately based social contracts among those we study (such as alternative therapy groups, or lone mothers) the very act of researching these social worlds places us in a different position and can remove us to the edges of that private and personal world, positioning us on the edge of another, public, world. (1998: 204)

Ribbens and Edwards alerted us to the dynamics and challenges of conducting feminist research on family lives in the academy, and they also pointed us to the complexities and problems in the kinds of public and private or personal knowledge that might be produced.

Reflections

I have argued that the changing social conditions and moves towards neo-liberalism in the early 1990s had complex and contradictory effects on our personal and professional lives and how we studied them. Feminism played a part in how political and social ideas were voiced, as did the more contradictory moves towards neo-liberalism. I argued that there has been some change in which women, mainly middle class and highly educated, and/or social scientists played a greater part in public life and in studying and theorising those changes. Feminist activities and theories have accounted for transformations in women's lives and their freedom/liberation from such constraints, as well as the economic and social obligations of women's dependency and autonomy.

Nevertheless, women's lives in families were not irrevocably changed for the better under these changing forms of liberalism. Sexual abuse, harassment and violence continued in many women and children's family lives, and many women's lives were constrained by family and family obligations for children, husbands, and other dependants. There remained ample evidence of how women's lives in families remain constrained, and indeed in which inequalities between families on the basis of class, 'race', ethnicity and family structures, may have increased under neo-liberalism and the changing social conditions of the 1990s. However, the knowledge and understanding that we created was more sensitive to the social conditions and constraints on women's public and personal lives.

CHAPTER SEVEN

The Political is Personal

Personal responsibilities and personal reflections about work-life balance

Introduction

In this chapter, using a feminist reflexive narrative interwoven with the methodological concepts adopted by sociologists, I reflect upon how the political and social transformations from the mid-1990s became deeply personal, incorporating notions about family lives, once held to be personal and private. Using popular and policy examples around transforming family lives as 'evidence' will illustrate Jamieson's point:

> Ours is a time of unprecedented exposure to public stories through the mass media . . . public stories about personal life both a cause and a consequence of a lack of separation between public and private life. (Jamieson, 1998: 11)

How these notions were entrenched in policies, no longer separate from the business of government, were complex and contradictory and affected different classes and diverse groups of women differently in different countries and cultures. Examples from Australia and New Zealand contrast remarkably with those from the US and UK, and with those from other parts of Europe. I pinpoint several American and British instances of these global policy shifts which, whilst attending to global family changes, have remained within the ambit of what was by then conventionally referred to as neo-liberalism. Critiques of the governments and policies of the 1990s, as I mentioned in the previous chapter, were part of the phase that I refer to, following Fraser (1997), as 'the post-socialist condition'. These notions have been contested over concepts of 'evidence' from traditional social sciences but I want to explore the uses of feminist theories in critiquing and understanding policy analyses.

Through this analysis, I thread my personal changing circumstances and how these mapped on to wider social and policy changes and our understandings of them. These feminist understandings drew upon critical reflections on emergent notions of governance as well as transformations in women's lives in terms of education, employment and public participation from 35 to 50 years ago. In the last decade, personal reflections upon these myriad shifts and transformations have become a core of social analysis, using, as I have mentioned in previous chapters, the tools of personal reflection, narrative and auto/biography. By the end of the millennium, these forms of analysis had become not only fashionable but entirely conventional, by feminists and social scientists alike, contested though they may be around notions of 'evidence', diversity and difference for classes and groups of women. They built upon the earlier reflections of second wave feminists to which I also draw attention.

I draw on examples from the USA and Britain and consider how the political figures that spearheaded the changes – President Bill Clinton and Prime Minister Tony Blair – were the very embodiment of the changes that they sought to achieve. Clinton presided over neo-liberal policy shifts towards embedding notions of personal responsibility as emblematic of women's family responsibilities, whilst at the same time turning intimate sexual personal matters into public debate. Blair also was responsible for neo-liberal policy shifts in what became known as 'work–life balance' as emblematic of women's work and family responsibilities whilst at the same time turning parental responsibilities into more private matters. Both Clinton and Blair also embodied the dramatic shifts in family lives that have taken place over the last 35 years, since the embedding of social liberalism in politics in the USA and UK. Clinton was of my generation coming of age during the Kennedy era and becoming part of the social movement for change and yet his life contrasted markedly with that of Kennedy as did the policies that he instigated. Blair was of the generation coming of age during the era of social democracy in the late 1960s and yet his life has contrasted markedly with those responsible for the initiation of sexual equality policies, as have the family-friendly policies that he instigated creating new work-life balances around the personal.

Personal reflections on shifts in my work-life balance

During the second half of the 1990s my personal and professional life, or work-life balance, changed dramatically, as mentioned in the previous chapter. My mother died in early 1996, timing her death for her funeral to coincide with my younger sister's birthday (which she shared with my ex-husband). She had always identified closely with my sister each being the youngest of three, although many commented upon my similarities in looks, interests, passions and personality with her. Her passing away seemed to split her family rather than meld it together. She had briefly suffered from Alzheimer's in the couple of years leading up to her death although it was nothing like the issues that John Bayley portrayed of his wife Iris Murdoch's process of disintegration (Bayley, 1998). We, her three daughters, had been disconcerted about how to manage the various processes of care at home and away. We had, however, become familiar with both Jewish and secular social services, and the uses of forms of health and social care, including brief bouts of respite care and employing a carer in her own home. My mother had herself been a diligent and stalwart provider of Jewish social care and 'meals on wheels' for elderly people in the 10 years leading up to her own needs. She initially resented having to be a recipient rather than provider and found moving from carer to cared for difficult, not least for the loss of independence and autonomy entailed. Feminist studies of such forms of care did little to help us with the daily problems but they provided a sound basis for understanding the continuing problems of social provision for elderly women. This has been most clearly articulated by Jane Lewis (1991). I found some succour in reading Ann Oakley's novel *Scenes from the Garden of Eden* the day on which I saw my mother for the last time and just hours before her passing away. Whilst obviously not specifically about my own unfolding drama it gave me some idea about how I wanted to spend my last moments with my mother, unconscious though these ideas were at the time.

Since my mother died my various family relationships have slowly changed, both those with my sisters and their families, and with my children. I have reflected upon these changes in such intimate and personal relationships, including the recognition of my own ageing and need for change in my conduct of my professional activities. Acknowledgement of these small steps and shifts in my consciousness is about all that I am consciously aware of although there have been major changes in my professional circumstances. Suffice it to say that 1996 seemed the nadir of my personal life, whilst it may have been the pinnacle of my professional life, being director of the Social Sciences Research Centre and research at South Bank University and on HEFCE's Sociology panel for the RAE. I was enmeshed in research on aspects of family life, both policy critiques and carefully crafted studies of aspects of family lives of children, young people and their parents, mothers especially. I was also extremely active in professional feminist groups such as *Through the Glass Ceiling* and the *Women's Studies Network Association* and I was co-editor with Dulcie Groves of the *Journal of Social Policy*. Combining social and feminist research, especially around complex policy-oriented, methodological and detailed issues about changing subjectivities of women as mothers and young people, and management seemed a good work balance. I had also been involved in providing critical policy evaluations (David, 1996;) and when New Labour were elected to power became more closely involved, as did others, in providing policy advice and critiques. (e.g. Smith Institute, 2000)

In 1997 I applied for and gained what seemed to be a senior position as Dean of Research at the London Institute, an amalgam of five art colleges. This seemingly enviable post gave no opportunities for either senior management for feminists nor for continuing to conduct good feminist research in the social sciences. The management was irredeemably sexist and patriarchal, fully committed to traditional forms of male management and the director seemed to be the embodiment of these traits. The post did offer the possibilities for learning about post-modernism and post-structuralism, including psychoanalytic perspectives in the humanities and creative arts, which has enhanced my expertise in developing aspects of postgraduate and professional education. Given that I could not accommodate my twin passions in this post, and that I had become what amounted to a victim of my own success, I negotiated a settlement with the very patriarchal management.[1] By mutual consent, I left for a period of study or 'garden' leave based at the Institute of Education, London University. I then acquired a post as professor at Keele University concentrating mainly on postgraduate and professional education and the opportunity to continue to conduct feminist social and educational research. This post offered the new opportunities to work with, both through teaching and research, mature women as students, at various levels and stages of higher education from undergraduate to postgraduate, rather than the historically traditional and conventional 18 to 24 year old school-leavers. It also provided the possibilities to continue to study, write and work reflexively and to think more carefully and consciously of transformations of knowledge within and across higher education. Transformations both in the knowledge economy and in family lives, and how we have been transforming our identities and subjectivity in relation to these wider contextual shifts is a critical part of feminist methodology and pedagogy.

Feminists writing their personal and family lives

During the 1990s, personal reflections and reminiscences reached an art form and many feminists wrote about both their personal and academic lives, producing intellectual and personal auto/biographies, increasingly for academic rather than more public audiences and part of the transformation in feminist theories, methodologies and pedagogies. The generations of women who helped to create second wave feminism through their writings wrote about their feelings about sexuality and sexual relations, alternatives to traditional marriage, maternity and motherhood, memoirs of significant milestones and reflected upon them as they were growing old. As already mentioned in previous chapters, Beauvoir had a great influence on feminist theorising but her writings on old age and growing old have, as yet, been far less influential (Beauvoir, 1977). A volume of Beauvoir's autobiography that Curthoys (2000) in her seminal millennial essay, for instance, did not consider was about Sartre and his death, called *Adieux: a Farewell to Sartre*. Perhaps this was because it did not touch her life 30 years ago and did not yet touch her life when she wrote her millennial essay (see Chapter Two) as it has not yet touched most feminists' lives.[2] Beauvoir also had reflected on her relationship with her mother and feelings about her mother through her death (Beauvoir, 1973 originally published in 1964; 1965 in English *A Very Easy Death*). This kind of personal writing about mother–daughter and father–daughter relationships mushroomed in the 1990s. In Britain, as we have already seen, Carolyn Steedman had been particularly influential in drawing upon her feelings about her relationship with her mother on the growth of this kind of writing. Two other significant elder feminists wrote eloquently and poetically about their mothers (Steinem, 1995 *Ruth's Song* also mentioned in Heilbrun, 1997; Friedan, 2001). Beauvoir also wrote about the processes of ageing and significant birthdays such as 60 (Beauvoir, 1970).[3]

Reflection on particular birthdays, such as fifty, sixty or seventy became quite usual in the 1990s as more feminists reached these milestones. Several highly significant American feminist reflections were penned (Friedan, *The Fountain of Age* first published in 1993, Vintage 1994; Jong, 1994/5 *Fear of Fifty*; Steinem, 1995; Heilbrun, 1997 *The Last Gift of Time: life after sixty*). Betty Friedan (1994) became 60 in the mid-1990s and in her essay she considered, like Beauvoir (1977), the wider social and cultural influences on how old age was treated within an advanced society. But unlike Beauvoir and in keeping with her changed political emphasis she saw this as a human rather than particularly female issue. Indeed she castigated Beauvoir for not recognising that it is a general rather than specific problem to women. Similarly she also castigated Germaine Greer for a similar failure and wrote how both 'Beauvoir and Greer . . . have expressed outrage at woman's victimization by this double standard. But it seems to me . . . that men are as victimised . . .' (1994, p. 224). Steinem was also 60 in the mid-1990s and wrote both personally and more programmatically about the need for strategies for old age. At the same time, however, she recognised just how the various generations of feminists might not appreciate such writings, as she herself had not until she began to grow older. She wrote:

> I still worry that putting 'sixty' in the title of the last essay may have the same effect on younger readers that it would have had on me. At their age, my generation regarded people over sixty, or even forty, as another species – and planned our lives very poorly as a result. But I hope this essay will help younger readers to see a long and adventurous life ahead, to worry less about early successes, failures or even advice to 'settle down' (which as it turns out we never do) . . . Most of all, I hope it's helpful to my beloved age peers, in whom I have the greatest faith. If our generation could survive coming of age in the 1950s, we can survive anything . . . (Steinem, 1995: 13–14)

She argued for more openness and understanding of the issues across the generations, continents, communities, classes and races, and for the continual recognition of changing lives and societies and for feminist considerations. Both Friedan and Steinem, despite their differing and changing politics, spent considerable time on understanding life changes in women's lives; interested as they were in the issues arising out of 'the change of life', namely the menopause and its impact upon women's changing lives. Both concerned themselves with issues of domestic violence and rape. But Friedan and Steinem were narrowly representative of white, middle class and public intellectuals rather than more academic and theoretical feminists.

Many of the older generation of academic feminists also began to reflect back on their personal lives. For instance Denise Riley (1996) wrote an account of her early life as a feminist writer as part of the contributing to feminist theorising around the political (in Butler and Scott, 1996). Carolyn Heilbrun (1997), a key feminist biographer, also wrote in her usual candid style about the processes of growing old entitled *The Last Gift of Time: life after sixty*. Heilbrun's essays were critical reflections on personal issues and methodologically sophisticated in arguing somewhat theoretically that such writing may be 'autobiographical fictions'. In an essay about her memories of past events in her student days and chance encounters, she commented:

> I was fortunate in that my biographer evoked only innocuous memories. Indeed without her I would not have learned that Simone de Beauvoir had visited Wellesley while I was a student there and had apparently decided she had nothing to say to me. At the time I had no idea who she was. *The Second Sex* was published three or four years later in France, and not in the United States until almost ten years after her Wellesley visit. Still, I was glad to discover that I had been in range of her, even if that knowledge provided only a memory missed . . .

> What one remembers is, I think, a clue to what one wants to be. I turned my back on involuntary memories, and refused to give them more than passing attention, because I did not wish to be a rememberer; . . . autobiographical fictions of childhood and backward-reaching memoirs certainly abound, as though the writers were trying not only to turn early memory into art but even to chase it back as far as it would lead. (1997: 118; 120)

Heilbrun's concerns were with individual women's rights and making the world better for women from a liberal feminist, white, and middle class perspective. Other academic feminists took an initial autobiographical standpoint to reflect on their theoretical, ideological or philosophical stance. Nell Noddings and Jane Roland Martin, eminent feminist philosophers and educationalists reflected on their personal and intellectual lives with Gloria Steinem providing the preface to Martin's narrative (1999) of her experiences, as a liberal feminist philosopher, in an elite university in the USA.

As part of this growing trend of personal writing in context, Diana Woodward and I put together a volume modelled on that perspective as noted in a previous chapter. In summarising the issues we wrote that we:

. . . presented 16 autobiographical accounts of women's careers in higher education
. . . we want . . . to argue that although women's lives in academia may be seen as a
unique blend of the personal and professional, from childhood, family and education matters through to subject, institutional and organisational questions, there
are some critical opportunities and obstacles and constraints which warrant particular attention . . . serendipity was a major theme in all the accounts . . . despite . . .
modern and progressive educational backgrounds, all the women told of how they
had been brought up with relatively traditional notions of family life, so that most
of them had assumed that the accepted paths of marriage and motherhood would
follow on smoothly from childhood and young womanhood . . . Indeed, for most
of the women, marriage and bearing children constituted a significant part of
their accounts. Moreover the vast majority of these women . . . had married (or co-
habited) at some point in their lives. Many of them, however, had also divorced
and/or were no longer living with their initial partner and/or husband (two as a
result of very early widowhood) but some had remarried . . . (David and Woodward, 1998: 212)

What emerged equally significantly from our personal reflections were the two
themes of the extent of family change emanating from relatively traditional
family backgrounds, whether upper middle class or more middle- and working-
class backgrounds of the second generation and the role of education, especially
academic education, in providing the challenges and sustenance for these family
changes. At the anecdotal level there has been a quickening of the pace of particular forms of family change, especially around marriage, divorce and cohabitation. Simone de Beauvoir's unique but influential pattern has become somewhat
less unique amongst these generations. However, these changes do not, as the
other accounts have already alluded to, mean a lessening of commitment but
rather a shift in the legal nature and understandings of marriage and family.

Influenced by theoretical developments of post-structuralism, post-modernism
and modernity, the growth of this reflective scholarship in the 1990s crossed
sexual, racial and class boundaries and created hybridised accounts and voices
(Butler and Scott, 1992). There have been many narrative accounts by black
(e.g. Lorde, 1990s; bel hooks, 1990s; Mirza, 1997; Phoenix 2002), ethnic
minority (Tsolidis, 2000) and working class women (Walkerdine, 1997). Phoenix
drew attention to the ways in which black women in early second wave feminist
politics created alliances, mentioning the statement from Combahee River
Collective 1977 about alliances (Phoenix, 2002). Middleton and Weiler (1998)
and Unterhalter (1998), deploying the methodological technique of autobiographies, applied this to accounts of women who were involved in writing
their own both personal and professional lives as teachers, as had Sikes (1996)
and others earlier. This enmeshed with work by Edwards and Ribbens (1998)
referred to in the previous chapter. Many feminists reconstructed their
'journeys' across class and professional boundaries (Weiner, 1994; Deem, 1996;

Williams in her inaugural professorial lecture at Leeds University, 2000 and Miriam Bernard and Gill Jones in their inaugural professorial lectures at Keele University in February and May 2001 respectively).

All these women located their theoretical and intellectual developments as feminists and social scientists in the wider social context, influenced by being part of a particular post-war generation and involved in second wave feminism in Britain. All reflected upon childhood memories rather than relations with parents, children or families as formative. What they sought to do was to show the impact of the wider changing social and economic context upon their own intellectual and professional developments, including choices of topics of study. They illustrated how they were part of a particular generation, constructed by wider political and social events, to develop their own values and conscious involvement in feminist politics and forms of academic work, reflecting on this experience. Weiner went further in demonstrating her formation as a daughter of a Jewish refugee, born towards the end of the war. There have also been other ethnically and culturally sensitive narrative accounts, such as about mothers' stories written by feminist daughters (Appignanesi, 1999; Karpf, 1996; Slovo, 1990; Bauman, 1986) and relationships with their mothers as daughters or with their daughters as children. There have been interesting attempts to theorise intergenerational issues, as with the example cited in Chapter Three of the mother–daughter duo – Marilyn and Fenella Porter. Subsequent generations of feminists have become interested in understanding the influences of feminism as a political project or ideology on the lives of younger women, born during its influence; thus attempting to link feminist politics with generations of expressions of lived experiences, as discussed in Chapter Six.

Yet others began to reflect upon the lives of women who might have been their mothers. Some of this work was particularly poignant as it looked especially at women and their sufferings during the Second World War. Much of this work built upon a particular genre of biography, and work of a more Freudian nature. Indeed, there was a particular attempt to consider the lives of very young children orphaned by the Nazis and who were brought to this country and brought up, without parents, under the watchful gaze of Anna Freud. Freud wrote about this work (Britzman, 2001) and more 'personal testimonies' from the children themselves were produced in a book edited by Sara Moskovitz (1983) entitled *Love Despite Hate*. In the 1990s feminist sociologists turned their attention to these matters with Dahlia Ofer and Lenore Weitzman (1998 *Women in the Holocaust*) editing a book which provided personal testimonies of women as survivors and memoirs of women living within Germany and Poland. They argued that although both men and women were treated badly by the Nazis they wanted to use theories of gender and difference to show how differently and specifically women were treated through sexism and patriarchy.

Biographical writing of personal and family lives

The theoretical and intellectual developments in personal reflections for second wave feminists also became important for similar generations of 'pro-feminist' men (Lingard and Douglas, 1999). Using somewhat different 'personal testimony' about the impact of Nazism and the holocaust on his family life, for instance Seidler also addressed these issues. In *Shadows of the Shoah: Jewish identity and belonging*, Seidler (2000), a pro-feminist, developed an analysis about his own personal experiences and the ways in which his particular family background influenced his development of his personal and political identity. He located his theoretical writing in a wider context and on a broad canvas, drawing upon theoretical developments in post-modernism, post-structuralism and identity politics, as well as from feminist thinking. He argued for writing about personal experiences that were theoretically informed and informative:

> This writing, which is both personal and theoretical, raises questions that I have been trying to express for a while. It is the beginning of an exploration, a first step in a continuing process. Although sharing a particular journey and reflecting upon a particular experience of Jewish identity I hopefully will reflect upon more *general themes of identity, memory and belonging* [*my emphasis*] . . . I wanted to be able to share it with the next generation, so that the possibly they will not feel so silently burdened by not knowing as we often were, being a second generation. But in writing for my own extended family, those who survived and have been able to grow up in relative security, I am also writing for other families who might know even less. (2000: x–xii)

Seidler showed us the complex relationships across and between generations and their separate and several struggles for finding their own identities, in particular through the wider changing notions of identities and the concept of 'difference'. It was the recognition of the notion of difference to concepts of gender and class that led to more theoretical and substantive sophistication in drawing out accounts of family lives in different locales, locations and places. Attempts to start accounting for ones lives that led into more theoretically and methodologically informed approaches as well as to more detailed autobiographically informed accounts. Most of these were not constructed for the sake of producing autobiographies, but for the more theoretically informed task of developed a carefully nuanced approach to the diversities and differences as well as the continuities in family lives.

David Morgan, an expert on the sociology of family life, from a pro-feminist viewpoint on masculinities and fatherhood, also wrote in an autobiographical vein as noted in the introduction. His presidential address to the British Sociological Association (1998) reminded us of continuities and change within sociology in these issues. Addressing *Sociological Imaginings and Imagining Sociology* he was keen to imbue a sense of adventure, with the subtitle *Bodies, Auto/ biographies and other mysteries* he argued that:

> I shall attempt to apply these reflections particularly to two recent areas of study. The first . . . deals with the body, while *the second deals with the growing interest in auto/biographical practices in sociology and many other social sciences and areas of humanities.* (1998: 648) (my emphasis)

He used three biographical 'family' accounts to show how these made socio-logical arguments; one was Etzioni's account of his wife's tragic car accident which meant that his community came to his aid, fuelling his arguments for communitarianism; secondly Gillies' discussion of family Christmas rituals resulting from the tragic loss of a family member over that period; and thirdly Lemert's use of family memoirs about crimes. By dint of the examples, Morgan 'proved' that much autobiography was about aspects of family life.

Moreover, many of the more autobiographical pieces within sociology and the broader humanities and social sciences had to do with aspects of intellectual biography or the locating of oneself in order to draw wider meanings and under-standings. In *Sociology*, (1998, 32(4)) there were also articles about aspects of family life; particularly on the theme of risk in relation to childhood and parent-ing (Scott, Jackson and Beckett-Milburn, 1998) and on methodological issues, including Oakley's prelude to her book (2000). They all mapped onto the theoretical and methodological transformations in sociology and in perspectives on to family lives. They illustrated the moves towards a more reflexive sociology, and one in which gender, class and race were more explicitly considered. Draw-ing on both theories of risk and post-structural approaches has become more central to sociological endeavour. In attempts to understand and theorise women's family lives, feminist sociologists and others have been increasingly drawn to drawing on their own personal experiences and formations in classed, raced and diverse cultural backgrounds. The autobiographical has assumed new forms of complexity in feminist sociology but it has led to a particular framing of ideas and understanding of subjectivities and experiences of diverse family lives.

Morgan (1996), Allan (1999) and Bernardes (1997) have all in their different ways shown how feminist perspectives have been integrated into sociology. Allan (1999) confirmed the point made by many feminists that the aim was to provide a critique rather than an acceptance of the traditional nuclear family, although the critiques were quite specific and about the organisation of the household and family, or domestic life:

> While there had been previous studies of inequalities within families, for example Blood and Wolfe (1960) in America and Gavron (1968) in Britain, the failure of much American sociology – especially its failure to adopt a critical perspective about the structural divisions within domestic organization, and their links to

wider social and economic inequalities – fostered a climate in which 'family research' became devalued. Although some influential studies in family sociology appeared (Voysey, 1975; Askham, 1984; Holme, 1985) in general, the 'action' lay elsewhere, for example in studies of gender and household inequalities, in debates about 'public' and 'private' boundaries, and in analyses of paid and unpaid work (Oakley, 1974, 1976; Barker and Allen, 1976a, 1976b (*sic*); Finch and Groves, 1983; Siltanen and Stanworth, 1984). Of course all these topics were pertinent to family sociology, but they were framed much more by feminist perspectives and understandings than they were informed by existing models from the sociology of the family. (1999: 2)

Allan (1999), Bernardes (1997) and Morgan (1996) all regarded feminist perspectives as integral to the sociology of family and no longer represented distinctive perspectives, in that they acknowledged the moves towards a methodological and theoretical stance that incorporated more biographical and personal perspectives. They all pointed to particular perspectives and developments from feminism and feminist sociology that have, in their view, been singularly important, namely female experience particularly in the domestic sphere.

Understanding the political as personal

The relatively new perspectives on personal lives in public have derived not only from personal reflections such as auto/biographies and narratives, but also from the use of post-structuralism and post-modernism in understanding shifting discourses about family, personal and public lives. Feminist perspectives have been threaded through all these diverse and exciting or challenging approaches to understanding social and gender changes towards the end of the millennium. Nicholas Rose (1990) in *Governing the Soul* was important for providing such a perspective on understanding public processes through the use of the concepts, drawn from Foucault, of governance and governmentality. Similarly Stephen Ball (1994) developed the notion of policy sociology drawing on Foucauldian perspectives. Weeks (1996; 1998) also applied these social constructionist perspectives to understanding sexualities and alternative families. These post-structuralist perspectives have been used in many recent studies of social welfare regimes and changing balances between families in personal and public life. As we have already seen, many feminists also derived their theoretical notions from a combination of post-structuralism and feminism, using these ideas to critique policy developments, in particular Fraser (1997) was a strong influence, drawing on the work of Butler and Scott (1992), Young (1992) *inter alia*. Williams (1999; 2000) also adopted these theoretical ideas to understand perspectives on social welfare in Britain.

However, forms of critical realism, drawn from Marxist thought, combined with feminism have also provided important conceptual tools for understanding shifts in the personal and political. Levitas' work (1998) on analysing the

168 Personal and Political

competing ideological assumptions underpinning New Labour's project, constructed whilst in opposition, has been of seminal importance. She looked at three contrasting ideologies that had drawn from different political traditions to understand developments in New Labour ideologies, namely the Moral Underclass Debate (MUD), the Social Integration Discourse (SID) and Redistribution Debate (RED). All of these ideologies focused more on social class and social inclusion/exclusion than on concepts of gender, and indeed the pursuit of these ideas in office has featured more of a class than gender perspective. Lister (1997) similarly identified these kinds of contradictory forces underpinning the discourses of citizenship and gender, whilst pinpointing how feminist debates were critical to deeper understandings. Other feminist researchers have pointed to how crucial certain aspects of social and family change have been underpinning the new discourses of New Labour, albeit from a limited perspective. Millar (2000), Kiernan, Land and Lewis (1998) Edwards and Duncan (1999) amongst others have looked at diverse kinds of lone parent families and the implications for social and family policies in Britain.

The social transformations in economic and family life to which we have referred and which are evidenced by the developments in social science critiques can also be signified by dramatic changes in types of involvement in government and politics. However, it must also be noted that despite these changes, and the particularly noteworthy impact upon women's public lives and transformations from traditional family lives, these have not usually translated into expressions of feminist politics. In many respects it could be argued that they have been the beneficiaries of feminist campaigning but have not contributed towards its further development. They are part of conventional political debates in ways that were inconceivable thirty years ago and even 15 years ago. For instance, when Caroline New and I published *For the Children's Sake: Making Child care more than women's business* this was seen as both a fascinating academic account but an utopian fantasy in terms of policy developments. Nowadays, they are commonplace and no longer confined to feminist writings. These arguments about the role of mothers in political life have been growing in frequency, illustrating the ways in which some feminist arguments have become part of the political discourse. For example *The Guardian* leader on May 15th 2000 (p. 19) also discussed issues such as the role of mothers and fathers with children and at work or in public life, entitled *Happy Families. The faces change, but not the ideal.* It asserted 'Britain may have the highest divorce rate in Europe, but we seem to have a deeply romantic yearning for happy family life . . .' It concluded however 'whether it is . . . the prime minister combining the red boxes with winding the baby while Cherie prepares a case, we are looking to these celebrity families to pioneer models of fatherhood and sexual equality – and most of us are fascinated'.

Shifts in policy and practice towards the personal have also been indicated by a diversity of 'evidence', not only 'evidence' about personal reflections or family policy issues. However, the traditional, statistical evidence about changing family lives has become very stark indeed not only nationally but also globally whether in terms of marriage and/or divorce and cohabitation or types of work and family lives and personal responsibilities for family care. This initially focused upon changing trends amongst adults in terms of their forms of sexual and social relationships, such as rates of marriage, cohabitation, divorce, separation, and including the creation of single households. Associated with these were the trends in parenthood and generational changes around types of family-household associated with particular instances and processes of family life, such as the changing role of fathers and grandparents in children's family lives. Both official government reports focused on these, as did political pundits, creating scandals and cause celebres, especially during the 1980s and 1990s with the focus on lone parents or female headed households. (David, 1998; Kiernan, Land and Lewis, 1999).

What has become most emblematic of these various and diverse family life changes, influencing family policies under neo-liberalism, however, has been the rate of births 'out-of-wedlock', to coin a traditional phrase. By the end of the 1990s in Britain this was virtually 40% or two babies out of five being born to people who were not legally and formally together although they may have been cohabiting or simply co-parenting. In the USA this figure had risen to over 50% (an article in *The Observer* Sunday 30th December 2001 by Susan Mauschart).

Policy instances of the political as personal

There are two public policy examples that illustrate the neo-liberal shifts in the global social context, dominated as it has been by American political initiatives and the response of governments to wider socio-economic and family changes. They illustrate how both personhood in relation to sex and gender and its implications for social and education policies are now understood and conceptualised. One was the passage of the Personal Responsibility and Work Opportunity Reconciliation Act in 1996 in the USA, encapsulating the transformations in the policy terminology by legislating for personal responsibility. This term was used to imply responsibilities for private and family matters, care of children especially by women without state subsidy. Given the tenor of the language, it might have been felt that this law had been passed by a conservative administration and yet it was one which the then Democratic President Clinton reluctantly had to ratify given that the two houses of Congress were both staunchly Republican. This Act transformed social welfare in the USA, albeit that it was aimed at a relatively small and target population, removing the system of Aid to Families with Dependent Children (AFDC) historically known as welfare and replacing it with Temporary Aid to Needy Families (TANF) (Schram, 2000). The majority of recipients of AFDC had been women, usually single, often young and black and referred to as 'welfare mothers' or more pejoratively as 'welfare queens' (Schram, 2000, chapter two). These programmes had been extensively studied by social and feminist researchers (Piven and Cloward, 1966; 1976; David, 1982; 1986 a and b; Fraser and Gordon, 1994; Sennett 2002, lecture at Keele University) and had led to some of the more enduring feminist critiques of social welfare policies (Kiernan, Land and Lewis, 1998). The new programmes, allied with the Defense of Marriage Act 1996, and with federal funds and policies on sexuality education re-inscribed traditional 'family values' of marriage, the 'family wage' and heterosexuality, with only temporary (short-term) aid to families, or rather single mothers (Stacey, 1996; Cass, 2002). They recommenced a punitive approach to particular working class and minority ethnic women in poverty or poor home circumstances, expecting them to take full responsibility for the care and upbringing of their children without any state support (Schram, 2000). They also required young people in school to learn about these values through a federally funded programme that required the teaching of 'abstinence-only before marriage' as a basis for states acquiring funding.

The second instance of these wider and global shifts in responses to family changes and policies about families, albeit more complex and contradictory, emerged from the landslide elections of the New Labour government in Britain in 1997 and in May 2001. Women figured strongly amongst the elected representatives in both parliamentary Labour parties. In the 1997 general election there was a historic shift in women's presence in Parliament, in that the Labour women elected as Members of Parliament constituted a quarter of the parliamentary Labour party. In the media they were referred to pejoratively as 'Blair's babes' and few were appointed to hold office in the government.[4] This media construction denied women full agency and reduced them to infancy. The one known feminist who was appointed in 1997 as Secretary of State for Social Security, and belatedly as Minister for Women – Harriet Harman – was given the task of taking through Parliament deeply unpopular policies on cuts to child benefits for lone parent families, inherited from the previous Conservative government.[5] This punitive policy offended many feminists and traditional Labour supporters and resulted in the first major back-bench revolt in the autumn of 1997. She barely survived a year as a government minister and was vilified in the media for her political stances around families and lone parents, although she had been active in several feminist campaigns, notably the National Child Care Campaign and writing on such issues (Coote, Harman and Hewitt, 1990).

The policies that the New Labour government adopted were announced as both 'family-friendly' and yet targeted on people who were deemed to be socially excluded from conventional education and employment (Levitas, 1998). These policies consistently failed to modify and in some cases exacerbated gender or social inequalities (Lister, 2000; Lewis, 2000). The discursive shifts in the language of such policies highlighted the ways in which there were moves away from a focus on women's employment and family lives towards a more general interest about both work as central to people's lives and the increasing long hours culture of work. From policies about family-life/work-life balance introduced in the first New Labour government through policy documents such as *Supporting Families* (1998) and the National Childcare Strategy there was a shift towards the dominant notion of 'work-life balance' by early 2001. This removed the notion of family from explicit policy consideration and emphasised instead notions of personal and private life as distinct from work, regardless of gender or sex. In other words, the term family had previously been used to apply to women's caring responsibilities but the discursive shifts implied ambivalence about women with more concern about the balance between work and issues such as leisure rather than family and caring responsibilities.

These shifting notions increasingly became the subject of feminist policy analysis and were remarked upon at a number of events. For instance, a seminar on public policies organised by Gender Research Forum in the newly named Women's Equality Unit (changed from the Women's Unit and itself a notable discursive shift) in the Cabinet Office in 2002 drew attention to these various discursive and rhetorical shifts that also had dramatic effects on women's lives. Ruth Lister and Joni Lovenduvski were particularly stringent in their critiques of the development of social and political policies under New Labour. They deployed relatively new forms of feminist analysis to illustrate the ways in which women's lives remained unequal and indeed inequalities were increasing under these regimes, despite the prominence of women within the parliamentary Labour party and government. This seminar also illustrated how contradictory the changes have been, in that there were many prominent feminist academics present, and presenting a wealth of social and feminist analysis of contemporary social issues, including detailed and nuanced studies of family, as parents, partners, children, childcare, work and family policies. Yet the thrust of the analysis was to demonstrate the persistence of social and gender inequalities despite the growth and pre-eminence of such a range and diversity of feminist academic studies around carefully crafted studies of the minutiae of family lives and policies to reinforce or support family diversities and differences.

Both feminists and social scientists had been part of the social changes and thus were influenced by them as much as they influenced them. As noted before, the processes of change had become embedded in how we conceived of ourselves, our subjectivities and identities. Much rested on how we thought through issues, made choices and were expected to make choices that in the past may have been much more structured into political and social processes. Thus neither feminist nor social scientific thinking was separate from the processes of change. This kind of process has increasingly been referred to as that of reflexivity; the continual process of thinking about one's identity as part of wider social change and transformation. The approach to 'evidence' and understanding has developed over the last decade, given that it is not only the 'facts' that may have altered, but also our understandings and interpretations of them. Giddens, with others, (1996) in talking of 'reflexive modernization' generalised a set of approaches initially adopted by feminists and others, to reflect upon changing social and family lives and their meanings, being constantly vigilant and reflecting upon our approaches to our subjectivity. He subsequently applied this perspective to developing a policy approach for New Labour, entitled *The Third Way* (1998; 2000) that balanced left and right, steering a course between private and public provision of social services in the context of a market and late modern society. This approach of the third way was adopted by New Labour in their first term of office as a method by which to steer between traditional conservative or liberal policies allowing for freedom of choice and traditional socialist policies which regulated public policy provision of social services.

British instances of transformations to 'the political is personal'

Several instances may be referred to as further evidence of the shifts and transformations in personal and family lives, as played out in the public arena. In particular they demonstrate the ways in which the original credo of second wave feminism 'the personal is political' has contributed to these transformations in such a way as to turn the credo on its head. These are instances of the political as personal. In Britain, for example, the contrast in the family lives of two Prime Ministers over a twenty year period puts some flesh on this argument. Even more dramatic instances, however, of this have been the ways in which the life and death of first Princess Diana and second the Queen Mother became the subject of intense media and public scrutiny, analysed frequently by journalists and pundits galore (Morton, 11997; *The Guardian*, April 9th, 2002). Princess Diana's life was extremely well analysed by feminists and others about how she was an icon of both a fairy tale princess and an 'oppressed' woman. Although she provided yet another instance of the importance of changing 'family values' in relation to feminist ideas and indeed ideals, given the amount of public analysis of Princess Diana I shall only refer briefly to it here (Bea Campbell, 1998; Julie Birchill, 1998). However, it was Princess Diana's growing realisation of her identity, gained partly through therapy with one of the leading feminist therapists and founder of the Women's Therapy Centre in London, Susie Orbach, that led to her being able to 'break out' of the icon of the patriarchal family in Britain. The royal family had been held up as a symbol of the traditional family to emulate but through Princess Diana's marital problems the general conflicts between men and women over divorce came to be debated very publicly. Her divorce also symbolised the extent of family change in British society such that it had become 'acceptable' for it to be tolerated rather than traditional 'suffer in silence' approaches being the norm. After her divorce, she came to represent many such women and public sympathy shifted towards her especially by women and as represented by the media. Such was this concern for her and her wellbeing that Blair on her tragic and untimely death talked of her 'the people's princess'. Despite the fact that Princess Diana was involved in a very public sexual liaison whilst not being married public sympathy remained with her.

Margaret Thatcher as Prime Minister tried to continue to lead a 'traditional' family life, albeit that she was a married 'woman' in a man's world. She viewed her family and child-care responsibilities as entirely her own private matter, rather than an issue for public policy and public resolution. Fortunately for her, perhaps, when she reached the office of Prime Minister, her child-bearing and child-rearing years were over, and the family concerns were more to do with her marital relationship. According to her autobiographical account, she justified her unusual and unique work in terms of her *laissez-faire* politics, which meant that her senior position did not, according to her, threaten her husband's senior managerial role in a company business (Thatcher, 1995). This contrasted quite remarkably with the family life of New Labour's Prime Minister, Tony Blair. He came to the Prime Ministerial office as a relatively young man, and the youngest Prime Minister for over 100 years. He was the father (then) of three school-age children and he had a professional working wife. Indeed, his wife Cherie Booth is perhaps the best exemplar of the family and social transformations to which we have been referring given her position as a working wife and mother of three young children. However, her successes as a professional woman lawyer and senior barrister marked her out as a relatively unusual working wife. In this respect her occupation is identical to that of Margaret Thatcher but the way in which it has been developed has been very different. Nevertheless, the pattern of their family lives is one that matches that of many professional and educated middle class women of her generation. The pursuit of a career rather than the use of a long career break for maternity and motherhood became one of the key instances of changing middle class family life at the millennium. The pattern of childcare and educational support that the Blairs employed matched that again of many middle class professional households and was no longer viewed as something unique to senior public office. In policy terms however it became quite controversial and known as 'the family-work' balance.

This became more public when there were changes in family circumstances for the Blairs. The need for new arrangements and parental care on the birth (in May 2000) of their fourth child, Leo, were the occasion for renewed publicity of what had traditionally been seen as private family matters. This event made the Prime Minister the first one to become a father in 10 Downing Street for over two hundred years. For both of them becoming parents was a major public event rather than a relatively private matter. And yet this confirmed the Blairs as a relatively traditional middle class couple in terms of family life. At the same time it also invited public policy debate about family life especially about early childcare and parenting. Indeed, on the announcement of the birth Cherie Booth, a fully committed working woman although not a self-declared feminist , put her name to a new campaign for working rights for parents and for education and training, given public authenticity to such a major change and policy proposal. The context of childbirth becomes a significant public issue in ways in which it had not been spotlighted before. However, six months before the birth, when the nanny that the Blairs had hired to help care for their three teenage children planned to publish her account of life in the Blair household, a legal injunction prevented these being made public on the grounds of respecting family privacy. The questions of the kinds of childcare provisions to be made both in the immediate aftermath of the birth and the longer term provisions when Cherie Booth would return to her demanding work as a senior barrister QC were all subject to debate and public scrutiny. The question raised by Ms Booth herself of whether her husband would take paternity leave after the baby was born was also subject to public and popular debate. This issue of fathers' involvement in early childcare was arguably so contentious that it was, initially, left to be resolved by popular discussion in the media rather than by a decision to take a lead in developing new approaches to paternal involvement in childcare.

Only days before the baby's birth another contentious issue about the so-called family-work balance was raised about more general questions of parental leave for parents of young children. As a barrister in court Ms Booth representing the TUC against the government raised questions about provision for parental leave for parents of children up to the age of five. The government had decided against the European Court's ruling on the implementation of the parental leave directive and was only making it available for children born in the last six months, rather than five years. The British government had sought to limit it to parents of children born at the start of the millennium. Cherie Booth presented the case in the week before her baby son was born, making the issue not only generally important but also a deeply personal one for her and her family. All of these issues signal massive changes in what has been called the family-work balance especially for women. Cherie Blair/Cherie Booth QC is the first wife of a Prime Minister (and even senior Ministers) to have professional paid employment in the last 35 years. What is also important is that she worked throughout the lives of her now teenage children and thus had to make childcare arrangements, like many other working parents.

This illustrates some of the wider changes in parental employment for women that have occurred over the last 25 to 30 years. However, these transformations in married women's working lives as instanced by Cherie Booth seem to pale in significance compared to the ways in which more sexually problematic issues have been revealed as on the public agenda. The creation by Blair of 'the people's princess' on Princess Diana's death in August 1997, shortly after Blair became Prime Minister, however transformed her to iconic status and removed her from public criticism of her sexually dubious life. Indeed, partly as a result of her having been involved in feminist therapy with Susie Orbach, she received iconic feminist status. Here she became perhaps the first woman to have her personal and private life so scrutinised in the public arena, illustrating the point about the transformations in personal versus political life.

American examples of the transformation to 'the political is personal'

Two major events in the USA during the summer of 1999 gave further confirmation of the ways in which family and personal issues moved on to the political agenda and subject to intense public scrutiny. 'Family values' (Stacey, 1996) as known in the USA became the subject of daily analysis, highlighting contrasting issues such as the eulogising of the American family in its patriarchal form, on the one hand, and the containment of issues such as sexual peccadilloes and abuse on the other. Thus the death of J F Kennedy junior, on the one hand, led to massive outpourings of grief about the latest tragedy from the Kennedy family dynasty. Hillary Clinton's defence of her husband, President Clinton's sexual peccadilloes from a childhood of abuse, (in *Talk* magazine, August 1999) led to intensive analysis of the intricacies of family life. These two events illustrated the transformations in the ways in which family lives, and particularly intimate biographies of famous public figures, were publicised. The Clintons were icons of the post-war generation, coming of age in the 1960s in the aftermath of President Kennedy's assassination. Their family lives were played out in the spotlight of history in ways not conceived of before, with Hillary Clinton able to reflect upon her life and that of her husband in the full glare of publicity. Given the public scrutiny and the impeachment of President Clinton on the grounds of his sexual peccadilloes with Monica Lewinsky the mere mention of it is sufficient to indicate the public transformation in the treatment of the personal and intimate details of a major politician's life. More interestingly from this point of view is the way in which Hillary Clinton, as a publicly committed feminist dealt with the issues, illustrating the social transformations in public life and her reflexivity about them. 'Family values' were also given added vibrancy with

the publication of Hillary Clinton's interview with *Talk* magazine (published on
August 3rd 1999) about her husband's family background, being subject to
sexual abuse and psychological abuse, caught between pleasing his mother and
his grandmother at a very young age. Interestingly Hillary Clinton managed to
appear above the issue of her husband's sexual dalliances and to put them into a
wider family history context, maintaining the issues nevertheless in the public
gaze:

> 'This,' she says, alluding to her husband's infidelity, 'has received an unprece-
> dented amount of attention. You know people have a lot of daily problems in rela-
> tionships. *Everybody has some dysfunction in their families.* (my emphasis) They
> have to deal with it. You don't just walk away if you love someone – you help the
> person . . . I don't believe in denying things. I believe in working through it. Is he
> ashamed? Yes. Is he sorry? Yes. But does this negate everything he has done as a
> husband, a father, a president?' . . . 'Bill has been subjected to so much abuse,' she
> continues, 'He doesn't make any excuses for what he did. But the reaction was
> unprecedented and harmful to the country . . . People are mean. I think it's a real
> disservice, the way we sort of strip away everybody's sense of dignity, of privacy.
> People need support, not disdain' . . . 'My husband is a very good man,' Hillary
> insists. 'They are jealous of him. Yes, he has weaknesses. Yes, he needs to be more
> responsible, more disciplined, but it is remarkable given his background that he
> turned out the kind of person he is . . . capable of such leadership . . . You know in
> Christian theology there are sins of weakness and sins of malice, and this was a sin
> of weakness.' I tell Hillary I read his mother's autobiography, in which she wrote
> about the atmosphere of alcohol, violence, and chaos that forced her son to be the
> man of the house while he was still a child. Hillary leans over and says softly,
> 'That's only the half of it. He was so young, barely four, when he was scarred by
> abuse that he can't even take it out and look at it. There was terrible conflict
> between his mother and grandmother. A psychologist once told me that for a boy
> to be in the middle of a conflict between two women is the worst possible situation.
> There is always the desire to please each one.' . . . I gained an insight into her
> much-tried loyalty as she spoke with emotion about her mother, Dorothy
> Rodham, a product of divorce who was put on a cross-country train at the age of
> eight with her three year old sister. 'My mother never had any education,' Hillary
> told me. 'She had terrible obstacles, but she vowed that she would break the
> pattern of abandonment in her family and she did.' Dorothy's daughter is a woman
> who does not advocate divorce, who counsels teenage sexual abstinence, and who
> stays with a man when no one can understand why – has learned her mother's
> lessons well. Hillary Clinton is clearly determined never to revert to the pattern of
> abandonment.' (Clinton, 1999: 174 and 248)

This story drew on Hillary's account of both her own family history, recounted
to her, presumably, by her mother and others, and that of her husband,
recounted to and distilled by her, through years of thought and reflection. Like
all memoirs it tells a particular account through one person's perspectives,
analyses and interpretations. The story, here presented, has many threads and

strands of meaning for both public and personal development. One overwhelming impression is of misogyny, despite it being recounted by a woman. Mothers and grandmothers feature as the major players in the families, giving abuse and abandonment. Yet another enduring impression and part of the interviewer's interpretation is of the other side of the coin of maternalism – Hillary as both a caring wife/mother – an education learnt at her mother's knee. Here we are given the firm impression of the double-sided nature of family-education. This double-sided interpretation also lends itself to a liberal feminist interpretation of Hillary as a strong woman who dared to speak about the intimate and painful details of family life, speaking frankly about both abuse and abandonment, and yet not falling victim to these issues. It also explained her passionate (and maternal) commitment to an 'un-feminist' or unfaithful man, and perhaps her frankness and openness redeem her in feminist and other liberal political eyes. They may also appear consistent, in some contradictory way, with enduring traditional family values to 'stand by your man'. Yet again by speaking out at this juncture, the story finally also squares the circle and provides some closure to an issue, from a family values perspective. On the other hand, it was argued that it could be seen as a cynical political ploy both to keep the Clinton family in the public spotlight and raise issues for political campaigns. She had recently decided to stand for the Senate seat held by Daniel Patrick Moynihan for New York State, which he had announced he intended to vacate. She initially ran against the Republican mayor of New York, Rudy Guiliani, but he eventually decided not to stand because of his own sexual peccadilloes and his wife's making them public. After the events of 9/11 he became a hero of New York as the personally involved mayor.

Reflecting on these two key American families allowed me to recall the ways in which my intellectual journey has been located in American academic life; more global and international than local.[6] What it also signalled was how both feminist analysis and family change had been transformed during this period of my life, perhaps best instanced by the fact that the Clintons were of the same generation as I am. The contradictory nature of the changes is indeed exemplified in the Clintons' lives. On the one hand Hillary Clinton represented a committed feminist and working life for educated middle class women and yet on the other hand she was subject to her own personal and intimate life being scrutinised in the full glare of publicity. However, her ability to express her commitment to feminism is indeed a contrast with Britain, where the term has not been acceptable in the political and public arena. Thus the desired changes have brought with them many instances of unintended and indeed unwanted consequences.

Ferdinand Mount (*The Sunday Times*, 9 May 1999, p. 19) writing a popular critique of Giddens' Reith lectures was highly critical of the arguments about social change and global transformations and the shifts from the private family to public democracy of emotions. However he acknowledged that there was some evidence of this through particular examples and he referred to Clinton as the prime exemplar of the shift in from private personal matters to public issues. Mount's argument about the Clinton family provided a useful instance of the transformations in family life and the ambivalent ways in which they could be viewed (Ferdinand Mount, *The Sunday Times*, 9 May 1999, p. 19).

'Evidence' of educational changes for women over 25 years

I have argued that the shifts that the transformations in family and women's lives over the last 35 years that have been theorised as shifts between the personal and political can also be exemplified through various forms of 'evidence'. So far, I have looked at theoretical and methodological developments as feminists and other social scientists have entered the academy. The 'evidence' about women's entry into the academy and their contribution to theories is equally dramatic, as the theories they developed.

In the years following the height of second wave feminism rates of women's enrolment in higher education increased significantly. According to U.S. Department of Education publications (www.ed.gov/pubs/TitleIX/part 2.html), in 1973, less than half (43%) of female high school graduates aged 16–24 were enrolled in college, compared to almost two thirds (63%) in 1994; and 17% of young women as compared to 26% of young men in 1971 had completed four or more years of college, as compared to 27% of both in 1994 (Figure 1). Similar trends appear in the UK albeit that the actual percentages are far lower than in the USA. In 1975/6 6.5% of girls had completed 1 or more GCE A levels (enabling them to enter higher education) as compared with 7.6% of boys, whilst the figures were virtually trebled and reversed by the year 2000. Eighteen percent of girls had achieved one or more A level, whilst only 15% of boys had. There were similar reversals in the numbers and proportions of female students of all ages entering higher education, with significantly more women than men in higher education on a part-time basis (Figure 2).

Figure 1. Rates of US women's enrolment in higher education

Year	Percentage US female high school graduates, 16–24 years, enrolled in college	Ratio US women to men completing four or more years of college
1973	43%	0.65 : 1
1994	63%	1 : 1

Source: http:www.ed.gov/pubs/TitleIX/part2.html. Retrieved 14 February 2002.

These statistics, and a host of others that described girls' successes in secondary education, were a direct outcome of activism directed toward changing national-level policy. This activism also led to the development of new forms of feminist pedagogy in the academy, as we have seen in Chapters Two and Three. It has also contributed to subsequent generations of women students as mature students and intensification of feminist theories and methodologies.

Figure 2

Year	Numbers of UK female students entering higher education (in thousands)	Ratio UK women to men in higher education
1975–6	264	0.56 : 1
1999–2000	683.2 (full-time)	1.15 : 1 (full-time)
	444.4 (part-time)	1.28 : 1 (part-time)

Sources: http://www.statistics.gov.uk and http://www.dfes.gov.uk and from Elizabeth.Cowen@ons.gsi.gov.uk

Feminist pedagogy in the academy

The dilemmas about personal and political have been highlighted by feminist writers considering how feminist research entered the academy (Bird, 2000) and become part of academic fare. Morley's work together with Walsh (1995; 1996), and Rassool (1999) gave detailed consideration to some of these issues as has the work on women's studies by Mayer and Trethault (1995). Morley (1999) writing in autobiographical mode demonstrated the diversity of ways in which feminist academics chose to research and teach, highlighting a variety of forms of pedagogy, mostly inimical to the traditions of academic life.

> The intellectual beginnings of this book can be found in an autobiographical account of my engagement with feminism and education as a student, a lecturer, a school-teacher, educational policy-maker and community activist. I taught women's studies for 11 years and from the moment I entered the academy, I have been attempting to theorise why universities are experienced as such alien territories by many women. I wish I could say that this was all a massive projection on my part . . . but the problems do not disappear that easily . . . This is an account of the academy as perceived from the margins . . . (1999: 1)

Curthoys' (2000) millenial essay was also part of a growing tradition of academic writing, used within women's studies and feminist sociology amongst other courses (Acker, 2000). Nevertheless, much of that pedagogy drew from traditional feminist ways of organising and emphasised a particular caring ethic in approaches, by contrast with men's ways of being academics (Blackmore, 1999). Finding our own voice – and a voice that is neither male nor merely personal and private – became increasingly urgent and the feminist literature is now replete with these kinds of debates about our intellectual and political journeys (St Pierre and Pillow, 2000). Moreover, the debates not only focused upon how our personal and private lives intersected with our professional lives. Personal experiences foregrounded how our studies were now conceived and written, balancing our personal and political lives and journeys across and through the generations. This was theorised within academic sociology to a greater extent than in the past although there were many earlier instances of personal and feminist testimony; Pauline Bart (1985) and Catherine Mackinnon (1989) told us of particular incidents of personal and family violence that drew them to their theoretical concerns with particular aspects of feminism.

There has also been an attempt to go beyond the merely personal reflections on our lived experiences and to consider how these influenced the kinds of knowledge that can be accumulated and presented publicly from the private sphere or arena. This became a growing intellectual debate about the nature of evidence about personal, private and family lives (St Pierre and Pillow, 2000). Some writers such as Alice Pitt (2000) have even begun to consider the complexity of using or being asked to use personal knowledge or experiences in public and educational settings, rendering the personal possibly subject to abuse and certainly not unproblematic. Pitt wrote about the complexities of realities and knowing about them:

> The elements of surprise and curiosity . . . are anticipated in Grumet's pedagogy, where autobiographical narratives serve, not to reveal the world, but to launch the possibility of finding things that matter and to sustain an appetite for the difficult work of teaching and learning with others and alone . . . the personal resists the stark opposition between public and private and between the individual and the social, but these apparent boundaries are not simply collapsed . . . we use the personal to make and renegotiate boundaries between ourselves and the world. (Pitt, 2000: 73)

Reflections

I hope to have shown the significant uses of writing auto/biography and personal lives and its current more complex uses in understandings of family and personal lives at the millennium. Throughout the 1990s there were many shifts, changes and transformations both in the public and social world and how generations of women particularly as feminists have understood, theorised and responded to those changes and transformations. Notions of personal, private or family and domestic, as opposed to public knowledge, and how we study and present our findings of these issues were increasingly subject to scrutiny and study. Beauvoir remained a shadow and influence on various developments and understandings in personal lives, particularly moving from merely thinking about how to changes our lives 'on coming of age' or as young adult women to thinking about the diversity of influences upon our personal and private lives throughout our lives.

Transformations in social and public life have been dramatic and the intimate and personal lives of key politicians have become the subject of public debate. Clinton and Blair, amongst others, exemplified the kinds of changes that have occurred. Yet they also provide examples of the extent of continuity, in that it is they, as men, who have been subject to the public gaze as the central players rather than their wives. Moreover, in so far as their wives have been subject to gaze, they indicate shifts amongst only some women, largely middle class, educated and white, and mainly in respect of the political and professional sphere, along with the changing role of social sciences themselves. Some anti-feminist critics go further in arguing the case for what they assert as post-feminism, for instance Natasha Walter (1998) and Naomi Wolf (1996). This is not my argument at all. I have showed the intertwined nature of social transformations, especially over the family and various aspects of family lives and the interpretations of them as made by social scientists and feminists together, thus accounting more for the rise rather than demise of feminism. Feminists and sociologists have theorised the political as personal.

There are numerous ways in which family life and changes in family life over the last several generations can be considered. However, the key feminist approach to these issues is to consider such developments from the point of view of personal experience. As noted, some of the main feminist writers who have influenced academic feminism and sociology have written about both their own personal and family experiences, and about how such experiences may or do impact upon women's lives both in the family and outside of it. The range of accumulated wisdom about economic and social transformations and their impacts on women's lives shows both continuity and change. This has over the last thirty years become central rather than peripheral to academic writings and in particular sociological and social scientific accounts in the academy. There is an intimate relationship between changes in family life through education and women's involvement in both campaigning and in the academy, which is changing and constructing our understandings and meanings about family and social changes. It is also methodologically important and significant. It is part of what has come to be known, as noted in the previous chapter, as the processes of reflexivity.

I have tried to set the context about how to think about and even how to 'measure' family changes and changes in family life, which have been both the basis of increasing amounts of academic feminist writing and also increasingly the butt of policy debates. Indeed, throughout the same period of time as that in which academic feminism has matured into an important interdisciplinary subject area/specialism in the academy, especially amongst social scientists and the humanities, political debates have centred upon the crisis of the family. Thus the changing forms of patterns of marriage were invoked as reasons for changes in the welfare state and social policy provisions, without recourse to the specificity of the nature of the changes. These trends occurred not only in Britain but also in the USA and other countries, following similar patterns of policy development.

Interestingly, however, although it is now clear that education, especially higher education has provided the means and the vehicle for understanding these complex developments and changes, and it has also been the means for bringing about further changes and developments, there has been no similar attempt to halt the developments in education provision, with perhaps the exception of particular curricula and support for particular feminist and radical initiatives. The links at all levels between family and education, and the complex yet challenging changes that they can bring about, has not been the target of a backlash. Rather a space has been opened up for lively and vigorous debate; and the further means provided through technological developments, including media, TV and IT for expanding and extending those debates into new arenas.

Notes

1. The director's approach had seemed deeply personal at the time. However, with the benefit of hindsight, his behaviour towards Estelle Morris, Secretary of State for Education and Skills confirmed it and led to his enforced resignation in October 2002.
2. At the time of writing I read of how a film was to be made on Beauvoir's life, about her apparently long-standing love affair not with Sartre but with Nelson Algren, an American novelist. The Observer 14.5.2000 p. 3 *Attenborough goes star-hunting for film on De Beauvoir's Left Bank Loves*. 'She was the arch-intellectual of the Left Bank and an early feminist heroine to generations of women. But now Simone de Beauvoir's softer side is to be exposed to the hard gaze of the world's cinema goers'.
3. Beauvoir's *Woman Destroyed* (1969) which was written and published when she was sixty was three short stories about the lives of three different middle-aged women and their relationships with husbands, partners and children. In particular she pinpointed the pains of growing older, loneliness and betrayals.
4. Yet they were powerful and important in their own right, many of them social scientists, sociologists or working in social and policy professions. They had been campaigners for women and children's rights before becoming politicians. The shift in gender relations was associated with women's involvement in the Labour party rather than the Tories or Liberal democrats. The numbers of women in Parliament remained very limited at 119 women MPs: 13 Tory, 3 Liberal Democrats and over 100 Labour MPs in 1997.
5. A clear illustration of New Labour's ambivalence to women was the initial appointment of a Minister for Women in 1997, a commitment through its election manifesto. Harriet Harman was a most prominent feminist MPs, who had worked as a lawyer for the National Council for Civil Liberties (NCCL) before successfully becoming an MP. She was a senior woman in the Labour party and a Labour cabinet member in opposition; and she was appointed as Secretary of State for Social Security, the most senior women's appointment in cabinet at the time. When all the ministerial posts (with attached salaries) had been filled

no-one had been offered the post as Minister for Women. Harriet Harman was asked to do it, with Joan Ruddock as her deputy but without a salary. This illustrated the enduring expectation that women would undertake serious tasks without payment and at the same time the oversight could hardly be put down as merely that given traditional expectations for women in the privacy of the family. Nevertheless, Harriet Harman made great strides to develop policies within a liberal feminist leaning, although her brief as Secretary of State for Social Security led her into contradictory positions, becoming the embodiment of New Labour's ambivalence towards women and feminism. She set up a women's unit, headed by a key feminist writer Anna Coote. She also instrumental in including in the New Deal training for poor lone mothers of young children and in persuading the Chancellor of the Exchequer to develop measures for poor mothers and their families: viz the working families tax credit and a childcare tax credit part of the National Child Care Strategy. This strategy covered provision of childcare services, nurseries and early childhood education measures as well as facilities for the out-of-school care of schoolchildren, whilst their mothers were involved in paid employment. She was removed from office in the summer of 1998 and her influence as a liberal feminist was relatively short-lived, although the NCCS, Sure Start and the working families tax credit, remained the cornerstone of new Labour's policies for children and their working mothers. Her replacement did not express even ambivalent commitment to women and liberal feminist values. Baroness Margaret Jay, a Labour appointee to the House of Lords, daughter of a former Labour Prime Minister and former wife of an ambassador to the USA, was made leader of the House and also responsible in cabinet for women's issues. Tess Jowell (a former social scientist) was appointed Minister for Health and also as her deputy as Minister for Women. Neither of these women made the same public commitments to feminism. Baroness Jay remarked publicly, at the time of her appointment, that she was not a feminist but committed to women's issues. Similarly the women's unit, in the Cabinet Office, responsible for developing policy proposals did not achieve a high public profile. After Labour's second election victory in 2001, Patricia Hewitt became both Secretary of State for Trade and Industry and Minister for Women. The newly-named Women and Equality Unit moved to the DTI in late 2001.

6. In part it is only with the benefit of hindsight, and particularly the curious and strange conjuncture of meeting up again with one of the first people I met at Harvard, introduced to me through the now Minister for Higher Education, who is now a faculty member in Wisconsin.

CHAPTER EIGHT

Conclusions

Feminist theorize the personal

Introduction

The argument of this book is that the global transformations in family lives, especially women's lives as, *inter alia* sexual beings, daughters, wives, partners, single, lone or married mothers and workers, have changed dramatically over the last thirty-five years, and that personal lives have become more public and acknowledged in political and economic arenas. At the same time women from all social classes and diverse social, ethnic and family backgrounds have been more involved in economic and educational activities. These transformations illustrate shifts from a past when personal, intimate and family lives were deemed to be private and separate from public support or responsibility and when women were held responsible for caring for families. The feminist political project from second wave feminism was about sexual and social emancipation and equality with the feminist credo that the personal is political used to change and account for power relations in sexual, family and economic relationships.

Alongside these changing personal and intimate family lives there have also been massive changes in how we, as feminists and social scientists, now understand and theorize changes in people's identities and subjective understandings of their lives. Indeed, I have used the various and changing methods of feminists to understand and theorize these shifting fortunes and perspectives on subjectivity and identities. I have relied on methods of personal experience, biography, auto/biography, voices, narratives and emergent ideas about insider as opposed to outsider perspectives and reflective practice (Chamberlayne, Bornat, Wengraf, (2000). I have related the changes to my own personal experiences of family and professional life and subjective understandings of the processes of political, social and educational changes linked to critical moments.

My argument has been that, over the last 35 years, feminists have theorized the personal as they earlier theorized the political (Butler and Scott, 1992). This process now is as much an educational as a political project, although in the initial stages of second wave feminism it was primarily a political project. It has indeed become very much part of academic and intellectual endeavour to understand changing lives and subjectivities as deeply embedded in academic theories in education, the social sciences and the humanities. There have been huge epistemological changes. I have also argued that these global transformations have been linked with economic, political and social changes, including major shifts in market economies, information technologies and what is now known as the 'knowledge economy' (Blackmore, 1999). The kinds of shifts and transformations in economic, social and family lives, and the attendant and emergent public policies to maintain or modify their effects have varied culturally and been different in national and political contexts according to particular critical moments. Nevertheless, the major transformations have been identified in the moves from modern societies, characterized by stable and democratic regimes committed to forms of family policies for social welfare and measures of social and economic protection for citizens, to late or post-modern societies, characterized by risk, diversity and differences. Ethical dilemmas have been posed about the character of such regimes (Bauman, 1993). Three critical phases were identified that I will elaborate on below.

Feminist and other theories within the academy

These wider socioeconomic changes have also mapped on to changing methods of understanding and interpreting the varied and multitudinous developments in politics and public policy of modernization or modern societies. Indeed, the social sciences together with cultural studies and the humanities have grown and mushroomed alongside these more global economic and social developments. Thus the traditional methods of objective social science as the key to explaining social change have given way to more diverse and varied perspectives, including more subjective accounts about identity, subjectivity, biography and cultural constructions and narratives (Chamberlayne Bornat Wengraf, 2000). Attending to subjective voices, stories and narratives have taken a major place in these new theories and reflective practices (Schon, 1993). The methods of ethnographic and imaginative pursuits have taken the place of more traditional objective accounts, relying on critical theories and critical moments. Equally importantly, shifts from social and economic protection to the risks that such transforming societies pose, have also been theorized, identified as creating both anxieties and the need for constant reflexivity or vigilance to the minutiae of social change (Scott and Jackson, 1999; Beck, 1992 and 1999).

The transformations in family and personal lives and the moves towards more public agendas that I identified have not just affected women but have also affected men and their subjective identities and personal experiences (Beck and Beck-Gersheim, 1995; Jamieson 1999). My argument has been that these shifts and changes in both family and personal lives and the wider socioeconomic contexts and public agendas have been complexly related to each other. The theories that have been used to explain these varied and diverse social and political transformations have borrowed from feminist theories but have also adapted and adopted social and critical theories in complex interwoven ways. Some have sought to explain the changes in terms of emotions around love and intimacy (Giddens, 1992; Hochschild, 1990) whilst others have concentrated upon discursive and textual analyses of public policies (Levitas, 1998; Land, 1990s; Fairclough, 1999; Popkewitz, 2000) and notions of changing forms of governance and governmentality (Rose, 1993; Hulquist and Dahlberg, 2000) or risks and reflexivity (Lash, Beck and Giddens, 1996). The explanations are as diverse as the transformations in personal and political lives that they seek to explain.

Three phases of liberalism: policy transformations over family life-work balance

I have argued that there have been three distinct sociopolitical phases over the last 35 years or so that help to explain the transformations in personal and political lives. I identified these three phases around the changing balances between personal and political and/or family and work linked with wider political and socioeconomic changes and ideologies around shifting and conflicting concepts of liberalism. Liberalism was defined as a democratic political theory tending towards either social or economic rights, and the balances between them. I also linked them with my own personal and professional experiences as one of the generation of women growing up in the aftermath of the Second World War, benefiting from widening educational opportunities on a social class basis and becoming involved in social and socialist movements for emancipation. In this context, these generations of women created the conditions for widening and deepening women's liberation and subsequently theorizing these issues as part of 'second wave' feminism.

Social Liberalism: 'the personal is political'

The first phase was that of *social liberalism* linked with social democracy and socialism. Critical moments by which to date this phase from the perspective of sexual, social and family changes and policies were the assassination of President Kennedy on November 22nd 1963 through to the rise of Reaganism and Thatcherism in the late 1970s. Two further sub-phases were identified as part of this, namely the rise of women's liberation, associated with social movements and sexual liberation, and second wave feminism, in the 1960s in Britain, France, the USA and later associated with Australia, Canada and other Western European countries such as Germany and Sweden. Secondly, I pinpointed the 1970s as the phase in which feminism entered the academy as a contested subject. I as part of that early generation of feminist academics struggled with the challenges of embedding feminist and socialist ideas within the academic subjects of the social sciences. Thus this also was the phase of embedding the project of 'the personal is political', identifying issues of family as about sexual, social and work lives of men and women and how they were regulated and maintained by social, economic and public policies.

Economic Liberalism: 'the personal and political'

The second phase was that of *economic liberalism* linked with the rise of the market economy, deregulation and the privatization of public services known as Reaganomics or Thatcherism. Critical moments by which to date this phase from the perspective of sexual, social and family changes were the election of Thatcher as British Prime Minister in May 1979 and President Reagan in the USA in January 1981. The end of this phase could be seen as either the demise of Thatcher on November 22nd 1990 or Reagan's replacement by President Bush in 1989. During this phase of the 1980s there were major changes, challenges and contradictions in women's working and family lives both outside and inside the academy, including the embedding of women's professional and feminist activities and more varied forms of academic feminism within the academy. The notion of 'femocracy' (Yeatman, 1990) was applied in some countries and contexts to indicate the professionalisation of equal opportunities and liberal feminism. In other contexts and countries there was the curious demise of traditional 'family values' in public policies. This was then the phase of developing critical feminist theories within and across subjects within the academy. During this phase one feminist project, with which I was closely associated, became one of providing critical theories about 'the personal and the political', notions of how personal and family lives were being constricted and constrained by the public policies of marketization and privatization and yet freed from regulatory mechanisms.

Neo-liberalism: 'the political is personal'

The third phase was that of *neo-liberalism* linked with the entrenching of a market economy and moves away from social welfare and family policies towards policies of personal and social responsibilities associated with 'the third way' balancing public and private (Giddens, 1998; 2000). Critical moments by which to date this phase from the perspective of sexual, social and family changes were the continuation of conservatism in Britain and the USA from 1990, and the decline of communism and socialism in Eastern Europe from the early 1990s. This is the phase that Fraser (1997) called 'the post-socialist condition'. The first sub-phase in Britain was Majorism, whilst in the USA it was associated with Clinton's rise as a New Democrat from 1993, going through until 2001. The second sub-phase was the rise of New Labour in 1997, copying the US public policies. This is the phase of entrenching diverse and different feminist theories, associated with post-structuralism, post-modernism or critical realism and theories of risk societies within the academy. During this phase feminist projects diversified and became multiple studies of subjectivity, cultural diversity and sexual and social difference.

It was this phase that could be associated with the notion that 'the political is personal', whereby social and political transformations had led to the theorizing of political changes in terms of personal, intimate and sexual lives being more publicly on the political agenda and also on educational agendas. Theoretical diversity became the hallmark of feminist pedagogy, whilst more women from diverse walks of life entered the academy, as mature and professional students, as the academy itself expanded. Yet it is important to note that, despite massive changes, masculinist agendas remain crucial in political and academic life.

Personal and critical moments in the work/life balancing act

For me personally, there have been several critical moments that I want to discuss as markers of the continuities and changes in personal and political life over the last 35 years. These are all about different aspects of my personal and professional life, around interwoven family cultural traditions, professional engagements and theoretical questions linking personal and political matters.

Feminist Seders

Over the last five years, I have held feminist Seders, in keeping with the Jewish family tradition of celebrating liberation from oppression. The Passover Seder is held by Jewish families to remember Jewish emancipation from slavery in Egypt over 3000 years ago. The Seder narrative mixes bitter memories with more fleeting sweet moments. This emancipatory theme has been seen as emblematic of other liberatory struggles, such as from Nazism, or for civil and social rights for oppressed minority ethnic people in countries such as South Africa or the USA. Since the 1970s, many Jewish women in Britain, the USA and elsewhere had used the opportunity to marry it with women's liberation (Letty Pogrebin, 1990; Betty Friedan, 2001). Given the cultural turn, it is now easier to express these personal and family matters in public.

The feminist Seder that I held at the time of penning this conclusion was even more of a bitter-sweet affair than we have celebrated in the recent past. We wanted to remember and remark upon both Jewish and women's emancipation but we were conscious of the violent conflict raging between Israel and Palestine and the struggles for peace and security for Israeli people and the struggle for political, civil and humanitarian rights of the Palestinian people.

The Seder was attended by 13 women, friends and family from across the generations – an interesting feminist take on 'the Last Supper' which was also a Seder. Most of the women had come to several of our previous Seders – two feminist friends and former colleagues from South Bank days brought their elderly mothers, who competed to be the eldest, both being 88. Two other feminists who came had been long-standing family friends, former students from Bristol days and friends of my daughter who was the youngest. It was a way for us to share our ambivalent love of Jewish family life and traditions, free from the constraints of some Jewish family traditions, which are essentially patriarchal. We wanted to share the traditions but modify them to take account of our feminist politics and ideas and we did so by recounting and revising the stories of the Rabbis, the patriarchs and matriarchs and the four sons as daughters, the main one being seen as transgressive like ourselves. One of us around the Seder table had been instrumental in organizing us to take political action about the escalating violence in the Middle East and had formed a network entitled *Jews for Justice for Palestinians*. This network was opposed to Israeli government policies that undermined the livelihoods of the Palestinian people, and supportive of Israeli people who wanted peace and security, and the growing number of Israeli army reservists who refused to serve in the occupied territories of the West Bank and Gaza strip. The occupied territories had been taken in the 1967 Six Day war and now constituted the major source of conflict and dispute over rights to homes and livelihoods. Over 1000 Israeli reservists had refused to serve with the Israeli army in maintaining and policing the occupation.

Thirty-five years ago I went to Israel as a volunteer as a result of the Six Day war, committed as I was then both to socialism and Zionism through my Jewish family background. It was just before the rise of the second wave of feminism, as I have already noted, but liberatory politics were in the air and then Israel was still seen as relatively oppressed and insecure young country, but committed to humanitarian and democratic values. Transformations in my personal and professional life and Israel's fortunes, economic and political power have been massive over that time, although the anxieties and fears about security and peace have continued and yet been challenged. The see-saw politics in Israel have demonstrated the fears and anxieties about security and safe borders of many Jewish families in Israel. The frequent lurches to the right in Israeli government policies have indicated insecurities, fears, anxieties and an abiding commitment to traditional Jewish family and religious values and an inability to reconcile Jewish humanitarian values with more religious views and right-wing policies of violence and militarism.

However, my transformations have been more dramatic in that my life course both personally and professionally has been varied and not followed a very traditional path. Back in 1967 I thought that I might pursue a more traditional family life and not become so professionally engaged, albeit that I wanted a political engagement with the politics of social change. My feminist persona was only embryonic at that moment but was shortly to be born. On my return from Israel, I took a post at the LSE and became deeply involved in socialist and feminist politics and met there a number of colleagues who have become constant and firm friends and political allies. In particular, I met my friend and colleague Hilary Land and together and separately we have forged our feminist politics and theoretical practices, including our ambivalent relationships with political, social and familial changes and policies. We have also constantly remained both academic and politically committed feminists, arising from those early years when we became academic colleagues at Bristol University, back in the early 1970s.

Feminists Retiring

A few days before the feminist Seder I had been to a seminar, hosted by the Nuffield Foundation, to celebrate Hilary Land's formal retirement from Bristol University and ostensibly from academic life at which we held a conversation about 'families and policies towards families, past, present and future'. What was particularly fascinating was the extent of change as well as continuity revealed during this conversation. There were about 30 friends and colleagues there from across at least two generations. There were the older generation of academic women, mainly those doughty and feisty feminists who had already retired – Dorothy Wedderburn, Dulcie Groves, Hilary Rose, Mary McIntosh and Sheila Allen. Several of them had contributed to autobiographical accounts to my edited collection (David and Woodward, 1998). There were also those of us who were still in post but represented now the older generation of feminist academics – Janet Finch, Ceridwen Hughes, Diana Leonard, Jane Lewis, Ruth Lister, Clare Ungerson, amongst others. A few friends and colleagues also came from abroad, namely Bettina Cass from Australia who was spending study leave in the USA studying current family and welfare policies and Arnlaug Leira the child-care expert from Norway. There was also a sprinkling of men, colleagues from the very early days, including Professor Roy Parker who had been our head of department at Bristol University during those early heady days of introducing feminist ideas into our subject of social policy (then known as social administration).

Hilary Land introduced the conversation with providing the first examination paper for our innovative undergraduate course in family and social policy back in 1975. She made the comment about how little seemed to have changed and what contemporary relevance the paper had with questions such as 'Do you agree that the welfare concerns of the State begin and end with the family?' and 'in what ways has social policy influenced the structure and activity of the contemporary family?' She also drew attention to the ways in which financial institutions, fiscal and economic policies had continued to dominate family and social policy considerations, in particular for children and women as wives and mothers. She also pointed to the importance to family change of developments in reproductive technologies. Her talk however was also peppered with personal reminiscences and references to her parents, her mother having died of multiple sclerosis and her father who was the epitome of a male breadwinner. She also referred to her early readings of key feminist texts, not unsurprisingly Simone de Beauvoir, and Doris Lessing's *The Golden Notebook*. She added, however, Eleanor Rathbone and her interest in feminism, which had sparked Hilary Land's passion for studying family policies.

The general conversation ranged over a variety of issues and questions about how to choose points of departure and change and how to measure and account for developments through a particular evidence-base. There were four presentations that variously addressed families and policies about family changes and the implications for the future. It was widely recognized that the conceptual apparatus for understanding changes remained complex but still importantly located in traditional notions of inequalities and social class. Similarly the contradictory moves across continents and countries towards a more market economy and the privatization of public and social policies had not led to more global social justice. They had been important in loosening traditional family ties around women's work but had not had a commensurate effect on women's caring responsibilities barely altering the family/work life balance. Indeed, although the USA was arguably more oriented to a market economy and women's personal responsibilities for caring (Cass, 2002), British and Australian shifts around the citizen as parent and worker through a new discourse of work-life balance had not increased social or sexual justice. Thus although it was recognized that women's labour force participation had increased particularly for women as parents, whether single, divorced, cohabiting or married over the last 30 years social policies had not modified sufficiently the burdens of women's continuing personal responsibilities for caring for families. Thus the discursive shifts in political language from families and social policies towards work-life balances and personal responsibilities were more emblematic of change than the complex and contradictory social evidence available about women's lives would indicate. However, the future for families and women within families and work remained class-based, complex, uncertain and contradictory, yet more on a public agenda about personal lives and new forms of social citizenship to be reinforced through education and politics.

Feminists and Sociologists

At about this time I also attended the BSA annual conference entitled 'Reshaping the Social'. I presented a paper on my work, with colleagues Pamela Alldred and Pat Smith on teenage parenthood, pregnancy and sex education. In this paper we pointed to the changing notions of sexual and social identities of young people through the growing literature on understanding subjectivity around masculinities and femininities. In particular we were exploring changing family identities and whether young people wanted to explore these issues in a public arena such as school or preferred home and parents for these personal discussions. Our preliminary analysis of young people's perspectives was that they preferred to learn about sex and relationships in personal and familial settings rather than in the more public locale of the school. They wanted access to information from professionals and experts rather than their teachers, whom they felt might use more personal views in other contexts, affecting their school and educational careers. They saw huge risks and a lack of trust associated with personal discussions within school contexts. (Scott, Jackson, Beckett-Milburn 1998; 2001)

Over the last decade or two, official policies on young and teenage parenthood had been moving towards more public displays and debates about personal, social and health education, including sex education, and now citizenship education, within the school curriculum. These moves had not only taken place in Britain (Isobel Allen 1984; Sue Lees, 1996; Louisa Allen, 2001) but also in Canada (Kelly, 2001) the USA (Burdell, 1995/6) and Australia and New Zealand (Allen, 2001, Middleton, 1998). However, there were different nuances to the debates about the central importance of marriage, and citizenship in the school curriculum. In the USA the policy of 'abstinence only before marriage' had been invoked as a central part of the curriculum and access to federal funds for education during the Clinton era. This contrasted with more liberal strategies in other countries where debate has centred more on questions of discussing sexual and social relationships in education (Bullen, Kenway and Hey, 1999; David, 2003 in press). In particular, some countries, such as the Netherlands, had a cultural norm of teaching about sexual and family relationships to very young people such that the social stigma of young parenthood was not invoked (Lewis and Knijn, 2002). These family policies were another indication of shifts around the personal and political and the extent to which the personal has been made political and public in terms of debate about sexuality and intimacy.

At this BSA conference I had also attended a keynote plenary lecture presented by Professor Bryan Turner of Cambridge University. He happened to be a contemporary student of mine in sociology at Leeds University back in the 1960s, again helping to invoke notions of continuity and change around families and feminisms. He gave a *tour de force* of a paper about 'the rights revolution' developing a sociology of rights around the idea of vulnerability and addressing the various sociological pressures towards rights in globalization, democratic movements and the civil society of NGOs. He also addressed epistemological questions. However, his presentation confirmed the continuity of masculinist agendas in sociology and possibly wider social life, despite the fact that he was addressing questions about social movements for change. In response to a question he reluctantly acknowledged that his central point about vulnerability derived from feminist theories as pointed out at a seminar at the University of Kent by Professor Mary Evans. However he had not inserted reference to her in the formal presentation of his paper. In her work on biographical and personal issues in women's lives Mary Evans (1993) pointed to the limitations in women's intellectual life and social ideas through the continuing need to attend to and engage with masculinist agendas, which remained dominant in public life. What greater confirmation of continuity than this instance.

Feminists envision the future

Nevertheless, there are some instances of changes for future generations of young people, and women especially, in that opportunities for work, albeit now required for women whether or not they have family and thus personal responsibilities, are more embedded in cultural and economic changes. Similarly shifting legal and quasi-religious regulations have led to greater women's choices around sexual and social relationships and rates of marriage versus consensual unions and childbearing dramatically altered in many late modern societies. Single motherhood no longer bears the opprobrium it once did, whilst teenage motherhood might remain a moral panic yet the shifts have been in terms of educational rather than economic opportunities.

Personal and professional lives are now part of public agendas, and scientific developments in terms of reproductive technologies offer a whole host of possibilities as well as potential nightmares were market economics to be applied. Hilary and Steven Rose, in a lecture about moves towards a 'geneticised culture' questioned

> the dystopic vision of Princeton molecular biologist Lee Silver who predicts (*Remaking Eden*) – in the context of the unregulated society that is the USA and towards which Europe may be moving – that Wnancially regulated access to presumed beneficial gene technology will lead to extensive genetic manipulation . . . his book threatens to become the *Brave New World* of our time . . . After all, he argues, if one can pay for one's child's education after birth, why not give it a helping hand before birth? And if one is free to buy a car or house, why not suitably endowed oVspring? Ultimately, he suggests, there will come about a divergence within the human population into separate races and eventually species – one 'Gen-rich', the other 'Natural'? (Rose and Rose, 2002, p. 2)

They remained more sceptical about such a disturbing future and yet envisioned a new role for scientiWc knowledge such as human genetic manipulation and argued for an ethical basis for these applications. 'We are arguing more broadly that the WHO goal of "adding years to life and life to years" will still primarily be achieved through access to the conditions through which good health is realizable: access to clean water and food, reduction of pollution, and the absence of war' (ibid, p. 3). Thus they envisioned a more ethical basis to a geneticised culture in the future.

Feminists theorize the personal

These various instances of continuity and change in women's lives in families, policies about families and theories about social and sexual changes lead me to the conclusions that transformations in personal and political and women's lives have been complex and contradictory. There has been more than a semblance and representation of change, in particular over how women as sexual and social beings have been presented and viewed. Shifts around personal and political in public and socioeconomic agendas have indeed been crucial. Whilst feminist theories, interwoven with critical, post-structural and/or post-modern theories have achieved an important place in pedagogies and theories within higher education and the academy they only serve to reinforce the continuing centrality of gender complexly linked with social class, race and ethnicity. Nevertheless, these changes have also been conceptualized in diverse and different ways but they have also implied changes for men too. Thus patriarchal and masculinist agendas have prevailed and remained dominant. More importantly, despite massive socioeconomic and technological change social class differences have remained and been retained; indeed reinforced in many contexts, as the evidence about young and teenage girls, their identities around sexuality, pregnancies and parenthood or motherhood might suggest. The need to educate such young women and new generations to resist such masculinist agendas and traditional conceptions of women's lives caring for others and taking 'personal responsibility' remains a vital task as Mikel Brown (1998) amongst others had argued. Whilst the global socioeconomic transformations in liberal agendas women's lives have irredeemably changed, the struggle to transform and equalize those lives remains. The political aims of social and sexual equality and emancipation and global sexual justice remain to be achieved although sociologists together with feminists have theorized the personal.

Bibliography and References

Abbey, S and O'Reilly, A (eds.) (1998) *Redefining Motherhood: changing identities and patterns* Toronto, Canada: Second Story Press

Acker, S (ed.) (1989) *Teachers, Gender and Careers* London: Falmer

Acker, S (1994) *Gendered Education* Buckingham: Open University Press

Acker, S (1999) *The Realities of Teachers' Work: never a dull moment* London: Avebury

Allan, G (1999) *The Sociology of Family Studies: a reader* Oxford: Blackwell

Allan, G (2002) *Commitments and Ties: solidarities in personal relations* Inaugural Lecture, Keele University, May 1st

Alldred, P, David, M E and Edwards, R (2002) Minding the Gap: children negotiating home and school, in: Edwards, R. (ed.) *Children, Home and School: autonomy, connection or regulation?* London: Falmer Press

Allen, I (1984) *Sex and Personal Education* London: Policy Studies Institute

Allen, L (2001) Closing Sex Education's Knowledge/Practice Gap: the reconceptualisation of young people's knowledge *Sex Education* 1 (2) 109–23

Altbach, P G and Kelly, G P (eds.) (1986) *New Approaches to Comparative Education* Chicago: University of Chicago Press

Althusser, L (1971) Ideology and Ideological State Apparatuses, in: *Lenin and Philosophy and other essays* London: New Left Books

Appignanesi, L (1988) *Simone de Beauvoir* London: Penguin

Appignanesi, L (1999) *Losing the Dead: a family memoir* London: Chatto and Windus

Arnot, M (2002) *Reproducing Gender? Essays in educational theory and feminist politics* Buckingham: Open University Press

Arnot, M, David, M and Weiner, G (1996) *Educational Reforms and Gender Equality in Schools*, Research Discussion Series No 17, Manchester, Equal Opportunities Commission

Arnot, M, David, M and Weiner, G (1999) *Closing the Gender Gap: post war education and social change* Cambridge: Polity Press

Arnot, M and Dillabough, J (2000) (eds.) *Challenging Democracy: international perspectives on gender, education and citizenship* London: Routledge/Falmer

Arnove, F, Altbach, P and Kelly, G (1992) (eds.) *Emergent Issues in Education: comparative perspectives* Albany, New York: SUNY Press

Ball, S J (1990) *Politics and Policy Making in Education: explorations in policy sociology* London: Routledge

Ball, S J (1994) *Educational Reform: a critical and post-structural approach* Buckingham: Open University Press

Ball, S J, Davies, J, David, M E and Reay, D (2001) Decisions, Differentiations et Distinctions: vers une sociologie du choix des etudes superieures, *Revue Francaise de pedagogique*, 136, Juillet–Septembre 20

Ball, S J, Davies, J, David M E and Reay, D (2002) 'Classification' and 'Judgement': social class and the 'cognitive structures' of choice of Higher Education *British Journal of*

Sociology of Education 23 (1) 51–72

Ball, S J, Reay, D and David, M E (2002) 'Ethnic Choosing': minority ethnic students, social class and higher education choice. Race Ethnicity and Education 5(4) 333–357

Banks, O (1986) *Faces of Feminism: a study of feminism as a social movement* Oxford: Blackwell

Banks, O and J (1964) *Feminism and Family Planning in Victorian England* Liverpool: Liverpool University Press

Barker, D L and Allen, S (1976a) (eds.) *Sexual Divisions and Society: process and change* London: Longman

Barker, D L and Allen, S (1976b) (eds.) *Dependence and Exploitation in Work and Marriage* London: Longman

Barrett, M (1980) *Women's Oppression Today: problems in Marxist feminist analysis* London: Verso

Barrett, M and McIntosh, M (1982) *The Anti-Social Family* London: Verso

Bart, P and Moran, E G (1993) (eds). *Violence against women; the bloody footprints* California: Sage

Barton, L and Walker, S (1983) (eds.) *Gender, Class and Education* Brighton, Falmer Press

Basit, T (1996) *Eastern Values, Western Milieu: identities and aspirations of adolescent British Muslim girls* Aldershot: Ashgate

Bauman, J (1986) *Winter in the Morning: a young girl's life in the Warsaw Ghetto and beyond* London: Virago

Bauman, Z (1993) *Post-modern Ethics* Oxford: Blackwell

Bauman, Z (2000) *Liquid Modernity* Cambridge: Polity Press

Bayley, J (1998) *Iris: a memoir* London: Abacus

Beauvoir, S de (1960) *The Second Sex* London: First Four Square Edition (First published 1949, England 1953)

Beauvoir, S de (1963) *Memoirs of a Dutiful Daughter* Harmondsworth: Penguin (First published 1958)

Beauvoir, S de (1968) *Force of Circumstance* Harmondsworth: Penguin (First published 1963)

Beauvoir, S de (1969/1971) *Woman Destroyed* London: Collins/Fontana

Beauvoir, S de (1970) *Prime of Life* Harmondsworth: Penguin

Beauvoir, S de (1973) *A Very Easy Death* New York: Warner (First published 1964 in French; 1965 in English)

Beauvoir, S de (1974) *Adieux: a Farewell to Sartre* Harmondsworth: Penguin

Beauvoir, S de (1977) *Old Age* Harmondsworth: Penguin (First published 1970)

Beck, Ulrich (1992) *The Risk Society: towards a new modernity* London: Sage

Beck, U (1999) *World Risk Society* Cambridge: Polity Press

Beck, U. (2000) *What is Globalisation?* Cambridge: Polity Press

Beck U and Beck-Gersheim, E (1995) *The Normal Chaos of Love* Cambridge: Polity Press

Beck, U, Giddens, T and Lash, S (1996) *Reflexive Modernisation* Cambridge: Polity Press

Belenky, M, Clinchy, B, Goldberger, N and Tarule, J (1986) *Women's Ways of Knowing: the development of self, voice and mind* New York: Basic Books

Belenky, M, Bond, L and Weinstock, J (1997) *A Tradition that has no name* New York and London: Basic Books

Benn, M (1999) *Madonna and Child: towards a new politics of motherhood* London: Vintage

Bernard, J (1973) *The Future of Marriage* London: Souvenir Press

Bernard, J (1975/6) *The Future of Parenthood* London: Calder and Boyers

Bernard, M (2001) *Women Ageing: old lives: new challenges* Inaugural Lecture, Keele University February 22nd. Published as: Women ageing: old lives, new challenges *Education and Ageing* 16 (3) 333–52

Bernardes, J (1997) *Family Studies: an introduction* London: Routledge

Bernstein, B (1990) *Class, Codes and Control, Vol. 4 The Structure of Pedagogic Discourse* London: Routledge

Bhatti, G (1999) *Asian Girls at Home and at School: an ethnographic study* London: Routledge

Bird, E (2001) Disciplining the inter-disciplinary: radicalism and the academic curriculum *British Journal of Sociology of Education* 22 (4) 463–78

Blackmore, J (2000) *Troubling Women: feminism, leadership and educational change* Buckingham: Open University Press

Blackmore, J (2002) Is it only 'what works' that 'counts' in new knowledge economies? Evidence based practice, educational research and teacher education in Australia *Social Policy and Society* 1 (3) 257–67

Blackmore, J and Kenway, J (1993) eds. *Gender Matters in Educational Administration and Policy: a feminist introduction* London: Falmer

Blackstone, T *et al* (1968) *Students in Conflict: LSE in 1967* London: Weidenfeld and Nicolson

Blair, T (2002) Speech at London School of Economics, March 10th

Blunden, G (1983) Typing in the Tech: in Gleeson, D (ed.) *Further Education* London: RKP

Bowe R, Ball, S J, and Gold, A (1993) *Reforming Education and Changing Schools* London: Routledge

Bowles S and Gintis, H (1976) *Schooling in Capitalist America* London: RKP

Bourdieu, P (1986) *Distinction: a social critique of the judgement of taste* London: RKP

Bourdieu, P (1988) *Homo Academicus* Cambridge: Polity Press

Bourdieu, P (1990) *The Logic of Practice* Cambridge: Polity Press

Bourdieu P (2001) *Masculine Domination* Oxford: Polity

Bourdieu, P and Passeron, J C (1977) *Reproduction in Education, Society and Culture* London: Sage

Brah, A (1996) *Cartographies of Diaspora: contesting entities* London: Routledge

Brah, A, Mac an Ghaill, M and Hickman, M (1999) (eds.) *Thinking Identities, Ethnicity, Racism and Culture* Basingstoke: Macmillan

Bristol Women's Studies Group (1979; 1984) *Half the Sky: an introduction to Women's Studies* London: Virago

Britzman, D (1991) *Practice Makes Practice: a critical study of learning to teach* Albany New York: SUNY Press

Britzman, D (1998) *Lost Subjects, Contested Objects: towards a psychoanalytic inquiry of learning* Albany, New York: SUNY Press

Britzman, D (2003) *After-Education: Anna Freud, Melanie Klein and psychoanalytic histories of learning* Albany, New York: State University of New York Press

Brown, L M (1998) *Raising their Voices: the politics of girls' anger* Cambridge, Mass. and London: Harvard University Press

Brown, P and Crompton, R (1994) (eds.) *Economic Restructuring and Social Exclusion* London: UCL Press

Bruegel, I (1979) Women as a Reserve Army of Labour: a note on recent British experience, *Feminist Review* 3: 12–32

Burchill, J (1998) *Diana* London: Weidenfeld and Nicholson

Burdell, P (1995/6) Teen mothers in high school: tracking their curriculum, in Apple, M. (ed.) *Review of Research in Education 21* Washington DC American Educational Research Association

Burgess, T and Pratt, J (1974) *The Polytechnics: a report* London: Pitman

Butler, J (1990) *Gender Trouble: feminism and the subversion of identity* New York and London: Routledge

Butler, J and Scott, J (1992) (eds) *Feminists Theorise the Political* New York and London: Routledge

Campbell, B (1987) *The Iron Ladies: why do women vote Tory?* London: Virago

Campbell, B (1988) *Unofficial secrets: Child Sexual abuse the Cleveland Case* London: Virago

Campbell, B (1998) *Princess Diana* London: Virago

Carling, A, Duncan, S, and Edwards, R (2002) (eds.) *Analysing Families: morality and rationality in policy and practice* London: Routledge

Cass, B (2002) Talk at Hilary Land's retirement seminar 20th March

Chamberlayne, P, Bornat, J and Wengraf, T (2000) (eds.) *The Biographical Turn in the Social Sciences* London Routledge

Chodorow, N (1978) *The Reproduction of Mothering: psychoanalysis and the sociology of gender* Berkeley and London: University of California Press

Cixous, H (1976) *La* Paris: Gallimard

Clinton, H (1999) interview with *Talk* magazine; premier issue September; 1 (1)

Collins, P H (1990) *Black Feminist Thought: knowledge, consciousness and the politics of empowerment* London: Unwin and Hyman

Comer, L (1974) *Wedlocked Women* Leeds: Feminist Books

Cooper, J E, Kendall, R and Sartorius, N (1972) *Psychiatric Diagnosis in New York and London* Oxford: Oxford University Press

Coote, A and Campbell, B (1982) *Sweet Freedom: the struggle for Women's Liberation* Oxford: Blackwell

Coote, A, Harman, H and Hewitt, P (1990) *The Family Way* London: Institute for Public Policy Research

Coote, A (2000) (ed) *New Gender Agenda* London: Institute for Public Policy Research

Curthoys, A (2000) Adventures in Feminism: Simone de Beauvoir's autobiographies, women's liberation and self-fashioning *Feminist Review* 64: 3–18

David, M. E (1975) *School Rule in the USA: a case study of participation in school budgeting* Cambridge, Mass: Ballinger

David, M. E (1977) *Reform, Reaction and Resources: the 3 Rs of educational planning* Windsor, Berks NFER

David, M E (1980) *The State, the Family and Education*, London, Routledge & Kegan Paul

David, M E (1983) The New Right, Sex, Education and Social Policy: towards a New Moral Economy in Britain and the USA, in Lewis, J (ed.) *Women's Welfare: Women's Rights* London: Croom Helm

David, M E (1986) Moral and Maternal: The Family in the Right, in Levitas, R (ed.) *The Ideology of the New Right*, Cambridge, Polity Press

David, M E (1987) On Becoming a Feminist in the Sociology of Education, in Walford, G (ed.) *Doing Sociology of Education*, Lewes, Falmer Press

David, M E (1989) Prima Donna Inter Pares: Women in Academic Management, in Acker, S (ed.) *Teachers, Gender and Careers*, London, Falmer Press

David M E (1991) Mothers and Education: Issues in Family-Education Policy, *European Feminist Research Conference, Women in a Changing Europe*, University of Aalburg, Denmark, August: 18–22

David, M E (1993) *Parents, Gender and Education Reform*, Cambridge, Polity Press

David, M E (1998) (ed.) *The Fragmenting Family: does it matter?* London, IEA Health & Welfare Unit Choice in Welfare

David, M E and Land, H (1983) Sex and Social Policy, in Glennerster, H (ed.) *The Future of the Welfare State: remaking social policy*, London, Heinemann

David, M E, Edwards, Hughes and Ribbens, J (1993) *Mothers and Education: Inside Out? exploring family-education policy and experience* London: Macmillan

David, M E, West, A and Ribbens, J (1994) *Mother's Intuition? Choosing Secondary Schools*, London: Falmer Press

David, M E, Davies, J, Edwards, R, Reay, D and Standing, K (1996) Mothering, Reflexivity and Feminist Methodology, in Morley, L and Walsh, V (eds.) *Breaking Boundaries: women in higher education* London: Taylor and Francis

David, M E, Davies, J, Edwards, R, Reay, D and Standing K (1997) Choice within Constraints: mothers and schooling *Gender and Education*, 9 (4): 397–410

David, M E (1998) Class and Gender Aspects of Higher Education in a London Polytechnic, in Floud, R (ed.) *Metropolitan Higher: the establishment of higher education in london*, London: Athlone Press, 96–122

David, M E and Woodward, D (1998) (eds.) *Negotiating the Glass Ceiling: senior women in the academic world*, London: Falmer Press,

David M E and Reay, D (2000) Equality in Action: Class, gender and race in education, in Stephenson, W (ed.) *Equality in Action: seminar 3: Addressing Inequalities in Education*. A seminar held on Wednesday 26th January 2000 at 11 Downing Street, London, London: The Smith Institute

David, M E (2002) From Keighley to Keele: personal reflections on a circuitous journey through education, family, feminism and policy sociology *British Journal of Sociology of Education* 23 (2)

David, M E, Ball, S J, Davies, J and Reay, D Gender Issues in Student Choices of Higher Education *Gender & Education* 15 (1) 23–39

David, M E (2003 forthcoming) Teenage Parenthood is bad for parents and children: a feminist critique of family, education and social welfare policies and practices, in Bloch, M N and Popkewitz, T. S (eds.) *Changing Governing Patterns of the Child in the Welfare State*, New York: St Martins Press and London: Palgrave Macmillan

Davis, M (1990) *City of Quartz: excavating the future in Los Angeles* London: Verso

Dawe, A (1970) The Two Sociologies *British Journal of Sociology* 21: 207–18

Deem, R (1996) Border Territories: a journey through sociology, education and women's studies *British Journal of Sociology of Education* 17 (2): 5–19

Dehli, K (1996) Love and knowledge: adult education in the Toronto home and school Council, 1916–1940 *Ontario History* 88 (3) September: 207–28

Dehli, K (1996) Unfinished business? The dropout goes to work in education policy reports, in Gaskell, J and Kelly, D (eds.) *Debating Dropouts: new policy perspectives* New

York: Teachers' College Press

Dehli, K (1996) Travelling Tales: education reform and parental choice in postmodern times *Journal of Educational Policy* 11(1) 75–88

Dehli, K (1997) Between market and state? Gender and power in the new educational marketplace *Discourse: Studies in the cultural politics of education* 17 (3) 363–76

Dehli, K (2000) *Feminist Views of Motherhood* Paper presented at AERA, annual meetings in Chicago

Dehli, K (2003) Making the parent and the researcher: genealogy meets ethnography in research on contemporary school reform, in Ball, S J and Tamboukou, M (eds.) *Genealogy and Ethnography* New York: Peter Lang (forthcoming)

Dehli, K (2003) An important archive of usefulness: regulating parents participation in schooling, in Brock, D (ed.) *Making Normal: moral regulation in Canadian Society* Neilson (forthcoming)

Delphy, C (1984) *Close to Home: a materialist analysis of women's oppression* London: Hutchinson

Delphy, C (1993) Sex as a category of social analysis *Women's Studies International Forum* 16 (1) 1–9

Delphy, C and Leonard, D (1992) *Familiar Exploitation: A new analysis of marriage in contemporary western societies* Cambridge: Polity Press

Dominelli, L (1987) Father–daughter incest: patriarchy's shameful secret *Critical Social Policy* 16 (1) Summer: 8–23

Dominelli, L and Mcleod E (1989) *Feminist Social Work* Basingstoke: Macmillan

Donzelot, J (1980) *The Policing of Families* London: Hutchinson

Downes, D M, Davies, B, David, M E and Stone, P (1976) *Gambling, Work and Leisure* London, Routledge and Kegan Paul

Du Bois-Raymond (1998) 'I don't want to commit myself yet': young people's life concept *Journal of Youth Studies* 1 (1) 63–79

Duchen, C (1986/7) Feminism in France: From May 1968 to Mitterand *French Studies* 61 (4)

Duplessis R, and Snitow, A (1998) *The Feminist Memoir Project: voices from Women's Liberation* New York: Three Rivers Press

Duncan, S and Edwards, R (1997) (eds.) *Single Mothers in an International Context* London: UCL Press

Duncan, S and Edwards, R (1999) *Lone Mothers, Paid Work and Gendered Moral Rationalities* London: Macmillan

Edwards R (1993) *Mature Women Students: separating or connecting family and education* London: Taylor and Francis

Edwards R (2002) (ed) *Children, Home and School: autonomy, connection or regulation?* London: Falmer Press

Edwards, T, Fitz, J and Whitty, G (1981) *The State or Private Education: an evaluation of Assisted Places scheme* London: Falmer Press

Ehrenreich B (1983) *The Hearts of Men: American dreams and the flight from commitment* London: Pluto Press

Ehrenreich B (1989) *Fear of Falling: the new middle class in America* New York: Basic Books

Ehrenreich B (2001) *Nickel and Dimed: On (not) getting by in boom time America* New York: Metropolitan

Ehrenreich B and English, D (1979) *For her own good: 150 years of the experts' advice to women* London: Pluto Press

Eichler, M (1980) *The Double Standard: a feminist critique of feminist social science* London: Croom Helm

Eichler, M (1988) *Families in Canada Today* Toronto: Gage

Eichler, M (1997) *Family Shifts* Oxford: Oxford University Press

Eisenstein, H (1984) *Contemporary Feminist Thought* Sydney and London: Allen and Unwin

Eisenstein, Z (1981) *The Radical Future of Liberal Feminism* New York: Longman

Eisenstein, Z (1982) The Sexual Politics of the New Right: on understanding the crisis of liberalism *SIGNS Journal of Women and Culture* 7 (3) 567–88

Eisenstein, Z (1996) Equalising Privacy and Specifying Equality, in Hirschman, N and di Stefano, C (eds.) *Revisioning the political: reconstructions of concepts in western political theory* Oxford: Westview

Ellsworth, E (1997) *Teaching Positions: difference, pedagogy and the power of address* New York and London: Teachers' College Press

Epstein, D and Johnson, R (1999) *Schooling Sexualities* Buckingham: Open University Press

Epstein, J (1990) School and Family Connections: theory, research and implications for integrating the two sociologies of education and family *Marriage and Family Review* 15 (1/2) 99–126

Etzioni, A (1993) *The Parenting Deficit* London: Demos

Etzioni, A (1993) *The Spirit of Community: Rights, Responsibilities and the Community Agenda* New York: Crown

Etzioni, A (1994) *The Spirit of Community: Reinvention of American Society* New York: Simon and Schuster

Etzioni A (1999) *The Limits to Privacy* New York Basic Books

Evans, M (1985) *Simone de Beauvoir: a feminist mandarin* London: Tavistock

Evans, M (1991) *A Good School: life at a girls' grammar school in the 1950s* London: The Women's Press

Evans, M (1993) Reading lives: how the personal might be social *Sociology:* special issue on biography and autobiography in sociology 27(1) February: 5–15

Evans, M (1997) Negotiating the frontier: women and resistance in the contemporary academy, in Stanley, L (ed.) *Knowing Feminisms: academic borders, territories and tribes* London: Sage

Evans, M (1997) *Introducing Contemporary Feminist Thought* Cambridge: Polity Press

Faludi, S (1991) *Backlash: the undeclared war against women* London: Chatto and Windus

Faludi, S (1999) *Stiffed: the betrayal of modern man* New York and London: Vintage

Fairclough, N (1999) *New Labour, New Language* Harlow: Longman

Featherstone, J (1974) Children and youth in America: review *Harvard Education Review* Special Issue part II 'The Rights of Children' 43(4) February 160–8

Featherstone, J (1979) Family matters *Harvard Education Review* 49 (1) February: 20–53

Finch, J (1983) *Married to the Job: wives incorporation into men's work* London: Allen and Unwin

Finch, J and Groves, D (1983) eds. *A Labour of Love: women, work and caring* London: Routledge

Fine, M and Weis, L (1998) *The Unknown City: the lives of poor and working class young adults* Boston: Beacon Press

Firestone, S (1979) *The Dialectic of Sex: the case for feminist revolution* London: The Women's Press

Fleming, S (1971) *Women Workers Struggle for their Rights* Bristol: Falling Wall Press

Fraser, N and Gordon, L (1994) A genealogy of 'dependency': tracing a keyword of the US welfare state *SIGNS Journal of Women in Culture and Society* 19 (2): 309–36

Fraser, N (1997) *Justice Interruptus: critical reflections on the 'post-socialist' condition* New York and London: Routledge

Freeman, J (1975) *The Politics of Women's Liberation: a case study of an emerging social movement and its relation to the policy process* New York: McKay

Friedan, B (1963) *The Feminine Mystique* Harmondsworth: Penguin

Friedan, B (1982) *The Second Stage* London: Michael Joseph

Friedan, B (1982) *It Changed my Life* London: Michael Joseph

Friedan, B (1994) *The Fountain of Age* London: Vintage

Friedan, B (2001) *Life so Far: a memoir* New York: Touchstone for Simon and Schuster

Frosh, S, Phoenix, A and Pattman, R (2001) *Young Masculinities: understanding boys in contemporary society* London: Palgrave

Gardiner, J (1974) Women's Domestic Labour *New Left Review* 89 Jan–Feb: 47–58

Gaskell, J (1992) *Gender Matters from School to Work* Milton Keynes: Open University Press

Gaskell, J (2002) *Discourses of Feminism: the Women's Movement in B.C, Ontario and education* Women's World 2002 Conference, Uganda: Kampala University

Gaskell, J and Taylor, S (forthcoming) The women's movement in Canadian and Australian education: from liberation and sexism to boys and social justice *Gender and Education* 15 (2)

Gavron, H (1966) *The Captive Wife: conflicts of housebound mothers* London: RKP

Gewirtz, S, Ball, S.J and Bowe, R (1995) *Markets, Choice and Equity in Education* Buckingham: Open University Press

Giddens, A (1990) *The Consequences of Modernity* Cambridge: Polity Press

Giddens, A (1991) *Modernity and Self-Identity: self and society in the late modern age* Cambridge: Polity Press

Giddens, A (1992) *The Transformation of Intimacy: sexuality, love and eroticism in modern societies* Cambridge: Polity Press

Giddens, A (1993) *Beyond Left and Right* Cambridge: Polity Press

Giddens, A (1998) *The Third Way: the renewal of social democracy* Cambridge: Polity Press

Giddens, A (1999) *Runaway World: how globalisation is reshaping our lives* London: Profile Books

Giddens, A (2000) *The Third Way and its Critics* Cambridge: Polity Press

Gilder, G (1981) *Welfare and Poverty* New York: Basic Books

Gilligan, C (1984) *In a Different Voice: psychological theory and women's development* Cambridge Mass. and London: Harvard University Press

Gilligan, C and Brown, L M (1992) *Meeting at the Crossroads: women's psychology and girls' development* Cambridge Mass. and London: Harvard University Press

Glazer, N and Moynihan, D.P (1967) *Beyond the Melting Pot?* Boston: MIT

Glazer-Raymo, J (1999) *Shattering the Myths: women in academia* Baltimore and London: The John Hopkins University Press

Glennerster, H (1980) ed. *The Future of the Welfare State: remaking social policy*, London,

Heinemann

Gordon, L (1977) *Woman's Body, Woman's Right* Harmondsworth: Penguin

Gordon, T, Thompson, R and Holland, J (1996) *The Male in the Head* London: Tufnell Press

Gordon, T and Holland, J (2000) *Making Spaces: citizenship and differences in schools* Houndsmill: Macmillan

Graham, H (1984) *Women, Health and the Family* Brighton: Wheatsheaf

Greer, (1970) *The Female Eunuch* London: Macgibbon and Key

Greer, (1999) *The Whole Woman* London: Paladin

Griffith, A and Smith, D.E. (1990) What did you do in school today? Mothering, schooling and social class, in Miller G and Holstein J (eds.) *Perspectives on Social Problems* vol.2 Greenwich CT: Jai Press

Griffith, A and Smith, D.E. (1987) Constructive cultural knowledge: mothers as discourse, in Gaskell, J and McLaren (eds.) *Women and education: A Canadian perspective* Calgary: Detselig

Hall, C (1992) *White, Male and Middle Class* Cambridge: Polity Press

Hall P, Land H, Parker R and Webb A (1975) *Change, Choice and Conflict* London: Macmillan

Hall, S and Jacques, M (1983) (eds.) *The Politics of Thatcherism* London: Lawrence and Wishart

Hanmer, J and Maynard, M (1987) (eds.) *Women, Violence and Social Control* London: Macmillan

Haraway, D (1990) *Simians, Cyborgs and Women* NewYork: Routledge

Harding, S (1986) *The Science Question in Feminism* Milton Keynes: Open University Press

Harding, S (1987) (ed.) *Feminism and Methodology* Milton Keynes: Open University Press

Harding, S (1991) *Whose Science? Whose Knowledge? Thinking from women's lives* Milton Keynes: Open University Press

Harrison, B and Lyon, E.S (1993) A note on ethical issues in the use of autobiography in sociological research *Sociology:* special issue on biography and autobiography in sociology 27 (1) 101–110

Hartman, H (1981) The unhappy marriage of Marxism and feminism, in Sargent, L (ed.) *Women and Revolution* Boston, Mass: South End Press

Hartsock, N (1998) *The Feminist Standpoint Revisited and other essays* Boulder, Colorado and Oxford: Westview Press

Haskey, J (1998) Families: their historical context, and recent trends in the factors influencing their formation and dissolution, in David, M E (ed.) *The Fragmenting Family?* London: IEA Health and Welfare Unit

Hass, A (1980) *Teen Parents* California: University of California Press

Hass, A (1990) *In the Shadow of the Holocaust: the second generation* Cambridge: Cambridge University Press

Heilbrun, C (1989) *Writing a Woman's Life* London: The Women's Press

Heilbrun, C (1993) *Towards a Recognition of Androgyny* New York: Knopf

Heilbrun, C (1997) *The Education of a Woman: the life and times of Gloria Steinem* London: Virago

Heilbrun, C (1997) *The Last Gift of Time: life after sixty* New York: Ballantine Books

Held, D (1999) *Global Transformations: politics, education and culture* Cambridge: Polity Press

Held, D (2001) September 11th: Violence, Law and Justice in a Global Age, Distinguished Lecture in the GSSS series at Keele University, November 29th

Heron, L (1985) (ed.) *Truth, Dare or Promise? girls growing up in the 1950s* London Virago

Hewlett, S A (1986) *A Lesser Life: the myth of women's liberation* London: Michael Joseph

Hewlett, S A (2002) *Baby Hunger: The new battle for motherhood* London: Atlantic Books

Hey, V (1996) *The Company She Keeps: an ethnography of girls' friendships* Buckingham: Open University Press

Hirschmann, N and Di Stefano, C (1996) (eds.) *Revisioning the Political: reconstructions of concepts in Western political theory* Oxford: Westview

Hochschild, A (1983) *The Managed Heart: the commercialisation of human feeling* Berkeley CA, University of California Press

Hochschild, A (1998) *The Second Shift* New York: Viking

Home Office (1998) *Supporting Families: a consultation document* London: HMSO

Hooks, b (1981) *Ain't I a Woman?* Boston: South End Press

Hooks, b (1984) *Feminist Theory: from margin to centre* Boston: South End Press

Hooks, b (1989) *Talking Back* Boston: South End Press

Horowitz, D (1998) *Betty Friedan and The Making of the Feminine Mystique: The American Left, The Cold War and Modern Feminism* Amherst, Mass: University of Massachusetts Press

Howe, F (2000) (ed.) *The Politics of Women's Studies: testimony from thirty founding mothers* New York: The Feminist Press

Hudson, B and Ineichen, B (1986) *Taking it Lying Down* London: Macmillan

Hultquist, T and Dahlberg, G (2001) (eds.) *Governing the Child in the New Millennium* New York and London: Routledge/Falmer

Humm, M (1992) (ed.) *Feminisms* Hemel Hempstead: Harvester

Irigaray, L (1977) *This Sex Which Is Not One* Paris: Minuit

Irigaray, L (1991) (ed. Whitford, M) *The Irigaray Readers* Oxford: Blackwell

Jackson, S (1982) *Childhood and Sexuality* Oxford: Basil Blackwell

James, S, and Della Costa, M (1975) *The power of women and the subversion of the community* Bristol: Falling Wall Press

Jamieson, L (1998) *Intimacy: Personal Relations in Modern Society* Cambridge Polity Press

Jencks, C, Bane, M-J, Cohen, D, Gintis, H, Smith, M and Acland, H (1973) *Inequality: a re-assessment of family and schooling in America* London: Allen Lane; New York: Basic Books

James, A , Jenks, C, and Prout, A (1998) *Theorising Childhood* Cambridge: Polity Press

Jewish Women in London Group (1988) *Generations of Memories: voices of Jewish women* London: The Women's Press

Jones, A (2001) (ed.) *Touchy Subject: teachers teaching children* Dunedin NZ: University of Otago Press

Jones, G (2001) *Youth research and youth policy: wholesome partnership or unholy alliance?* Inaugural Lecture, Keele University 2nd May

Jong, E (1971) *Fear of Flying* London: Hart-Davis

Jong, E (1994) *Fear of Fifty: a mid-life crisis* London: Vintage

Karpf, A (1996) *The War After* London: Hart-Davis Minerva

Kelly, G (1982) Women's Education in the Third World, in Elliott, C (ed.) *Comparative perspectives* Albany, New York: SUNY Press

Kelly, G.P and Slaughter, S (1991) (eds.) *Women's Higher Education in Comparative Perspective* Dordrecht and London: Kluwer Academic Publishing

Kelly, D (2000) *Pregnant with Meaning: teen mothers and the politics of inclusive schooling* New York: Peter Lang

Kenway, J (1990) (ed.) *Gender and Education Policy: a call for new directions* Geelong, Vic: Deakin University Press

Kenway, J and Willis, S with Blackmore, J and Rennie, L (1997) *Answering Back: girls, boys and feminism in schools* St Leonards, NSW and London: Allen and Unwin

Kenway, J (2000) *Designing Generations and Hybridising Entertainment* Talk given at the Gender and Education international conference, London University Institute of Education, April

Kenway, J, Bullen, E and Hey, V (1999) New Labour, social exclusion and education risk management: the case of gymslip mums *British Educational Research Journal* 26 (4) 441–56

Kenway, J and Bullen, E (2001) *Consuming Children: Education – Entertainment – Advertising* Buckingham: Open University Press

Kiernan, K, Land, H and Lewis, J (1998) *Lone Motherhood in 20th Century Britain* Oxford: Oxford University Press

Komarovsky, M (1967) *Blue Collar Marriage* New York: Vintage

Kristeva, J (1984) *Revolution in Poetic Language* New York: Columbia University Press

Kuhn, A (1990) *Alien Zone: cultural theory and contemporary science fiction cinema* London: Verso

Laing, R D (1965) *The Divided Self* Harmondsworth: Penguin

Land, H (1976) Women: Supporters or Supported? in Barker, D L and Allen, S (eds.) *Sexual Divisions and Society: process and change*

Land, H (1977) The Myth of the Male Breadwinner? *New Society* 9 October

Lareau, A (1989) *Home Advantage: social class and parental interventions in elementary Education* London: Falmer Press

Lather, P (1991) *Getting Smart: feminist research and pedagogy with/in the post-modern* London: Routledge

Leach, Sir E (1967) *A Runaway World?* London: BBC Reith Lectures

Lees, S (1986) *Losing Out? Sexuality and adolescent girls* London: Hutchinson

Lees, S (1993) *Sugar and Spice: Sexuality and adolescent girls* London: Penguin

Lees, S (1997) *Ruling Passions? Sex and violence, reputation and the law* Buckingham: Open University Press

Lees, S (1997) *Carnal Knowledge: rape on trial* London: Penguin

Leonard, D and Hood-Williams, J (1988) *Families* Basingstoke: Macmillan

Lessing, D (1972) *The Golden Notebook* London: Grafton Books

Levin, J (2001) Obituary for Professor Jill Forbes *The Guardian* July 20th

Levitas, R (1998) *The Inclusive Society? Social exclusion and New Labour* London: Macmillan

Lewis, J (1991) On the menopause and HRT *Feminist Review 43* Spring: 38–57

Lewis, J (1980) *The Politics of Motherhood: child and maternal welfare in England 1900–1939* Beckenham: Croom Helm

Lewis, J (1983) (ed.) *Women's Welfare, Women's Rights*, London: Croom Helm

Lewis, J and Knijn, T (2002) The politics of sex education policy in England and Wales and The Netherlands since the 1980s *Journal of Social Policy* 31(4) 669–95

Littlejohn, G, Smart, B, Wakeford, J and Yuval-Davis, N (1978) (eds.) *Power and the State* London: Croom Helm

Lingard, B and Douglas, P (1999) *Men Engaging Feminism: pro-feminism, backlashes and schooling* Buckingham: Open University Press

Lister, R (1996) (ed.) *Charles Murray and the Underclass: the developing debate* London: IEA and Sunday Times: Choice in Welfare 33

— Lister, R (1997) *Citizenship and Feminist Perspectives* Basingstoke: Macmillan

Lister, R (2002) Plenary presentation to *Gender Research Forum* of the Women and Equality Unit, Cabinet Office, April

Lorde, A (1994) *Sister Outsider* Trumansberg, New York: The Crossing Press

Luttrell, W (1997) *School Smart and Mother Wise* New York and London Routledge

Luxton, M (1997) (ed.) *Feminism and Families: critical policies and changing practices* Halifax, Nova Scotia: Fernwood

Lyon, E S (2000) Biographical constructions of a working woman: the changing faces of Alva Myrdal *European Journal of Social Theory* 3 (4) 407–28

— Mackinnon, C (1989) *Towards a Feminist Theory of the State* Cambridge, Mass. And London: Harvard University Press

Mackinnon, A, Enquist, I Salzman and Prentice, A (1998) (eds.) *Education into the Twenty-first Century: dangerous terrain for women* London: Falmer Press

Maher, F and Trethault, M J (2001) *The Feminist Classroom, Dynamics of Gender, Race and Privilege*, expanded edition, Boulder, CO, New York and London, Rowman and Littlefield

Malos, E (1980) *The Politics of Housework* London: Alison Busby

Marks, E (1973) *Simone de Beauvoir: encounters with death* New Brunswick NJ: Rutgers University Press

Markowitz, R J (1993) *My Daughter, The Teacher: Jewish teachers in the New York City Schools* New Brunswick NJ: Rutgers University Press

Martin, J R (1999) *Coming of Age in Academia* New York and London: Routledge

Marwick, A (1999) *The Sixties* Oxford: Oxford University Press

McCrindle, J and Rowbotham, S (1977) *Dutiful Daughters: women talk about their lives* London: Allen Lane

Mcleod, J (2000) Subjectivity and schooling in a longitudinal study of secondary students *British Journal of Sociology of Education* 21 (4) December 501–23

Measor, L, Tiffin, C and Miller, K (2000) *Young People's Views of Sex Education* London: Routledge

Medawar, J and Pike, D (2001) *Hitler's Gift: scientists who fled Nazi Germany* London: Piatkus

Middleton, S (1998) *Disciplining Sexuality: Foucault, life histories and education* New York: Teachers' College Press

Middleton, S and Weiler, K (1998) (eds.) *Telling Women's Lives* Buckingham: Open University Press

Millar, J (1994) State, family and personal responsibility: the changing balance for lone mothers in the United Kingdom *Feminist Review* 48 Autumn: 24–40

Millar, J (2000) *Families and Social Policy* London: Hutchinson

Miller, J (1996) *School for Women* London: Virago

Miller, N (1991) *Getting Personal: feminist occasions and other autobiographical acts* New York: Routledge

Miller, N and Morgan, D (1993) Called to account: the CV as an autobiographical practice *Sociology* Special issue on biography and autobiography in sociology 27 (1) 133–44

Millett, K (1977) *Sexual Politics* London: Virago

Mirza, H (1992) *Young, Female and Black* London: Routledge

Mirza, H (1997) (ed.) *Black British Feminism* London: Routledge

Mirza, H and Reay, D (2000) Black Women Educators and the Third Space, in Arnot and Dillabough (eds.) *Challenging Democracy* London: Routledge/Falmer

Mitchell, J (1969) Women: the longest revolution *New Left Review* 40 November–December: 11–38

Mitchell, J (1971) *Woman's Estate* Harmondsworth: Penguin

Mitchell, J (1984) *Women: the longest revolution: feminism, literature and psychoanalysis* London: Virago

Mitchell, J (1974) *Psychoanalysis and Feminism* Harmondsworth: Penguin

Mitchell, J and Oakley, A(1976) (eds.) *The Rights and Wrongs of Women* Harmondsworth: Penguin

Mitchell, J and Oakley, A (1986) (eds.) *What is Feminism?* Harmondsworth: Penguin

Mitchell, J and Oakley, A (1997) (eds.) *Who's Afraid of Feminism? Seeing through the backlash* Harmondsworth: Penguin

Mitchell, J and Rose, J (1982) *Feminine Sexuality* London: Palgrave

Moi, T (1985) *Sexual/Textual Politics: feminist literacy theory* London: Methuen

Moi, T (1986) (ed.) *The Kristeva Reader* Oxford: Blackwell

Moi, T (1987) (ed.) *French Feminist Thought: a reader* Oxford: Blackwell

Moi, T (1990) *Feminist Theory and Simone de Beauvoir* Oxford: Blackwell

Moi, T (1994) *Simone de Beauvoir: the making of an intellectual woman* Cambridge Mass: Blackwell

Moi, T (1999) *What is a Woman? and Other Essays* Oxford: Blackwell

Morgan, D (1996) *Family Connections: an introduction to family studies* Cambridge: Polity Press

Morgan, D (1998) Sociological imaginings and imagining sociology: bodies, auto/biographies and other mysteries *Sociology* November 32 (4) 647–665

Morley, L (1999) *Organising Feminisms: the micropolitics of the academy* London: Macmillan

Morley, L and Rassool, N (1999) *School Effectiveness: fracturing the discourse* London: The Falmer Press

Morton, A (1997) *Diana: her true story in her own words, 1961–1997* London: Michael O'Mara

Mount, F (1982) *The Subversive Family: an alternative history of love and marriage* London: Unwin Counterpoint

Mount, F (1999) Column on the Reith lectures *The Sunday Times* May 9th

Moynihan, D.P. (1965) *The Negro Family* New York: Basic Books

Moskovitz, S (1983) *Love Despite Hate: child survivors of the Holocaust and their adult lives* New York: Schocken Books

Murray, C (1996) in Lister, R (ed) *Charles Murray and the Underclass: The Developing Debate*

Myrdal, A and Klein, V (1956) *Women's Two Roles: Home and Work* London: RKP

Nathan, P R and Gais, T L (1997) *Implementing the Personal Responsibility Act 1996: A first look* New York: SUNY Albany

New, C and David, M E (1985) *For the Children's Sake: making child care more than women's business*, Harmondsworth: Penguin

Noddings, N (1984) *Caring: a feminine approach to ethics and moral education* Berkeley: University of Canada Press

Oakley, A (1972) *Sex, Gender and Society* London: Maurice Temple Smith

Oakley, A (1974) *Sociology of Housework* London: Martin Robertson

Oakley, A (1976) *Housewife* London: Penguin

Oakley, A (1979) *Becoming a Mother* Oxford: Martin Robertson

Oakley, A (1980) *Women Confined: towards a sociology of childbirth* Oxford: Martin Robertson

Oakley, A (1981) Interviewing Women: a contradiction in terms, in Roberts, H (ed.) *Doing Feminist Research* London: Routledge

Oakley, A (1982) *Subject Women* London: Fontana

Oakley, A (1984) *Taking it Like a Woman* London: Jonathan Cape

Oakley, A (1995) *Scenes originating in the Garden of Eden* London: Flamingo

Oakley, A (1998) Gender, methodology and people's ways of knowing: some problems with feminism and the paradigm debate in social science *Sociology* 32(4) 707–31

Oakley, A (2000) *Experiments in Knowing: gender and method in the social sciences* Cambridge: Polity Press

Ofer, D and Weitzman, L (1998) (eds.) *Women in the Holocaust* Oxford: Oxford University Press

Okely, J (1986) *Simone de Beauvoir* London: Virago

Okely, J (1987) Privileged, schooled and finished: boarding school education for girls, in Ardener, S (ed.) *Defining Females* London: Croom Helm

Oram, A (1989) Serving two masters? The introduction of the marriage bar in teaching, in London Feminist History Group: *The Sexual Dynamics of History* London: Pluto

Oram, A (1996) *Women Teachers and Feminist Politics 1900–1939* Manchester: Manchester University Press

Owen, U (1986) (ed) *Fathers: reflections by daughters* London: Virago

Ozga, J (ed.) (1993) *Women in Educational Management* Buckingham: Open University Press

Perry, P (1993) From HMI to Polytechic Director, in Ozga (ed.) *Women in Educational Management* Buckingham: Open University Press

Peters, M (2001) National Educational Policy Constructions of the Knowledge Economy *Journal of Educational Inquiry* 2 (1)

Petchesky, R (1984) *Abortion and Women's Choice* New York: Basic Books

Phillips, M (19991) *The Sex Change Society: Feminised Britain and the neutered male* London: The Social Market Foundation and Profile Books

Phoenix, A (1990) *Young Mothers* Cambridge: Polity Press

Phoenix, A, Woollett, A and Lloyd, C (1991) (eds.) *Motherhood: meanings, practice and ideologies* London: Sage

Phoenix, A and Tizard, B (1993) *Black, White or Mixed Race? Race and racism in the lives of young people of mixed parentage* London: Routledge

Phoenix, A (2002) Mapping present inequalities to navigate future success: racialisation and education. Review essay *British Journal of Sociology of Education*, 23(3) 505–15

Pilcher, J and Wagg, S (1996) (eds.) *Thatcher's Children? Childhood and Society in the 1980s and 1990s* London: Falmer

Pitt, Alice J (2003) *The Play of the Personal: psychoanalytic narratives of feminist education* New York: Peter Lang Publishers

Piven F. F and Cloward, R (1970) *Regulating the Poor* New York: Basic Books

Piven F. F and Cloward, R (1976) *Poor People's Movements* New York: Basic Books

Piven F. F and Cloward, R (1979) *The New Class War*. New York: Basic Books

Pogrebin, (1990) *Rachel, Golda and Me* New York: Basic Books

Popkewitz, T. S (1988) What's in a research project: some thoughts on the intersection of History, Social Structure, and Biography *Curriculum Inquiry* 18(4) 379–400

Popkewitz, T. S (2001) (ed.) *Educational Knowledge: Changing Relationships between the State, Civil Society and the Educational Community* New York: SUNY Press

Porter, M and F (1999) *Feminist Voices. Making New Feminisms: a conversation between a feminist mother and daughter* CRIAW/CREF March

Puttnam, R. (2000) *Bowling Alone: the collapse and revival of American community* New York: Basic Books

Rassool, N (1999) *Literacy for Sustainable Development in the Age of Information* Clevedon: Multilingual Matters

Reader, K and W. Khursheed (1993) *The May 1968 Events in France* London: Macmillan

Reader, K (1999) Personal voices, personal experiences *French Cultural Studies* 10 (3) 20: 265–75

Reay, D (1998) *Class Work: Mothers' involvement in their children's primary schooling* London: UCL Press

Reay D and Ball, S J (1998) Making their minds up: family dynamics of school choice *British Educational Research Journal* 24 (2) 431–48

Reay, D, Davies, J David M E and Ball, S J (2000) Degrees of choice and choice of degree: social class, race and the Higher Education choice process, *Sociology* 35 (4) 855–74

Reay, D and Mirza, H (2000) Black women educators and the third space, in Arnot and Dillabough (eds.) *Challenging Democracy: international perspectives on gender, education and citizenship* London: Routledge/Falmer

Reinharz, S (1992) *Feminist Research Methods* New York and London: Oxford University Press

Reynolds, T (1997) Class matters, 'race' matters and gender matters, in Mahoney, P and Zmorczek, C (eds.) *Class Matters: 'Working-Class Women's Perspectives in Social Class* London: Taylor and Francis

Reynolds, T (2001) Black fathers and family lives in Britain, in Goulbourne, H and Chamberlain, M (eds.) *Families and the Trans-Atlantic World* London: Macmillan

Reynolds, T (2001) Black mother, paid work and identity *Journal of Ethnic and Racial Studies* 24, November

Reynolds, T (2002) Re-thinking a Black feminist standpoint *Journal of Ethnic and Racial Studies*, 26, June

Reynolds, T (2002) Reflexivity and power in the research process: the relationship between Black female researchers and Black female research participants, in May, T (ed.) *Companion to Qualitative Research* Milton Keynes: Open University Press

Ribbens, J (1993) Facts or fictions: Aspects of the uses of autobiographical writing in undergraduate sociology *Sociology* Special issue on biography and autobiography 27 (1) February 81–93

Ribbens, J and Edwards, R (1998) (eds.) *Feminist Dilemmas in Qualitative Research: public knowledge and private lives* London Sage

Ribbens, J, Edwards, R and Gillies, V (2002) *Step Parents* Durham: The Sociology Press

Rich, A (1976) *Of Woman Born: motherhood as experience and institution* New York: Bantam and London: Virago

Rich, A (1980) *On lies, secrets and silence* London: Virago

Riley, D (1984) *War in the Nursery: theories of the child and the mother* London: Virago

Riley, D (1983) 'The serious burdens of love?' Some questions on childcare, feminism and sociology, in Segal, L (ed.) *What is to be done about the Family?* Harmondsworth: Penguin

Riley, D (1992) A Short history of some preoccupations, in Butler and Scott (ed.) *Feminists Theorise the Political* London: Routledge

Robbins, Lord (chair) (1963) *Committee on Higher Education* Cmnd 2145 London: HMSO

Roberts, H (1981) (ed.) *Doing Feminist Research* London: Routledge

Rose, H (1994) *Love, Power and Knowledge: towards a feminist transformation of the sciences* Cambridge: Polity Press

Rose, H and Rose, S (2002) *A geneticised culture?* Gresham lecture at Gresham College, London, May

Rose, N (1990) *Governing the Soul: the shaping of the private self* London: Routledge

Rowbotham, S (1972) *Women, Resistance and Revolution* London: Penguin

Rowbotham, S (1973) *Hidden from History: 300 years of women's oppression and the fight against it* London: Pluto Press

Rowbotham, S (1973) *Woman's Consciousness, Man's World* London: Pelican Books

Rowbotham, S (1977) *A New World for Women: Stella Browne, Socialist Feminist* London: Pluto Press

Rowbotham, S, Segal, L and Wainwright, H. (1979) *Beyond the Fragments: feminism and the making of socialism* London: Merlin

Rowbotham, S (1983) *Dreams and Dilemmas: collected writings* London: Virago

Rowbotham, S (2000) *Promise of a Dream* London: Allen Lane/Penguin

Ruddick, S (1989) *Maternal Thinking: towards a new politics of peace* London: The Women's Press

Savage, M and Witz, A (1992) (eds.) *Gender and Bureaucracy* Oxford: Blackwell

Savage, M (2000) *Class Analysis and Social Transformation* Buckingham: Open University Press

Sayers, J (1986) *Sexual Contradictions: psychology, psychoanalysis and feminism* London: Tavistock

Sayers, J (1991) *Mothering Psychoanalysis* Harmondsworth: Penguin

St Pierre, E.A and Pillow, W (2000) (eds.) *Working the Ruins: feminist post-structuralist theory and methods in education* New York and London: Routledge

Schon, D (1987) *The Reflective Practitioner: how professionals think in action* Aldershot: Avebury

Schon, D (1991) *The Reflective Turn: how professionals think in action* New York and London: Teachers' College Press

Scott, S and Jackson, S (1999) Risky Children and risky childhoods: childhood and sexuality in Lupton, D *Theorising Risk and Culture* Cambridge: Cambridge University Press

Scott, S and Jackson, S (2001) *Gender* London: Routledge

Scott, S, Jackson, S and Beckett-Milburn, K (1998) Swings and Roundabouts: risk

Bibliography and References 213

anxiety and the everyday world of children, in *Sociology* 32(4): 686–750 reproduced in Jones, A (2001)

Schram, S (2000) *After Welfare: the culture of post-industrial social policy* New York and London: Basic Books

Seccombe, W (1974) The housewife and her labour under capitalism *New Left Review* 83: 3–24

Segal, L (1983) (ed.) *What is to be Done about the Family? Crisis in the eighties* Harmondsworth: Penguin

Segal, L (1987) *Is the Future Female? Troubled thoughts on contemporary feminism* London: Virago

Segal, L (1997) ed. *New Sexual Agendas* Basingstoke: Macmillan

Segal, L (1999) *Why Feminism? Gender, psychology, politics* Cambridge: Polity Press

Seidler, V J (2000) *Shadows of the Shoah: Jewish identity and belonging* Oxford: Berg

Seller, M (2001) *We Built Up our Lives: education and community among Jewish refugees* London: Eurospan

Sennett, R (1998) *The Corrosion of Character: the personal consequences of work in the new capitalism* New York and London: Norton

Sennett, R (2002) *Excavating issues of poverty and welfare* Distinguished lecture series for GSSS, Keele University April

Shaw, J (1994) *Education, Gender and Anxiety* London: Taylor and Francis

Sikes, P (1997) *Parents who Teach: stories from home and from school* London: Cassell

Skeggs, B (1997) *Formations of Class and Gender: becoming respectable* London: Sage

Skolnick, A (1978) *The Intimate Environment: exploring marriage and the family* Boston: Little Brown

Slovo, G (1990) *Ties of Blood* London: Headline

Smart, C and Silva, E.B (1999) (eds.) *The New Family?* London: Sage

Smart, C and Neale, B (1999) *Family Fragments* Cambridge: Polity Press

Smart, C. Neale, B and Wade, A (2001) *The Changing Experience of Childhood: families and divorce* Cambridge: Polity Press

Smith, D E (1987) *The Everyday World as Problematic* Milton Keynes: Open University Press

Smith, D.E. (1990) *Texts, Facts and Femininity: exploring the relations of ruling* London: Routledge

Smith, D.E. (1998) The Underside of Schooling: Restructuring, privatisation and women's unpaid work *Journal for a Just and Caring Education* 4(1) 11–30

Smith, D E and Griffith, A (1990) Coordinating the uncoordinated: mothering, schooling and the family wage, in Miller, G and Holstein, J (eds.) *Perspectives on Social Problems* vol. 2 Greenwich CT JAI Press

Smith, D E: The standard North American family: SNAF as an ideological code *Journal of Family Issues* 14 (2):50–65

Snitow, A, Stansell, C and Thompson, S (1984) *The Politics of Sexuality* London: Virago

Snitow, A (1992) *Feminist Review* (40) Feminism and motherhood: an American reading: 32–51

Snowman, D (2002) *The Hitler Emigres* London: Chatto and Windus

Somerville, J (2000) *Feminism and the Family: politics and society in the UK and USA* London: Macmillan

Stacey, J (1996) *In the Name of the Family* Boston: Beacon Press

Stambach, A and David, M E (2003, in press) Feminist Theory and Educational Policy: How Gender has been 'Involved' in Family-School Choice Debates *SIGNS: Journal of women in culture and society*

Standing, K (1997) Scrimping, saving and schooling: lone mothers and 'choice' in education *Critical Social Policy* 17 (2): 79–99

Standing, K (1999) Lone mothers and 'parental' involvement: a contradiction in policy? *Journal of Social Policy* 28(3): 479–97

Stanley, L (1992) *The Autobiographical I. The theory and practice of feminist auto-biography* Manchester, Manchester University Press

Stanley, L and Wise, S (1983) *Breaking Out: feminist consciousness and feminist research* London: RKP

Stanley, L and Wise, S (1993) *Breaking Out Again. Feminist Ontology and Epistemology* London: RKP

Stanley, L (1997) (ed.) *Knowing Feminisms: academic borders, territories and tribes*, London: Sage

Steedman, C (1986) *Landscape for a Good Woman* London: Virago

Steinem, G (1994) *Moving Beyond Words* London: Bloomsbury

Stott, M (1971) *The Guardian* March 31st p. 11

Swindells, J (1995) (ed.) *The Uses of Autobiography* London: Taylor and Francis

Thatcher, M (1995) *The Path to Power* London: Harper Collins

Tizard, B and Hughes, M (1984) *Young Children Learning: talking and thinking at home and at school* London: Fontana

Tomlinson, S (1990) *The 1944 Education Act and I* Inaugural Lecture, Goldsmith's College: London University

Tomlinson, S (1991) *Education in a Post-Welfare Society* Buckingham: Open University Press

Trustram, M (1985) *Women of the Regiment: marriage in the Victorian Army* Cambridge: Cambridge University Press

Tsolidis, G (2001) *Schooling, Diaspora and Gender: being feminine and being different* Buckingham: Open University Press

Ungerson, C (1987) *Policy is Personal: sex, gender and informal care* London: Tavistock

Unterhalter, E (2000) Transnational visions of the 1990s: contrasting views of women, education and citizenship in Arnot, M and Dillabough, J (eds.) *Challenging Democracy* London: Routledge/Falmer

Walby, S (1990) *Theorising Patriarchy* Oxford: Blackwell

Walby, S (2001) Against Epistemological Chasms: The science question in feminism revisited *SIGNS Journal of Women in Culture and Society* 26 (2) 485–509

Walford, G (1987) (ed.) *Doing Sociology of Education* London: Falmer

Walkerdine, V, and Lucey, H (1989) *Democracy in the Kitchen: regulating mothers and socialising daughters* London: Virago

Walkerdine, V (1997) *Daddy's Girl: young girls and popular culture* London: Macmillan

Walkerdine, V, Lucey, H and Melody, J (2001) *Growing Up Girl: psychosocial explorations in gender and class* London: Macmillan

Walkerdine, V (2002) Lecture on neo-liberalism, at London School of Economics, February 14th

Wallace, C (1997/2000) *Untamed Shrew: Germaine Greer* London: Richard Cohen Books

Walter, N (1998) *The New Feminism* London: Virago

Webster, F (1999) On Anthony Giddens *Times Higher Educational Supplement*, May 1st

Weedon, C (1987) *Feminist Practice and Post-Structuralist Theory* Oxford: Basil Blackwell

Weeks, J (1981) *Sex, Politics and Society* London: Longman

Weeks, J (1983) *Sexuality and its Discontents* London: RKP

Weeks, J (1995) *Invented Moralities* Cambridge: Polity Press

Weeks, J (2000) *Making Sexual History* Cambridge: Polity Press

Weiler, K (1998) *Country School Women Teaching in Rural California 1850–1950* Stanford, Ca.: Stanford University Press

— Weiner, G (1994) *Feminisms in Education* Buckingham: Open University Press

Weis, L (1990) *Working Class without Work: high school students in a de-industrialising economy* New York and London: Routledge

West, A, Edge, A, Noden, P and David, M E (1998) Parental Involvement in and out of school *British Educational Research Journal* 24 (4)

Whitty, G, Edwards, T and Gewirtz, S (1993) *Specialisation and Choice in Urban Education* London: Routledge

Whitty, G, Power, S and Halpin, P (1998) *Devolution and Choice in Education: The school, the state and the market* Buckingham: Open University Press

Williams, F (1989) *Social Policy: A Critical Introduction: issues of race, gender and class* Cambridge: Polity Press

Williams, F (1999) Good-enough Principles for Welfare *Journal of Social Policy* 28 (4): 667–89

— Williams, F (2000) *Travels with Nanny, Destination Good Enough: a personal/intellectual journey through the Welfare State* Inaugural Lecture, Leeds University May 11th

Wilson, E (1977) *Women and the Welfare State* London: Tavistock

Wilson, E (1983) *Mirror Writing* London: Virago

Wilson, E (1987) (ed.) *What is to be done about violence against women?* London: Penguin

Wolf, N (1991) *The Beauty Myth* Toronto: Vintage Books

Wollstonecraft, M (1970) *Vindication of the Rights of Women* London: Dent

Wyn, J, Acker, S and Richards, E (2000) Making a difference: women in management in Australian and Canadian faculties of education *Gender and Education* 21: 435–49

Yates, L (1993) *The Education of Girls: policy, research and the question of gender* Australian Council for Educational Research

Yates, L and Mcleod, J (2000) Social justice and the middle class *Australian Education Researcher* 27 (3)

Yeatman, A (1990) *Bureaucrats, Technocrats, Femocrats: essays on the contemporary Australian state* Sydney and London: Allen and Unwin

Yeatman, A (1994) *Postmodern Revisionings of the Political* New York and London: Routledge

Young, I M (1990) *Justice and the Politics of Difference* Princeton: Princeton University

Young-Bruehl, E (1998) *Subject to Biography: Psychoanalysis, Feminism, and Writing Women's Lives* Cambridge, Mass. and London: Harvard University Press

Yuval-Davis, N (1978) Women: Bearers of the Collective, in Littlejohn, G *et al* (eds.) *Power and the State* London: Croom Helm

Yuval-Davis, N and Anthias, F (1989) (eds.) *Woman–nation–state* Basingstoke: Macmillan

Zellman, G (1981) *The Response of Schools to Teen Pregnancy and Parenthood* Santa Monica, Ca.: Rand Corporation

Index